THE SOVIET UNION:
Socialist
or
Social-Imperialist?

*Essays Toward The Debate
On The Nature Of Soviet Society*

Compiled by the Editors of
<u>The Communist</u>
*Theoretical Journal of the
Revolutionary Communist Party, USA*

RCP Publications, Chicago

Copyright © 1983 by RCP Publications
ISBN 0-89851-062-7

First Printing: April, 1983
Printed in U.S.A.

Published by:
RCP Publications
P.O. Box 3486 Merchandise Mart
Chicago, IL U.S.A. 60654

Table of Contents

The 'State Capitalist' and 'Bureaucratic-Exploitative'
Interpretations of the Soviet Social Formation:
A Critique
    by David Laibman 9

Soviet Socialism and
Proletarian Internationalism
    by Al Szymanski 35

Soviet Economic Relations With India
and Other Third World Countries
    by Santosh K. Mehrotra and Patrick Clawson 79

The "Tarnished Socialism" Thesis
or The Political Economy
of Soviet Social-Imperialism
    by the Revolutionary Communist Party, USA
        NEW INTRODUCTION 135
        ARTICLE 153

Preface

In the summer of 1982, the Revolutionary Communist Party initiated a call for a conference and debate to be held in May 1983 on the nature and role of the Soviet Union, focusing on the question: "The Soviet Union: Socialist or Social-Imperialist?" In order to sharply delineate the issues at stake, the editors of *The Communist* invited several scholars with opposing perspectives to present their views on crucial aspects of the question. The essays making up this collection offer both the specialist and non-specialist reader a wide-ranging discussion of the controversies surrounding Soviet society and the role of the Soviet Union in the international arena.

Few other contentious political topics so concentrate profound theoretical questions about mankind's future and are so intimately bound up with basic practical choices throughout the world. The question of the Soviet Union pushes to the fore in any debate over the possibilities for radical social transformation and over the nature and potential of the developing international situation. Does the state-owned and centrally planned character of its economic system mean that it is inherently a social advance over capitalism, or does it simply reflect the encasement of capitalist relations of production in a more collective ownership form? Is the Soviet Union a progressive force in the world today, or an imperialist superpower, like the United States, compelled by its nature to wage a war of world redivision? Is it a natural ally of oppressed nations, or is it one more in a series of aspiring exploitative powers?

In the first essay, David Laibman formulates a critique of the position that an historically specific form of state capitalism exists in the Soviet Union. He argues that the categories of class and exploitation reflecting the structure and mechanisms of capitalist society can neither meet the theoretical requirements of Marxism nor stand up to empirical test if applied to the Soviet Union. Albert Szymanski, in the second essay, pursues a similar line of argument and review of evidence. He contends that the Soviet Union is not a stratified society comparable to those of the West, that a high level of worker participation and security exists in that society, and that its external relations are of a qualitatively different order than those of the Western imperialist states. The third essay, by Santosh K. Mehrotra and Patrick Clawson, examines Soviet trade and aid relations with India and other "third world" countries. The authors maintain that the Soviet Union derives substantial benefits from these ties and that India's economic relations with the Soviet Union have reproduced its pattern of dependency on foreign powers. In the final essay, the RCP critiques several pro-Soviet positions. The article stresses the persistence of class struggle in socialist society and the continual attempts of new bourgeois forces to seize power. It argues that the Soviet Union is today an imperialist power where the economy functions according to the laws of capital and where a bourgeois ruling class holds power.

This debate is assuredly not one of "mutual incomprehension" on both sides. Its implications go far beyond the empirical validity of particular claims. At issue methodologically lies the question of how Marxism uncovers the essence of social relations that underlie various appearances and forms. Politically and ideologically, the debate turns on an understanding of the very nature of the process of revolution and counterrevolution in the modern epoch. We live in an era of turbulence and upheaval, one that has seen the proletariat seize power in Russia and China and begin the unprecedented task of ripping up the roots of exploitation and oppression, yet has shown that the march to the future is not a unilinear advance. How to sum these experiences up, indeed what kind of revolutionary struggle and transformation is required to eliminate classes and class divisions on a world scale, is at the heart of this controversy.

The Editors of *The Communist*
April 1983

The 'State Capitalist' and 'Bureaucratic-Exploitative' Interpretations of the Soviet Social Formation: A Critique

David Laibman*

I.

In recent years, sections of the left in the United States and Western Europe have tried to provide a theoretical underpinning for their positions of antagonism toward the USSR. This has resulted in essentially two approaches (with, of course, variations of interpretation and emphasis within each approach). They are, first, the "capitalist restoration" view, which holds that capitalism either has been, or is in process of being, restored in the USSR in the historically specific form of "state capitalism" in which bourgeois relations of exploitation adopt the form of state ownership. The second approach is the "bureaucratic-exploitative" one, which designates the ruling bureaucracy as a class with the power to extract surplus value, i.e., establish itself in an exploitative relation to the subordinate working class.

David Laibman teaches economics at Brooklyn College, City University of New York. Reprinted by permission of the *Review of Radical Political Economics*, This article originally appeared in their Vol. 10, No. 4 (Winter 1978).

* The author acknowledges criticisms and comments from Renate Bridenthal, Don Van Atta, and several referees of the *RRPE*; remaining weaknesses probably result from failure to follow their advice.

This paper formulates a critique of both of these conceptions. Since the critique rests on an elaboration of the Marxist categories applicable to capitalist societies, the question of the nature of Soviet society serves as a test of the degree of our comprehension of these categories; this indeed is one of the reasons why the discussion of this issue is important for the US left today.*[1]

The next section will consider the categories of class and of capitalist exploitation insofar as they bear on the issues at hand. In section III the theoretical positions developed in section II will be used to develop operational (empirical) criteria that can, in principle, be applied to determine, in the USSR or anywhere else, the existence or non-existence of a) class; b) specifically capitalist exploitation. In section IV a *preliminary* sketch of an empirical test for the Soviet Union is drawn. Section V summarizes and concludes.

To state succinctly the conclusions reached: The term "state capitalism" cannot be used to describe *any* social formation in its entirety — and therefore to characterize the mode of production underlying that formation — without serious distortion of the concept of capital and mystification of capitalist production relations. Similarly, it is inadmissible to define any identifiable leadership group as an exploitative class without careful delineation of the means of coercion in that group's possession and the reproduction of those means *within* the production relation. All available data on social stratification and economic functioning in the USSR belie the claim that Soviet society today embodies capitalist *or* general-exploitative principles when the data are evaluated using theoretically substantiated criteria.

---

* Since the critique will be concerned with the theoretical adequacy of the basic conceptions underlying the two approaches, rather than with specifics, no attempt will be made to summarize the "state capitalism" or "exploitative bureaucracy" arguments in detail here. The reader is referred to Charles Bettelheim, *Class Struggles in the USSR. First Period: 1917-1923* (Monthly Review Press, 1976), especially the preface, for the most recent, and most ambitious, statement of the "state capitalist" position.

A statement of the "bureaucratic-exploitative" position will be found in Paul M. Sweezy, "The Nature of Soviet Society," *Monthly Review*, November 1974 and January 1975; "More on the Nature of Soviet Society," *Monthly Review*, March 1976.

II.

The key concepts, for the "capitalist" and "bureaucratic" hypotheses, respectively, are *capital* and *class*.

Without attempting anything like a survey of the literature on the capital concept [2] we may say that it describes a social relation in which class exploitation assumes an outward form of equality and reciprocity through exchange. Coercive power, exercised systematically by a ruling class and resulting in its appropriation of part of the product of the working class, takes on the guise of a sum of self-expanding value and is made effective through the impersonal working of market relations, outside of any human agency. This mystification of the class relationship is made *possible* by the fact that products take the form of commodities; the theory of surplus must be a theory of surplus *value*. It is made *necessary* by the advanced state of the productive forces, which renders inadequate the less subtle, more visible means of coercion, characteristic of earlier forms of class society. The mystification is therefore not merely a matter of ideology; it is an inherent and indispensable component of the process which goes by the name of capital.

The power of capital consists not only in the fact that its physical elements take on a value form, but also in the extended appropriation of that value as property. The class monopoly of the means of production is coercive because of the legitimacy of property ownership in general; the latter, in turn, is reproduced through widespread ownership as property of commodities which, by virtue of their nature as use-values and their failure to be aggregated to a critical size, cannot function as capital. In short, it is not only the value form but also the private-property form which set into motion and perpetuate capital's power to exploit the working class. [3]

Looked at from another angle, the power of capital appears as the valorization of labor-power: the reproduction of labor-power as a commodity. An important basis for this is the "radical separation of the direct producers from the means of production"; [4] it is, however, necessary to elaborate the specific mechanisms by means of which this separation is brought about in the capitalist mode of production. Here we may single out the role of the reserve army of unemployed and the threat of unemployment; the absence of reliable institutions supporting the indigent and elderly, and the threat of poverty; in general, the pervasive insecurity surrounding the "labor market," that intricate piece of social machinery which brings labor and the conditions of labor together temporarily under the aegis of an irresponsible and autonomous owning class.[5] It is the ownership-as-commodities of the conditions of labor, and of labor-power itself during the period when it is set into motion, that establishes the sway of capital.

When we move from the underlying categories of capitalist relations of production to their institutional embodiment we find, especially in advanced capitalist societies, a high degree of subtlety. Thus Marx consciously posits "Mr. Moneybags" as an abstract embodiment of those relations, aware that on the level of institutions the role in question is mediated through a complex set of interlocked institutions.[6]

In particular, we may distinguish three institutional complexes whose interaction establishes the power of capital: ownership, management and the social upper class. Ownership, as noted above, is the essential function which fragments and depersonalizes the capitalist function, establishing the laws of accumulation as objective laws independent of human will or agency. Management, of course, is the function which transmits the power of capital to workers in the way most directly experienced: the coercive, controlling force at the point of production. The social upper class with a distinctive and legitimated life style and a sense of cohesion and common purpose, establishes a terrain on which the informal interaction among representatives of the capitalist class, or of particular segments of that class, can take place. It also organizes the systematic drawing upward of talented and ambitious individuals from the working class and middle strata. This "upward mobility" is an important safety valve guaranteeing the reproduction of capitalist class relations.[7]

Something more should be said about the middle strata: small property owners, independent professionals, etc. While accumulation has a well-known tendency to eliminate these strata and draw their members toward the capitalist and proletarian poles, there is a contradictory dialectic at work. The middle strata play a positive role in capitalist reproduction as a goal for working-class mobility and source of ideological derailment, and as a buffer that mystifies the origin and nature of the antagonistic principle that workers experience continually. To play this role, the middle strata must actually have a qualitatively distinct class position, based either on autonomy and control over the work process or on property ownership. This distinction will be embodied in different forms of organization than those of the working class. In short, it makes a difference whether unskilled or semiskilled workers can aspire to become more highly paid workers, but workers all the same, or to join the ranks of a different order of society with a different life style and set of defining values.

The power of capital, then is exercised through a heterogeneity of institutional structures no one of which, taken in isolation, manifests that function. Taken as a unity whose parts are interdefined but cannot be reduced to each other, they constitute the mainspring of the capitalist production relation. Adequate comprehension of capitalism requires this complex structuring of concepts in which the capitalist function is determinant at the level of the production relations but is simultaneously constituted by the proximate forms in which it is manifested. This approach must be contrasted with a rationalist methodology of ideal types which focusses on "essences" or "deep structures" as uniquely "real" and the proximate forms as mere illustrations "at a lower level of abstraction." No more than the Hegelian Absolute Idea can the capital concept exist in disembodied form. Capital is not reducible to its forms of existence; but neither is it separable from these forms.

An important illustration of the rupture of this dialectic, and one germane to the present topic, is provided by Bettelheim:[8]

> Changes in legal forms of ownership do not suffice to cause the conditions for the existence of classes and for class struggle to disappear. These conditions are rooted, as Marx and Lenin often emphasized, not in legal forms of ownership but in *production relations*, that is, in the form of the social process of appropriation, in the place that the form of this process assigns to the agents of production — in fact, in the relations that are established between them in social production.

The existence of the dictatorship of the proletariat and of state or collective forms of property is not enough to "abolish" capitalist production relations and for the antagonistic classes, proletariat and bourgeoisie, to "disappear." The bourgeoisie can continue to exist in different forms and, in particular, can assume the form of a state bourgeoisie.

The counterposition of "juridical" and "real" relations has a textual basis in Marx, who spoke of "property relations" as "but a legal expression for" the real relations of production.[9] Nevertheless, I submit that the category "property relations" encompasses more than a superstructural expression, namely, an aspect of the "real relations" themselves: the *legitimated fragmentation* of basic control. In this sense, the juridical relation is the proximate form of the production relation and for all the reasons adduced above, essential to its existence and functioning. Capitalist production relations, and in particular the existence of a capitalist class or bourgeoisie, are not like a disembodied spirit that can inhabit one or another juridical form — i.e., state vs. private property — at will. As an important application of the dialectic of the production relations as a complex structure, one can neither merge the property form and the "social process of appropriation" and mistake the form for the real relation itself; nor separate them, and speak of the underlying class relation as one of real "appropriation," etc., without explaining the source and reproduction of the power to appropriate.

Finally, the possibility or impossibility of a "state bourgeoisie" is to be decided on the basis of a substantiated conception of the state. Without "overdetermining" this paper via an extended discussion of a complex subject, suffice it to say that the state is not a primary body in capitalist society.[10] In contradistinction to precapitalist (and post-capitalist) societies, in which the state operates directly as a component of the production relation, the production relation in capitalist society exists independently of the state which in turn derives its social function and power from those of the dominant class. The term "state capitalism" refers to economic activity under government ownership in societies where the capitalist social relation

— the power of capital — is generated in a substantial sector of private capitalist ownership. Here "substantial" implies an entrenched capitalist social structure complete with all necessary institutional proximate forms and capable of its own reproduction, which then transmits to the state sector the social relations that are part of its own functioning.

In short, state capitalism refers to state activity in capitalist societies, where the capitalist quality of that activity is determined by the dominance of private capitalist relations. In any society where the bulk of economic activity takes place under state ownership, the means of systematic coercion of a ruling class over an exploited producing class — if they exist — must be identified. The institutionalization of force in precapitalist modes of production has been described in a variety of settings; they have all required the existence of a social upper class. The class determination of the agents of state activity in "postcapitalist" society will be considered below. For the present, the important point is that *there is no such thing as a state-capitalist mode of production* consistent with a Marxist conception of the requirements of reproduction in capitalist relations.

If this line of reasoning holds, it follows that proponents of the "state capitalism" view of Soviet reality will have to demonstrate the existence of a *complex structure of capitalist social relations;* otherwise, any group identified as a "capitalist class," in particular Bettelheim's "state bourgeoisie," is hanging in mid-air, so to speak, without the power of capital to exercise.

But, equally important, a rigorous understanding of the nature of social classes *in general* reveals the poverty of the alternative "bureaucratic-exploitation" view as well. The holders of offices in a hierarchical structure of control are representatives of the management function; but this function derives its content from the totality of the production relations in which it is embedded. It is sheer illusion to imagine that, in terms of their administrative roles alone, "bureaucrats" can, by a pure act of will, transform themselves into an exploiting class. The power exercised by bureaucrats is, in the last instance, derivative, and its quality depends on the nature of the dominant class from which it is derived. To substantiate the concept of "state capitalism," or of the anomalous "bureaucratic mode of production," one would have to specify the nature of the systematic coercive power wielded by the "state bourgeoisie" or the "bureaucracy" *as a class*. This would have to be done without resort to metaphysical explanation or tautology; i.e., statements like "the top leadership secured for itself a monopoly of decision-making power" do not meet the requirement. Further, the mechanism of the *primary accumulation* of that class position would have to be identified.

III.

While these theoretical requirements seem strict — and of necessity they must be — it is possible to derive from them a set of *operational criteria* that can serve as the basis for an empirical test.

1) *Sources of the power of capital.* Of central importance in this connection is the separation of workers from the means of production. This can be tested directly, by examining available evidence on the organization of worker activity at the point of production and through representative institutions at higher levels of the decision-making structure as well. The organization of the labor assignment process can be examined to see whether anything like a *market* for labor-power exists. The latter entails unaided spontaneous search as the dominant method of finding jobs, the statutory existence and exercise of the power of enterprise management to fire workers at will — in short, a socially irresponsible, anarchic job-providing system. It would also imply, as *necessary* supporting mechanisms, persistent unemployment; pervasive insecurity and irresponsibility in the provision of the elements of social security (education, medical care, housing, basic subsistence); and inflation (a late-capitalist mechanism for undermining workers' savings).

Of utmost importance in establishing the existence of capital is the *valorization*, not only of the separate means of production, but also of the enterprise itself. This would mean that a sum of value functions as capital; i.e., is embodied in the enterprise but is independent of it and is therefore transferable from enterprise to enterprise. Thus, enterprises, together with their physical equipment or separably, can be bought and sold. This valorization of the means of production presupposes fragmentation or dispersion of ownership. The objectivity of values arising out of impersonal forces independent of human agency requires uncoordinated, simultaneous micro-decisions and aggregates which are unknown before the fact, indeed, the secrecy and duplication of information-gathering systems characteristic of unplanned, competitive accumulation. The quest for profit at the micro level must be shown to determine the composition of output rates of growth, the path of technical change, and the distribution of income. Moreover, profits accruing to enterprises must appear as the result of a spontaneous struggle, not as the outcome of socially planned activity. Thus, the prices which govern profitability must form spontaneously.

2) *The ruling class.* A first step on the way to establishing the existence of a ruling class in the USSR, whether "capitalist" or "bureaucratic," would be the identification of a stable elite with a distinct upper-class lifestyle as a base for informal communication and differential socialization. A partial list of ingredients: qualitatively significant income differentials, where the differentials are linked to positions of authority in the political-administrative structure; the ability to acquire equity control over natural and produced resources by investing this income; residential segregation; differential access to education; evidence of significant intermarriage among the elite; evidence that most positions of authority in the political-administrative hierarchy are occupied by people who have had elite socialization, i.e., of non-working-class backgrounds.

Pursuant to the more limited claim that the job-holding elite forms a ruling or exploiting class simply by virtue of the offices they hold, we remind ourselves that if the leading offices confer power, the social *source* of that power must be established. Nevertheless, certain operational criteria may be developed. We may ask, for example, whether positions are filled in a class-exclusive manner; i.e., whether there is widespread nepotism. We may ask whether positions can be bought and sold. We may ask whether there is any evidence that top decision-makers are held within fixed statutory limits; whether they are subject to evaluation, and, where necessary, recall or removal through action on the part of those at lower levels; whether there are institutional mechanisms for significant input from lower levels into the content of decision making and execution at the higher levels. Above all, we first note that in the USSR there are not one but several parallel hierarchies with different functions:

economic management, trade union, political (territorial), educational, and party. We then ask whether these pyramids of authority link up in a systematic way, i.e., whether the same people occupy the leading posts in each.

3) *Capitalist laws of motion.* Finally, a "state-capitalist" society should show signs that the characteristic forms of motion of capitalist society are at work. Care must be exercised in setting down a list of these forms as many are controversial in the context of societies whose designation as "capitalist" is not in doubt. The following have been mentioned: the falling tendency of the rate of profit; tendency to diminished efficiency; a falling rate of growth; cyclical growth; periodic crises of overproduction; polarization of classes and increasingly uneven distribution of income; progressing concentration and centralization; and prior development of light and consumer industry, with heavy industry following not leading.

IV.

An exhaustive test of Soviet reality, based on the criteria enumerated in Section III, is beyond the scope of this paper. Moreover, some of the criteria require interpretation and the end result will depend in any case on a weighting of the results of the tests of the separate criteria considered in isolation. In any ultimately meaningful sense, a definitive empirical test of the "state capitalist," "bureaucratic," and "socialist" hypotheses is beyond our grasp. This section should be considered a preliminary commentary on the empirical issues raised by the application of our criteria to the Soviet Union.

We begin with Chavance's[11] claim to find a "radical separation of the workers from the means of production" although he does not tell us exactly what this means. There is much evidence for the existence in Soviet enterprises of widespread worker participation in production planning, decision making and execution, control and check-up, primarily but not exclusively through the 113.5-million-member trade union movement.[12] Under the direction of the trade unions, some 5.5 million workers have currently been elected to the standing committees of permanent production conferences. These standing committees participate in generating and administering the annual Collective Agreement signed at each enterprise; long and short term planning; safety inspection; invention and rationalization; labor disputes; interpreting and applying existing plan targets and guidelines, especially in the areas of work norms and disposition of material incentive funds, housing and cultural development funds, etc.

It is difficult, if not impossible, to "prove" that these institutions — whose existence and functioning has never been disputed by any observer of the Soviet economy — operate in a way that ensures qualitative worker control over the economic process at the point of production.[13] Soviet labor legislation concerning these activities is relevant. Before quoting from legislation, however, its role as evidence must be clearly specified. It is certainly not true that because something is on the books it exists in reality as well. It is also not true that the existence of statutory rights and definitions is totally irrelevant. Since any society in which legislation and practice are totally at odds would be suffering or courting a massive "legitimation crisis," it is reasonable to assume that Soviet statutes at least influence the practice of the rights which they embody.

With only this cautious interpretation in mind, we cite passages of the Fundamental Labor Legislation of the USSR and the Union Republics, passed in its present form in 1971.[14] Article 97 in its entirety:

> Factory workers and office employees have the right to take part in discussing and deciding on questions of developing production; they have the right to submit proposals on improving the work of enterprises, institutions and organizations as well as suggestions pertaining to social, cultural and other services.
>
> Factory workers and office employees participate in the management of production through the trade unions and other public organizations, people's control bodies, general meetings and other forms of public activity open to them.
>
> It is the duty of the administration of an enterprise, institution or organization to provide conditions which ensure the participation of the factory workers and office employees in the management of production. The officials of enterprises, institutions and organizations must promptly

consider proposals and criticism made by the factory workers and office employees, and inform them regarding the steps taken on these matters.

And from article 96:

> Trade unions participate in the drawing up and realization of state economic development plans; in determining matters bearing on the distribution and utilization of the material and financial resources; they enlist the factory workers and office employees in the management of production; they organize socialist emulation, mass-scale participation in promoting new ideas in technology, and help to promote production and labor discipline.
> The establishment of working conditions, the fixing of wages and salaries, the application of labor legislation, and the utilization of public consumption funds...are the functions of the enterprises, institutions and organizations and their superior bodies effected together with the trade unions or with their agreement.

The Fundamental Labor Legislation bears on another matter of importance in deciding whether the "separation" claim has a basis in fact: the existence of a market in labor-power. This would be indicated by the existence of a) significant unemployment; b) an irresponsible job-provisioning system, including the power of management to "fire" workers. With regard to the latter, we cite Article 9, "Guarantees of Employment": "Unfounded refusal to grant a job is prohibited by law." Article 17 lists grounds for dismissal of an employee, valid only "if it is impossible to transfer the employee concerned to another job with his consent." And Article 18: "The administration of an enterprise, institution or organization cannot terminate a labor agreement on its own initiative without the consent of the factory, works or local branch trade union committee (this consent must be secured in advance)..."

With regard to unemployment, social insecurity, and inflation, it would be superfluous to elaborate here, given the consensus as to the essential absence of these phenomena in the USSR. Notwithstanding some efforts in scholarly and media circles to establish the existence of "disguised" unemployment and "suppressed" inflation,[15] and to belittle the impact of minimal-cost housing as a statutory right, free medical care, education and special support services for the elderly, the facts remain. I add only an emphasis on the *theoretical* importance of these facts.

As noted in the previous section, capital becomes "separated" from the workers, a force above them and antagonistic to them, only if it is *valorized* by a spontaneous market process. One would have to imagine a Soviet enterprise that can, of its own accord, close down; move to the sunbelt, or to Taiwan; acquire ownership in another enterprise, perhaps by making a tender offer to the holders of shares in that enterprise; or, more generally, acquire a book value by entering into spontaneous unplanned competition with other enterprises. Quite simply, everything that is known about the organization of the Soviet economy runs counter to that picture. Soviet enterprises (of course with the exception of the collective farms) are state property under indivisible ownership. Their managements are salaried employees carrying out planning and administrative functions. Large-scale investments, reorganizations, or relocations affect larger branch and territorial units, and are determined by planning bodies at the level of those units — with the participation of enterprise management and trade union bodies. All decisions, large and small, are embedded in the annual, five-year and perspective (15-year) plans of the enterprise and of all higher organizational units concerned. These plans, once ratified and operational, are on public record, a fact which all but eliminates the possibility of strategic, oligopolistic behavior, secrecy, etc. Major shifts are carried out with foreknowledge, and therefore without devastating impact on cities or regions, well known in capitalist countries as by-products of unprincipled movements of capital.[16]

Since supporters of the "state capitalist" hypothesis refer to the recent formation of industrial associations, a word about them is in order. These associations now number about 3,000; they are middle-level bodies which provide centralized research, planning, procurement and marketing facilities for the enterprises which comprise them. They receive control figures from ministries, and are responsible for working out detailed plans. These then constitute control figures for the enterprises, which work out the plan details at their own level. What is essential in relation to the claim that the associations represent a "form of competition" in which the "weak are gobbled up by the strong"[17] is the little-known fact that the associations are run by a board composed of representatives of the enterprises on a one-enterprise-one-vote basis. Given that the associations were formed to take over many planning functions originally performed by the ministries, they represent a marked increase in participation in planning by collectives at the operating level.[18]

An aspect of the recent economic reforms that has captivated the "capitalist restorationists" is the heightened emphasis on profit and profitability (the rate of profit) as indicators of performance, both for enterprises and for their superior organizations. This emphasis has led to the interpretation that profit has become "the objective and principal criterion of industrial activity and production in general."[19] Against this, Sweezy observes, correctly in my view, that the Soviet stress on heavy industry shows profit to have a minor role in overall investment and growth decisions. Sweezy also points out that the goal of maximizing profit is carried out by the enterprise under conditions of planned levels of output and planned prices. He might have added that, as an aspect of long-term planning decisions, the planned levels of profitability vary from sector to sector. Thus, the coefficient of general effectiveness (something like an output-to-investment ratio) differs by a factor of 5-6 as between light industry and heavy and extractive industry (coal).[20] In sum, no evidence, so far as the present writer is aware, has ever been presented showing enterprise profits to be a determining factor in output, growth, or technical change. It should also be mentioned that prices are planned with social policy in mind; the massive housing subsidy, greater in magnitude than the Soviet military budget, is perhaps the best example of this.

Opinion differs among "capitalist restorationists" as to the precise location of the state bourgeoisie (or, alternatively, of the bureaucratic ruling class). As a guide to thinking about the problem, the above census data may be helpful (Table 1).

In absolute numbers, there were 1,976,000 people in the

TABLE 1.

	% of total employed population		number in each category, 1970 as
	1959	1970	% of 1959
Total employed population	100	100	116.2
Physical labor	80.5	72.7	105.0
Mental labor	19.5	27.3	162.6
Workers in state administration	0.249	0.183	85.4
Party, Y.C.L., trade union	0.147	0.169	133.6
Economic management	1.108	1.363	143.0
Engineers and technicians	4.081	7.335	208.9
Teachers and counselors	2.542	3.639	166.3
Scientists and higher school instructors	0.319	0.659	240.2
Planning and record-keeping personnel	3.533	4.404	144.9

SOURCE: Adapted from data in *Current Digest of the Soviet Press*, Vol. XXVI, No. 49.

state, Party and economic management categories in 1971. All three categories grew more rapidly than the labor force as a whole, although much less rapidly than scientists, technicians and engineers. Using the term "state" more loosely than do the Soviet statisticians, the "state bourgeoisie" must reside somewhere in that base of two million people. They exercise the function of management — one of the three legs of the three-legged stool of bourgeois power described in Section II of this paper. One of the other legs, private ownership, is well known to be non-existent in the Soviet Union.

What about a social upper class? All studies of personal income distribution in the USSR show a spread among statistically significant sectors of the employed population in the neighborhood of five to one.[21] "It is recognized among the Soviet public that individuals can earn much more if they occupy one of a few thousand top ministerial or Party posts, or are famous for their endeavors in the arts or sciences."[22] The question at issue is not the effect of the relative handful of high-income individuals on Soviet life in general, nor the historical or other explanation for their income. It is, rather, whether those individuals occupy a unique and uniform position in the production relations of Soviet society, so that their income, whatever its nominal form, is determined to be essentially a surplus drawn from the labor of the rest of society. On this basis they would qualify as a "bourgeoisie" of some sort. Note that the ratio of "surplus" consumption to wages would be negligible; using Matthews' figures as a rough guide, on the order of .0002!*

Further, the trend in income distribution has, by all accounts, been toward greater equality. Thus, "in 1968, average money earnings for industrial workers were reported to be approximately 156 per cent of their 1955 level. For minimum wages, the corresponding figure is in the range of 255-286 per cent."[23] The tendency to raise the lowest incomes while holding

---

* Of course, proponents of the "state capitalist" interpretation will insist that the investment fund as well as the personal income of the elite is to be included in surplus value. To avoid misunderstanding, recall that this section is concerned only with the personal income distribution. However, an important implication of the conception of the capitalist class put forward in Section II of this paper is that the share of surplus value devoted to capitalists' consumption must be non-negligible, so that the social upper class can have a viable existence.

the upper ones constant diminishes the impact of the higher incomes on the overall quality of income distribution. It must also be remembered that no part of the high incomes can be *invested* — there simply are no securities markets in the USSR, and investment abroad is prohibited by law — except in the unimportant sense of savings in the state-owned bank, which pays a uniform (but real!) interest rate of 3%.

The question whether the income differentials are linked to positions of authority must be answered in the negative. The top government and management jobs pay well, but the really high incomes, as Matthews and others make clear, are in the top scientific posts and in the arts. These incomes, in short, are more in the nature of "quasi-rents," returns to scarce talent, than the result of membership in an elite managing class.

Turning to the issues of residential segregation and differential education, suffice it to say that no evidence has ever been forthcoming which purports to establish these facts. Soviet cities are not divided into "restricted" and working-class districts. Soviet educational curricula and investment per child are uniform; there are no private schools. (The special physics-math schools for talented children raise another problem, of differential backgrounds of children of intellectuals and of workers doing physical labor; but this hardly amounts to an example of elite education for the elite.) The overall impact of education is equalizing. Between the census years 1959 and 1970, the proportion of the population with a higher or (complete or incomplete) secondary education rose by 34 per cent. During the same period, the proportion of production workers with this level of education increased by 60-65 per cent. [24]

Evidence on the class background of the occupants of administrative posts is not supportive of the concept of a self-reproducing elite. Data on leading cadre in all three sectors — state, Party, economic management — indicate that the great majority, typically 75-90 per cent, came from working class or peasant backgrounds and started their careers as production workers or farmers. Studies of CPSU membership show that the working class proportion is steadily rising: 41.6% of the total membership in 1976, workers account for about 58% of new members. [25] ("Working class" in this usage is a narrow category; the other categories are office employees, scientists, etc.) Finally, there is some evidence that intermarriage among different occupational strata is increasing; one source reports that "one in every three marriages is contracted between people belonging to different classes and social groups."[26] The home, to this extent, does not become a vehicle for imposing a stratified conception of society in the minds of children.

Much of the evidence on education, inter-marriage, etc., has too wide a sweep to serve as *direct* evidence against the hypothesis of a very small elite minority. I believe it does constitute *indirect* evidence against that hypothesis, however, for the simple reason that in a society whose broad strata are gradually evening, it becomes harder to envision any plausible mechanism for insulating and perpetuating a tiny upper-class layer. In the capitalist United States, an extremely wealthy social upper class is rooted in a soil of broad-based stratification. The theorists of a Soviet "ruling class" should explain how the Soviet elite manages to reproduce itself without the paraphernalia of a society based on stratification from top down.*

All this seems fairly definitive. Nevertheless, we must pursue the concept of a Soviet "state bourgeoisie" to its highest degree of rarified disembodiment. We must imagine a bourgeoisie that does not receive surplus value in the form of personal income, that does not form a distinct social upper class, that does not own property, that is constituted from the ranks of the working class and peasantry.** Apparently, we must accept as a matter of definition that the present holders of high office simply *are* the capitalist ruling class! And we must forget to ask how their power to rule is reproduced in the production relations of their society.

---

* Remembering the role of a middle class in the reproduction of class relations in capitalist societies, we note that nothing like a middle class exists in the USSR, in the sense of autonomous, small property owners. In spite of the fact that Soviet literature and practice carefully acknowledge the still-existing distinctions among strata, the professional workers in the USSR have forms of organization largely determined by the forms characteristic of production workers — i.e., trade unions — and integrated with them.

**An important qualification is necessary, however. Since there have been barely three decades of uninterrupted peacetime construction and succession of the generations, it could be argued that inheritance of position within a definable stratum of job-holding rulers has not yet had enough time to emerge. In a rapidly industrializing society, it is natural that the present leadership come from non-elite backgrounds.

There are simply no operational criteria that are exactly relevant to this claim which therefore borders on tautology. Some tentative observations and questions about the organization and impact of administrative posts in the USSR may, however, be formulated. I know of no evidence that suggests that high offices in the Soviet Union are held within single families (nepotism); that present office holders can choose their successors; or that offices can be bought or sold. There is considerable evidence that the statutory rights of recall and control by lower bodies are exercised.† The historical record seems to indicate that the top leadership is rather strictly bound by consensus as far as policy making is concerned and that the success of an individual in a leading position depends on his/her ability to formulate policy, to convince, to organize and delegate responsibility in a way that enhances the morale of the political or economic unit or units within his/her jurisdiction. In short, there appear to be strict limits to the exercise of arbitrary personal authority — as N.S. Khrushchev discovered.

Finally, we observe that the hypothesis of a stable bureaucratic elite depends on whether the same individuals occupy the leading positions in the several hierarchies. For example, do the trade union leadership and the economic management leadership coalesce? Do the top office holders in these areas interact with each other significantly more than with their own memberships or constituencies? Unless solid evidence is produced to the contrary, the answer seems to be no. It is unheard of, for example, for a member of management at an enterprise to be head of the trade union or even to hold high office in the trade union (although management personnel must be *members* of the trade

---

† For example, summing up her discussion of the handling of labor disputes, Emily Clark Brown writes: "In spite of continuing reports of violations and of reprisals against critics, workers, with their increasing education and experience, show signs of more independence in their protests. When they persist they can elect local and regional officers who will function responsibly. And they have channels through which they can bring pressure on higher authorities to support their demands" (Brown, *op. cit.*, p. 229). On the statutory right of recall, from article 107 of the Constitution: "Deputies who have not justified the confidence of their constituents may be recalled at any time by decision of a majority of the electors in accordance with the procedures established by law." Soviet sources claim that, in the 1971-76 period, more than one thousand deputies in the Russian Federation (of a total of one million) were indeed recalled under this provision (*USSR '77, Sixty Soviet Years*, Novosti Press Agency, 1977, p. 29).

union and subject to the discipline of membership). Thus, management confronts a trade union leadership from the ranks of the workers, and one which can invoke the authority of the higher trade union bodies. Needless to say, the people in positions of authority in both trade union and management are overwhelmingly members of the Communist Party. But they derive the power of their offices from the organizations where those offices are located, not from Party membership, which is widely shared. In general, they will not be members of the same Party branch or unit.

The main point, of course, is that Soviet society is constituted in such a way that leaders of trade unions *must* function to fulfill the tasks of trade unions and leaders of enterprises *must* function to fulfill the tasks of enterprises. In the absence of spontaneous competition and the social irresponsibility of private accumulation, any antagonism or elemental conflict emerging from these roles immediately becomes a political problem which requires a political solution.

We come, finally, to the question of the existence of capitalist laws of motion. We will ignore "laws of motion" which are controversial in the context of unambiguously capitalist societies, such as the law of the falling tendency of the rate of profit.

The absence of significant unemployment, inflation and cyclical growth must be mentioned again in this context. The attempt to portray Soviet society as one in which polarization and relative immiseration are occurring would seem to come to grief against the trend toward equalization in income distribution, already cited. The economic reforms of the 1960s with their Statute on the Rights of Enterprises, and the recent devolution onto the industrial associations of planning tasks previously carried out by central bodies show a trend toward decentralization of control, within the framework of comprehensive planning. This is small comfort to theorists of centralization and "accumulation of capital" in the USSR; although Marx's concept of *concentration* — aggregation into larger and larger producing units — seems to apply to the development of productive forces in Soviet society as well as in capitalist ones. We have already noted the priority development of heavy industry, unlike any known capitalist development experience.*

One point of interest in this connection, however, refers to the view that there is "widespread anarchy of production"[27] in the USSR, a claim that Sweezy accepts, and interprets to mean that "conformity to plan may be diminishing with the passage of time." This is likely because the Soviet citizenry are as likely to "try to circumvent or thwart the plan as to conform to it."[28] No evidence is adduced. Certainly conformity to the 8th, 9th and 10th five-year plans is greater than to the 1st, 2nd and 3rd. The twin sources of non-conformity — inconsistent obligatory indicators and general economic scarcity — have both been reduced in importance by the growth of the productive capacities of the Soviet economy and by the decentralization of detail planning and use of generalizing efficiency indicators. Sweezy mentions "dealing in stolen state property" as though it can be taken for granted that this is a major component in Soviet gross domestic product; even if it were, one would be tempted to remind those who would base social and historical explanation on this circumstance that "the objects of plunder must be continually reproduced."

V.

In conclusion: the "state capitalist" hypothesis is false. The absence of private ownership of means of production in the Soviet Union is *material;* citing it is not a matter of confusing juridical relations with real relations, but of establishing the *necessary* proximate forms of *capitalist* real relations of production. The concept of a state capitalist mode of production is a category which betrays a total misunderstanding of the nature, genesis and requirements of the power of capital.

To the extent that the "state capitalist" hypothesis can be operationalized into an empirical test, the Soviet Union fails grandly. The overwhelming weight of the evidence establishes the absence of all of the necessary conditions for the existence of a ruling upper class: a social upper class with a distinct life style,

---

* In this connection Sweezy writes: "If profit had been the main consideration...there would have been much more investment in agriculture and consumer-goods industries than there actually has been.... How can this be explained if the USSR is indeed to be considered capitalist and profit is the dominant factor in the functioning of the economy?" *Op. cit.,* p. 16.

a legitimated claim to privilege via property-owning status, and the capacity to reproduce a continuous and antagonistic leadership through control over the filling of the top administrative posts. To the extent one sees "capitalism" when one looks at the Soviet administrative apparatus, one fails to understand the inner nature of capitalism. This is perhaps the most serious implication of the "state capitalist" hypothesis and its acceptance in left circles.

It is appropriate to ask the proponents of the "capitalist restorationist" view to state the conditions under which their claim would be falsified. What changes would have to occur in the USSR in order for the political and administrative leadership there to escape characterization as a "state bourgeoisie"? If this characterization rests upon the simple fact that the USSR has a central state and hierarchical organization of authority, then it rests on a foundation of classical anarchism, identifying the ruling class with state authority in general and mystifying the origin of the social power wielded by the state — a theory quite consistent with libertarian conservatism, but hardly with Marxism. If it rests on other grounds, those grounds must be stated. If the "capitalist restorationists" fail to state them in a manner consistent with a Marxist approach to social classes, we will be forced to conclude that their position boils down to a pure expression of hostility; its social-psychological origin in the ideological pressures exerted by our own capitalist society is not hard to detect, and its political expression is revealed as the most elementary utopian idealism.

The "exploitative bureaucracy" hypothesis is little better off. More sensitive to the precise quality of capitalist exploitation, it nevertheless fails to produce a convincing explanation for the capacity of the Soviet "bureaucracy" to draw unto itself the power to exploit, unless one succumbs to the illusion that the power resides in the "office" itself — surely a confession of theoretical bankruptcy. As in the case of the "capitalist" view, the "bureaucrats" come to personify an evil which almost appears to have mystical origins.* It should be stressed that the

---

* The related concept of a "degenerated workers' state" fails on similar grounds. Its hollowness can be revealed by simply asking, "degenerated from what?" The utopian character of the "golden age" psychology embedded in the concept becomes clear.

Marxist critique of the "bureaucratic class" notion is fundamental to the critique of the "capitalist" interpretation, since the latter ultimately rests on the conception of a disembodied state bourgeoisie that draws its capitalist qualities out of the ether, so to speak. The heart of the matter is the basic Marxist perception that power does not *reside in* its empirical loci; but rather, that the observed exercise of power, through the offices of state, managerial function, etc., is a manifestation of underlying class relations. Without a thorough-going critique of the "bureaucratic mode of production," the inadequacy of the "state capitalist" approach cannot be fully established.

The evidence, then, when evaluated in a consistently Marxist way, appears to be at least consistent with the view that the Soviet social formation is socialist, and inconsistent with any of the proposed alternatives.* It need hardly be said that neither this conclusion nor the very preliminary evidentiary basis on which it rests preclude a wide range of views on the state of health of Soviet society and on the nature of challenges to socialist development presented by bureaucratic malfunctioning, corruption, etc.

We must recognize that movements for revolutionary change in capitalist societies cannot be divorced from the practice of socialist construction in all parts of the world. That element of realism, which often seems to be a barrier to acceptance of the left in this country, may actually prove to be the only basis on which the left can acquire a major role. The U.S. working class will demand a socialism that is *of* this world, and will reject the implicit utopianism of those who attack all existing socialist societies from idealist positions. Thus we learn from the Soviet Union two vital lessons about our own society: the

---

* To avoid encumbering this paper with a long discussion of the formal definition of socialism, I simply state two salient characteristics: A socialist society is one in which the determinant production relation (that which dominates the mode of production) is non-antagonistic, i.e., does not involve class exploitation. Stated positively, this means that the working class rules, and determines the character and functioning of state power and the economic and cultural institutions. Moreover, reflecting the emergence of socialism on the historical basis of capitalist productive forces and relations, production and distribution are governed by conscious, political, *intentional* control, in the form of comprehensive planning, which contains and determines the social content of the subordinate commodity-money relations.

nature of the capitalist principle that dominates its development, and the nature of the path to revolutionary change. Utopian-idealist positions which take the guise of "Marxist" analyses of the USSR are major obstacles on that path.

NOTES

[1] Additional contributions to this literature may be cited: Bernard Chavance, "On the Relations of Production in the USSR," *Monthly Review*, May 1977; "Paul Sweezy Replies," *Monthly Review*, May 1977. See also H. H. Ticktin, "Towards a Political Economy of the USSR," *Critique*, Vol. 1, No. 1, Spring, 1973; Ernest Mandel, "Some Comments on H. H. Ticktin's 'Towards a Political Economy of the USSR'," *Critique*, Autumn, 1974.

[2] A good source of recent expositions of the classic Marxist concepts is Jesse G. Schwartz, ed., *The Subtle Anatomy of Capitalism* (Goodyear, 1976). A more detailed formulation by the present writer will be found in Part III of "Values and Prices of Production: The Political Economy of the Transformation Problem," *Science & Society*, Winter 1973-74, pp. 404-36.

[3] Cf. Sweezy, *op. cit.*: "... what distinguishes capitalism is not only the existence of wage-labor (i.e., the capital-labor relation) but also the division of capital into a multiplicity of units, each one seeking to expand both absolutely and relatively to the others ... [A]ll of what Marx called capitalism's 'laws of motion' depend in a crucial way on this underlying fragmentation of capital ... in no way superceded or overcome by the kind of state 'planning' which exists in even the most advanced capitalist countries of the West" (p. 18).

[4] Chavance, *op. cit.*, p. 2.

[5] In conditions of late monopoly capitalism, inflation must be added to this list.

[6] I.e., Marx's Preface to the first edition of *Capital*, where "individuals are dealt with only in so far as they are the personifications of economic categories, embodiments of particular class-relations and class-interests" (*Capital*, Vol. I, Kerr ed., p. 15).

[7] "The more a ruling class is able to assimilate the most prominent men of the dominated classes, the more stable and dangerous its rule." Marx, quoted in E. Digby Baltzell, *The Protestant Establishment* (Random House, 1964), pp. 3-4.

[8] Bettelheim, *Class Struggles in the USSR*, Vol. 1, p. 21.

[9] Marx, Preface to the *Critique of Political Economy* (Kerr, 1913), pp. 11-13.

[10] Except in transitional instances where two or more social classes achieve rough parity of power and the state achieves a relative autonomy in the balance. Cf. Ralph Miliband, *The State in Capitalist Society* (Basic Books, 1969); Nicos Poulantzas, *Political Power and Social Classes* (New Left Books, 1975).

[11] See note 1.

[12] A seminal source on Soviet trade unions and their activities is Emily Clark Brown, *Soviet Trade Unions and Labor Relations* (Harvard University Press, 1966). See also Leonard Joel Kirsch, *Soviet Wages: Changes in Structure and Administration Since 1956* (MIT Press, 1972).

[13] "... the industrial relations system in the Soviet Union, however imperfect in application, tends toward a constitutional system with large elements of worker-participation. At best the result in union-management cooperation within the framework of central planning and a common communist ideology .... The trend is toward an industrial relations system combining strong feelings of collective responsibility and common interests with opportunity for individuals to develop their capacities." Brown, *op. cit.*, pp. 327-328.

[14] *Labour Legislation in the USSR* (Novosti Press Agency Publishing House, Moscow, 1972).

[15] On "inflation" in the USSR, see David Laibman, "Seven Ways to Find Inflation in the Soviet Union," *New World Review*, July-August 1975.

[16] A recent useful description of Soviet economic organization will be found in Joseph S. Berliner, *The Innovation Decision in Soviet Industry* (MIT Press, 1976), Chapter 2.

[17] Chavance, *op. cit.*, p. 10.

[18] A description of Soviet production and industrial associations will be found in Hans-Hermann Hohmann, Michael C. Kaser and Karl C. Thalheim, eds., *The New Economic Systems of Eastern Europe* (University of California Press, 1975), p. 8ff.

[19] Chavance, *op. cit.*, p. 6.

[20] Frank A. Durgin, "The Soviet 1969 Standard Methodology for Investment Allocation Versus 'Universally Correct' Methods," *ACES Bulletin*, Vol. XIX, No. 2, Summer 1977, p. 41.

[21] Mervyn Matthews, *Class and Society in Soviet Russia* (Walker and Company, 1972), p. 92.

[22] *Ibid.*, p. 93.

[23] Kirsch, *Soviet Wages*, *op. cit.*, p. 183.

[24] Calculated from data in the *Current Digest of the Soviet Press*. Vol. XXVI, No. 49.

[25] *Pravda*, April 9, 1976.

[26] M. Rutkevich, "The Intelligentsia in Socialist Society," *Pravda*, May 16, 1972; translation in *Daily Review* (Novosti Press Agency), May 16, 1972, p. 5; M. Rutkevich, "Social Structure of Developed Socialist Society," *Pravda*, July 4, 1975; translation in *Daily Review* (Novosti Press Agency), July 4, 1975, p. 5.

[27] Chavance, p. 7.

[28] Sweezy, p. 16-17.

Soviet Socialism and Proletarian Internationalism

Al Szymanski

It is peculiar that the R.C.P. (as well as others) talk about Mao Tse-tung's "revolutionary scientific analysis of the process of capitalist restoration." Nowhere have Mao or the Chinese Communist Party ever provided a systematic analysis of what is alleged to be the process of capitalist restoration. Mao's comments as well as Chinese Party documents on "Soviet Social Imperialism" limit themselves exclusively to a few very broad generalities about leaders "taking the capitalist road" supplemented by exposés of specific abuses, e.g., such and such a leader has a Dacha, so and so accumulated a million rubles in the underground economy, etc.*

Albert Szymanski, author of *Is The Red Flag Flying? The Political Economy of the Soviet Union Today*, teaches sociology at the University of Oregon.

*For the Chinese position see, for example, "How the Soviet Revisionists Carry out All-Round Restoration of Capitalism in the U.S.S.R." (Peking: Foreign Languages Press, 1968), "Down with the New Tsars!" (Peking: Foreign Languages Press, 1969), *Social Imperialism: Reprints from Peking Review* N.O. edited by Yenan Books, Berkeley, California and *Social Imperialism: The Soviet Union Today*, 1977, Yenan Book Ed., Berkeley, California.

The suggestion in some of the 1960s and early 1970s Chinese documents that because of the existence of material incentives in the USSR, the appointment of managers by central ministries, the relative centralization of decision making (or the relative autonomy of decision making given some managers), the degree of income inequality, or the degree of commodification of the necessities of life, the USSR is capitalist, is seriously faulty, both because none of these things speak to the Marxist definition of socialism (workers' power with distribution according to work) and they are inconsistent, since at the time, such countries as Korea, Albania, Rumania (countries the Chinese considered socialist at the time) had very similar institutions. Further, China before 1965, to say nothing of the Soviet Union in the pre-1956 period, had pretty much the same institutions. All in Maoist eyes were considered to be essentially socialist. Other Chinese Maoist statements on the matter consist solely of undocumented assertions clearly contrary to empirical reality, such as income inequality has increased, workers' job security has significantly decreased, the plan is not really effective, the party elite passes its top positions on to their children, etc.

The ad hoc and unscientific presentation of the position of capitalist restoration by the Chinese Maoists was manifested in Western Maoists attempting to do the work never done by the Chinese themselves, i.e., attempting to present a systematic and documented analysis of the nature of the USSR based in Marxist theory.

The analysis that follows will critique many of the notions most common to such Maoist attempts to prove the USSR capitalist and imperialist. I will not focus exclusively on the R.C.P. analysis, (in my opinion, the best argued and documented of the attempts), but rather on the most common Maoist arguments (as found for example in Sweezy [1981], Bettelheim [1975], and Nicolaus [1975] as well as the R.C.P. [1974]).

Unlike the Chinese and most Western Maoist attempts to construct a systematic argument that supports the 1960s Chinese claims, the R.C.P. correctly defines the essence of socialism as workers' power over the state and economy (not as a question of markets). The R.C.P. analysis, however, like almost all Maoist attempts to support Mao's claim, is fatally flawed by *de facto* slipping into a syndicalist/anarchist definition of socialism as well as by grossly distorting the empirical evidence on the USSR.

This critique of the Maoist position on the USSR will attempt to do four things: (1) point out its unreasonable and un-Marxist definition of socialism; (2) argue that while its categorization of state capitalism is for the most part internally coherent, compatible with Marxist thinking, and viable as a social type, the empirical evidence is incompatible with the USSR being such a society (or anything remotely resembling it); (3) show that the USSR, in spite of its travails of the 1920s, 1930s, and 1940s, has made considerable progress in constructing an authentically socialist society; and (4) show that the USSR's relations with the less developed countries of Asia, Africa and Latin America, as well as with Eastern Europe, are qualitatively different than those of the USA with the Less Developed Countries, i.e., the USSR is *not* imperialist.

The Soviet Social Formation

Maoists seem to argue that a truly socialist society would not rely on material incentives or emphasize private consumption, instead emphasizing collective consumption (e.g., communal cooking and eating, neighborhood laundries, mass transit, etc.), and further that it of necessity must be highly politicized (i.e., the concerns and motivations of individuals should not be focused on private affairs, careers and consumption levels). Such a claim both confuses the traditional Marxist categories of socialism (where distribution is according to work) and communism (where distribution is according to need), and the Marxist concept of socialism as workers' control of the *means of production* (in contrast with utopian socialism's emphasis on collective *consumption*). It further seems to impose an unrealistic criteria for an authentically revolutionary society in the technologically backward regions of a predominantly capitalist world (at least during the first generations after a revolution). The desire (in good part induced by knowledge of Western life styles) which large portions of the working people of socialist countries have for consumer goods cannot be attributed to the lack of working class power (i.e., to a state bourgeoisie). Whether or not middle-class Marxists in the affluent West approve, most workers in the socialist countries authentically desire a car, a bigger apartment, more meat on the family table, etc. And there is no reason why this desire is logically incompatible with the traditional Marxist notion of working class power and control of the means of production (even if our model of what workers *should do* with their power is more ecologically sound or collective than theirs).

More importantly, Maoism often confuses the traditional anarchist and syndicalist positions on the role of direct producer's control of the workplace with that of Marxism, thereby confusing the question of the degree of *centralization* of decision making with the question of which class has state power. Socialism means *workers' power* over the economy and state. It is certainly logically possible for such power to be exercised in a highly centralized manner, for example by workers formulating or approving a central plan, with all the details worked out by hired employees whose job is merely to implement *the how* of realizing the workers' goals (and who, of course, would have to have considerable operational discretion in each enterprise to do so). The realization of a central plan (which in principle is most definitely a Marxist notion) would seem to imply severe limits on the autonomy of workers in any given enterprise to make decisions about what is produced, what prices are to be charged, the inputs necessary and even the essential organization of the production process (since such decisions must be deduced from the democratically established plan), e.g., once the working class *as a whole* decided it wanted mass transit instead of private cars, transport equipment workers cannot have the right to decide to produce cars instead of buses, or once they decide they need a house for every family within five years, construction workers cannot refuse to use the most efficient building materials.

It is also logically possible for a socialist society to be decentralized and to operate without a central plan. Here the workers of every enterprise *would be free* to decide what to produce, how to produce it and what prices to charge. The problems incumbent on such a mode of socialism in practice are immense, i.e., the re-establishment of markets and all their corollaries of unemployment, advertising, inflation, inequities in income, irrationalities in production, etc. There are a whole range of intermediate models of authentically socialist societies with different combinations of highly centralized planning and decentralized participation. In fact, every existing socialist society known to this author has combined the two in some degree. It is a mistake, as for example, both Bettelheim and Sweezy do, *a priori* to dismiss a society as not socialist if central planning prevails over workers' participation in enterprise management. The essential question is which class establishes the central plan and which class does it serve, not how much say in day-to-day operational decision-making workers have in an enterprise.

Another common Maoist mistake is to confuse the traditional Marxist position that the division of labor between mental and manual work will ultimately be abolished in communist society with the Marxist (and reasonable) position that this need not be the case in socialist societies. The task of socialism is to raise consciousness (as well as the productive forces) to such a level that the division of labor between supervision, planning and manual work can eventually be abolished. But this is the long term task of socialism, not part of its definition. Again, Maoism seems to accept the traditional anarchist position that the distinctions between engineers, administrators and workers can disappear more or less immediately after a revolution, rather than the far more realistic view that the long project of socialist construction will require the maintenance of such differences for some time before they wither away. Again, socialism means workers' power with distribution *according to work* (which implies different work for different people), *not* the abolition of the manual-mental division of labor.

A Look at the Evidence

The Maoist position argues that the USSR is a stratified society, with a deep chasm between the ruling stratum of bureaucrats and managers on the one side and the working people on the other, in which the state bourgeoisie allegedly exploits the working class in a manner comparable to the capitalist class in the West. While it is true that there are significant variations in income and privileges in the USSR, the range is far less than has existed in any known class society (capitalist or pre-capitalist), and certainly qualitatively less than exists in contemporary U.S. society. For example, in 1975 the ratio of the wage exceeded by the top 10% in the USSR to the wage exceeded by the lowest 10%

was 2.9 (compared to 6.2 in the U.S.) (Hough, 1974: 12). The highest incomes in the USSR are those of top educators, scientists and artists who make a maximum of 1,200 to 1,500 rubles a month; top government officials earn about 600 rubles a month (about 3-4 times the wages of industrial workers), and leading enterprise directors from 190 to 400 rubles a month (exclusive of bonuses), about 1.3 to 2.5 times workers' wages (Matthews, 1972, p. 91-3). In the U.S., on the other hand, the spread between top managers and leading capitalists and average workers' wages are of the order of 200 to 1. The income spread between the very top political and economic positions and the average industrial wage in the USSR is, in fact, approximately the same as that between self-employed professionals and the average industrial wage in the U.S. (where the ratio of physicians' income to the industrial wage is about 2.5). Thus, the equivalent of the economic and political elite in the USSR appears to be upper *middle class* professionals in the U.S., and not the top managers and capitalists (i.e., the Soviet "power elite" appears to have privileges equivalent only to the middle class in the U.S.). This is a radical contrast with any known class society.

It is commonly claimed that the distribution of real income in Soviet society is considerably more unequal than the distribution of money income. However, the distribution of real goods is, in fact, *more* equal than the income distribution suggests. While enterprise managers receive bonuses (averaging about 25% of salaries) and access to certain fringe benefits such as cars of the enterprise (as do state officials) as well as somewhat better goods in their trade union run shops, the working class receives, in addition to *their* bonuses, a wide range of free and heavily subsidized services (day care, university education, medicine, public transport, housing, etc.) as well as for many categories of workers (miners, heavy industrial workers) well stocked union shops, whose net effect is to make the distribution of material goods considerably more egalitarian in practice than the income statistics indicate. Further, Soviet pricing policy, which sets the costs of necessities such as basic food stuffs at below their cost of production, while setting very high prices for such luxury goods as automobiles, has a significant effect in equalizing the distribution of Soviet consumer goods more than income statistics suggest. Studies of the effect of the "social wage" (i.e., free services and goods) on the distribution of income within heavy industry in the USSR have found that the spread of about 2 to 1 in take home wages is reduced to about 1.5 to 1 because of the egalitarian effect of goods provided on the basis of need. (Osborn, 1970:32). Studies of the distribution of housing and automobiles, as well as goods available differentially in trade union stores (the so-called "special stores"), find that there is no tendency for there to be a high concentration of privilege (Osborn, 1970:Ch. 6).

Further, contrary to the claim that the Soviet Union has undergone a period of increased material inequality during which productive resources have been channeled into satisfying the wants of a privileged minority, the USSR has experienced a rather radical equalization of both incomes and actual living standards in the last generation. For example, the ratio of the wage exceeded by the top 10% to that exceeded by all but the bottom 10% *declined* from 4.4 in 1956 to 2.9 in 1975. Soviet policy since the mid-1950s has been to freeze the highest salaries while rapidly bringing up the lowest (especially those in rural sectors) (Hough, 1974). Further, the significance of the social wage has continually grown. It stood at 23% of average earnings in 1940, 29% in 1950 and 35% through the 1960s (Osborn, 1970, p. 32). One would hardly expect such a radical equalization in living standards just after the time Maoists claim the state bureaucracy consolidated themselves as a new ruling class. One should reasonably expect a class that controls production and exploits the working class, as well as controls the state, to *use* its power; and further, for its rule as exploiter to be manifested in a high and growing income (in money as well as social benefits). That neither is the case is a strong argument that the theory of a state bourgeoisie can not apply to the USSR.

If a state bourgeoisie is a true ruling class then it must be able to pass on its privileges to its children. There is no evidence at all that the group usually designated as the state bourgeoisie, (the upper echelons of the party, state and military apparatuses), have any significant tendency of passing on their top positions to their children. It is true, however, that children of the intelligentsia have a 1.5 to 2.0 greater chance than manual working class children of beginning higher education (but it should be noted that this differential has been steadily shrinking since 1950) (Hough, 1974). It should also be noted that this differential is lower than that for any advanced capitalist country.* In the mid-1960s, of the 47 government ministers of the USSR (the nearest Soviet equivalent to the richest owners and top managers of the West), 40% had parents who were manual workers, 27% parents who were peasants and only 18% parents who were in the intelligentsia. Of Central Committee members, 36% had manual working class parents, 47% peasant parents and only 16% nonmanual (both intelligentsia and white collar worker) parents, i.e., about 90% of top party officials come from humble backgrounds (Azrael, 1966, pp. 157-67; Lane, 1971, p. 122-36; Rigby, 1968, p. 11). Studies of the backgrounds of Politburo members show that there is no tendency for the proportion of top leaders recruited from the intelligentsia to increase over time. It should be noted that in contrast to the top political and economic positions, which are recruited very heavily from the working class and peasantry, scientific and professional positions do have a strong intergenerational linkage. About half of Soviet professionals and scientists had professional and scientist parents.

This situation contrasts strongly with that in the capitalist countries where the probability approaches 100% that if one's parents were corporate wealthy one will be as well. The Rockefellers, Fords, Mellons, etc., pass their wealth and position on from generation to generation. Further, the members of the boards of directors of the leading corporations tend to come predominantly from those who *inherit* large sums of wealth. Very, very few top managers, government officials, and even fewer wealthy businessmen, have working class parents. The contrast with the Soviets on these scores is extreme. Thus, in conclusion, although there is a tendency for children of the intelligentsia to themselves enter the intelligentsia, this is a linkage of essentially *middle class* positions and says nothing about the linkage of the top economic political positions. The vast majority of these are filled in each generation from people of humble backgrounds. There are very, very few cases of the children of former top ministers or party leaders becoming themselves top ministers or party leaders (where are the

---

*See Szymanski (1979) for an elaboration of this argument.

children and nephews/nieces of Lenin, Stalin, Khrushchev, Brezhnev, etc?).

These facts, and a multitude of other Western studies of the USSR,* force us to the conclusion that: (1) there is no wealthy class which has a living standard or wealth remotely comparable to that of the economic elite of the capitalist countries; (2) the top positions in Soviet society, unlike as in capitalist societies, are largely filled by people of common origins; (3) no privileged elite social stratum exists with its own highly distinctive life style, exclusive intermarriage patterns and virtual certainty of passing on its positions to its children, as *is* the case in the capitalist countries; and (4) the differences in income, life style and passing on of privileges to children is very much like the differences between the working class and the professional middle class in the U.S., indicating that those in "power elite" positions in the USSR are much more like middle managers and professionals in the West than they are like an owning or ruling class. In sum there is no evidence that a "state bourgeoisie" exists in the USSR.

The claim that a state bourgeoisie is drawn from a reasonably homogeneous group with all the essential attributes of a class, including the ability to reproduce itself, that the individuals at the top of Soviet society have been shaped into a self-conscious and essentially self-reproducing ruling class, and the assertion of the existence of a deeply class divided society in which consciousness of the we-they division on both sides of the great divide is as strong as it is in Western capitalist societies, could not be further from the truth.

Maoists claim that the Soviet working class is as powerless and as exploited as the working class in Western societies, and further that it is essentially exploited in the same way, i.e., it is forced to sell its labor power as a commodity to the state bourgeoisie who *de facto* owns the economic enterprises and allocates labor power and its product in their own class interest. Again, a careful study of relations of production in Soviet enterprises can not sustain such a claim.

It is virtually impossible to dismiss a Soviet worker. While

---

*See chapter 4 of my book *Is The Red Flag Flying?* (1979) for a much more thorough review of these studies.

the working class in the Soviet Union pretty much has lifetime job security, all workers are able to quit their jobs, and with no difficulty (because of the extreme labor shortage, a product of economic planning) they can easily find many comparable alternative employments. There is no reserve army of labor putting pressure on workers. This makes the Soviet labor system extremely advantageous to the producers, and sharply differentiates the Soviet labor system from both capitalist and precapitalist labor systems. Wage differentials by regions, industries, occupations and skill levels are established by the central plan in order to encourage workers to take those positions and develop those skills that the economy most needs, as well as to realize conceptions of social justice, e.g., coal miners, for example, are paid more than most doctors. The highly advantageous position of Soviet workers should not be underestimated as both an indicator of the class power of Soviet workers and a means for workers to exert influence over the administrators in their particular enterprises (given the lack of a reserve army of labor, the quitting of a significant number of workers to take jobs elsewhere could be devastating to a manager's bonus prospects). In fact, mass resignations have been known to occur.

Maoists often claim that Soviet workers are a mere instrument in the hands of a powerful state and lack any meaningful control over what is produced, how it is produced, and to what uses it is put. Bettelheim, for example, argues that "the factories are run by managers whose relations with 'their' workers are relations of command and who are responsible only to their superiors." In fact, Soviet workers have a multitude of institutionalized forms by which they influence the decision making processes within the enterprises where they work. Further, the role of worker participation has been continually growing since the mid-1950s. There is near consensus among Western social scientists who have seriously studied the USSR that workers' participation in the USSR goes considerably beyond that found in American firms. (See Granick, 1961, chapter 13; Conquest, 1967, chapter 5; Wilczynski, 1970, p. 209.) Soviet trade unions (especially since 1956) play an important role in most aspects of enterprise management, especially on issues having to do with job allocation and safety and workers' welfare, but also including workers' input to all aspects of decision making. (See Conquest, 1967, p. 157-59; Wilczynski, 1970, p. 100-02; Sherman, 1969.)

Production conferences elected by all workers in the enterprise (as well as general meetings of all workers), established in the early days of the revolution and revitalized in 1957, play an important role in the day-to-day management and operation of enterprises from the drafting of the economic plan through the establishment of wage rates and labor allocation to increasing productivity and protecting workers' rights.

Perhaps the most important channel of worker influence is the plant Communist Party organization (whose role in enterprise management was greatly strengthened in 1957). The party organizations which are very heavily production worker in composition have fundamental responsibility for overall political guidance on all levels of enterprise activity. Branch meetings of the party hear reports on all aspects of the enterprises' performance, as well as the criticisms of non-party workers. They play a central role in the selection and evaluation of enterprise directors (the appointment of all managerial personnel has to be ratified by the plant party committee, which typically takes place only after a plant-wide discussion with the workforce as a whole). Further, the local party, together with representatives from the trade union and the Young Communist League, form an "Attestation Committee" which monitors administrators' performance. This powerful committee is able to have managers removed for unsatisfactory performance. (See Lane and O'Dell, 1978, pp. 24-25.)

It is of considerable interest to note that in the 1970s there was a significant public debate in Soviet society about whether the workforce of each enterprise as a whole should have the right to actually elect their enterprise's administrators, rather than to merely be consulted as part of the process of selection. (Yanowitch, 1977.) In general, it is clear that Soviet workers are *qualitatively* more than mere providers of labor power to a new *de facto* owning class which includes enterprise managers.

Maoists claim that a state bourgeoisie is the ruling class of the USSR and that the working class has no access to political power, no rights of self-expression, no say in who occupies the positions of power in the Party and the government and is deprived even of any channels or methods of discussing and debating policies.

First, although elections are no more the most important mechanism of exerting power in the USSR than in any Western parliamentary "democracy," it should be pointed out that Soviet elections and legislative bodies are *not* the farce that they are portrayed in the West to be. The Soviet practice of one candidate per office, with the electorate voting yes or no, is preceded by a long process of nomination in which all kinds of popular bodies are consulted in the process of narrowing down a long list of nominees from various organizations and individuals to a single candidate that is likely to get a majority of yes votes. In the event a candidate fails to get a majority approval at the *final stage* of the election process, a new candidate must be selected after another long nomination process. In 1969, it should be noted that there were rejections of candidates at the final stage of 145 local Soviet elections. Western Sovietologists agree that there has been a significant increase in both the political role of the Soviets (the legislative bodies) and in popular participation in them since the mid-1950s. This is especially true of local and city-wide Soviets which have come to play a rather central role in local government. The standing committees of the Soviets, including those of the Supreme Soviet, play a real role in both monitoring administration and formulating resolutions for the meetings of the general bodies (i.e., they are not mere "rubber stamps" for preformulated party policies). (R. Hill, 1977, chapter 5, 6; Skilling and Griffiths, 1971; Hough, 1976.)

Authentic workers' democracy implies a real opportunity for conflicting ideas to confront one another so that working class interests can be correctly formulated. Public debate on most of the issues confronting society occurs on a far vaster scale than in the U.S. (contrary to Western and Maoist prejudices). The Soviet press is full of debates on a very wide range of issues: literary policy, economic and legal reforms, city planning, crime, pollution, farm problems, the role of the press, women's role in the economy, access to higher education, etc. The only issues that are more or less immune from open debate and concerted criticism are the basic institutions of Soviet society (e.g., the leading role of the Communist Party, the existence of a military, the desirability of socialism) and the *persons* (but not the policies) of the top leaders of the party. The consensus of those who follow the Soviet media is that the breadth and depth of public debate has been growing and that in recent years there has been virtually no proposal for gradual change in the policy of the Communist Party which has not been aired in the mass media. (Hopkins, 1970; Skilling and Griffiths, 1971; Hough, 1974, 1976.)

In addition to extensive letters to the editors in the Soviet newspapers and diversity of editorial opinions in the major Soviet papers, extensive debates occur in specialized journals and conferences and at meetings of workers in factories as well as within the party. It is standard practice to submit drafts of legislation on policy changes to a lengthy period of public debate. These periods of public discussion have often produced considerable change in the original drafts. (Skilling and Griffiths, 1971.)

Some of the concrete issues that have provided the strongest and sharpest public debates in the USSR in the last 25 years have included Khrushchev's attempt to proletarianize higher education from the late 1950s until 1965, the long and ongoing debates about greater access of children of the intelligentsia to higher education, the debate over the role of the Communist Party in the military which occurred between 1958 and 1962, the perpetual question of centralization-decentralization of economic decision making, the debate over pollution of Lake Baikal (and other similar environmental questions), the discussion over whether the birthrate can best be increased by paying mothers a wage for housework or improving day care services (prominent in the 1970s), as well as the debate about the election of managers. (Yanowitch, 1977; Skilling and Griffiths, 1971.)

The working class is involved in all aspects of local self-government including "comrades courts" with nonprofessional elected worker judges that deal with minor crimes; elected "People's Control Commissions" (invigorated in 1962) whose sole function is to inspect enterprises and state institutions and expose abuses; "auxiliary police" (volunteer worker police) which have come to have increasing responsibility for local crime control since the 1950s. (Hough, 1974, 1976.)

Probably the most important organization of working class power in the USSR is the Communist Party organization. Since the mid-1950s there has been a steady tendency for the proportion of manual workers in the party to increase (in 1956 they were 32% of the party, in 1976, 42%). Since the Twenty-Third Party Congress in 1966 well over 50% of *all* new recruits have been industrial workers and in the major industrial areas the proportion has been about 65%. (Rigby, 1974.)

Since the mid-1950s there has been renewed emphasis on democratization and rank-and-file initiative in the party. There is considerable evidence that inner-party democracy is real and that it includes wide ranging criticism and self-criticism (which both fills the party press and is expressed at party meetings). (Hough and Fainsod, 1979.)

Other structural factors which serve to guarantee that the "power elite" in the USSR is rooted in the working class include the not to be downplayed fact that the vast majority of the top "decision makers" comes from working class and peasant backgrounds (and were promoted under party supervision on the basis of their political orientation), as well as the necessity for the party to maintain legitimacy and actually inspire people to work hard for its goals (the disaster in Poland is evidence of what happens when the party loses its legitimacy and ability to inspire respect).

In conclusion, there is a very high level of both worker participation in the political processes and a multitude of institutional channels by which the working class (together with the intelligentsia) exercises control over those in "power elite" positions. If there is a ruling class in the USSR it is clearly not the individuals who at any given time find themselves in the top positions, but rather some combination of the industrial workers and intelligentsia that control them.

It should be noted that the technical and professional intelligentsia play a disproportionate role in both the public debates and in the political process. While democractic life in the USSR is real, there appears to be disproportionate influence over state and party policy exerted by those in highly skilled and relatively privileged professional and scientific positions. Therein appears to lie the principal distortion in Soviet socialism.

In summary, Maoist claims that the working class has no rights of self-expression and no access to political power are totally mistaken. Unfortunately, Maoists generally rely on "common sense," (colored by the anti-communist values that permeate Western culture) and journalistic anti-communist reports, rather than doing a careful study of what even most Western experts know about Soviet reality.

The Nature of Socialism

There seems to be no *a priori* reason why a post-revolutionary state bureaucratic society such as that outlined by the R.C.P. could not have evolved in the USSR. In fact, if the transition to socialism is as fragile and difficult as both the Maoist and Trotskyist traditions have maintained, it is most difficult to see how Soviet socialism could have survived the grievous travails it faced from 1918 through the 1950s to institutionalize authentic socialist forms. Maoist historical arguments about the degeneration of Soviet socialism are, in fact, compelling. The party and working class were decimated during the Civil War, when most class conscious workers either were killed or became officials. In the early '20s the working class itself largely dispersed back to the countryside. The working class of the 1930s was composed mostly of ex-peasants without Marxist traditions. The old Bolshevik leaders were largely purged in the late 1930s. Agriculture was forcibly collectivized against the wishes of the majority of peasants (and a substantial repressive apparatus thus had to be built up). Almost everything was subordinated to industrializing and defending the country in the 1930s. An extreme concentration of decision making power in the top echelons of the party and state occurred in the 1930s.

There seems to have been every opportunity for those in the leading positions of the Soviet party and state to consolidate their position and transform themselves into a state bureaucratic class. In the tradition of such conservative sociologists as Roberto Michels, Vilfredo Pareto and Max Weber, as well as the Trotskyist traditions of Marxism, Maoism argues that power corrupts and that those in positions of privilege and authority necessarily hold onto their positions and attempt to find ways of stabilizing, protecting, and perpetuating their favored status in society.

The fact that Soviet society passed through the shoals of the 1918-1950s period without becoming a state bureaucratic society, instead in the last generation experiencing a blossoming (albeit somewhat distorted) of socialist institutions, means that many of these basic assumptions must be re-evaluated. The Trotskyist and Maoist theories of the fragility of socialist transition, the notions imported into Marxism from bourgeois sociology such as Michels' "Iron Law of Oligarchy," and the traditional anarchist (and New Left) notion that power necessarily corrupts, and that those in positions of authority will always attempt to consolidate privilege and dominate those that have entrusted them with operational decision making authority, must be rejected. In spite of the lack of vital democratic working class life, and in spite of the extreme concentration of decision making powers in the 1930s and 1940s, the structure in which the leaders operated led to the consolidation of socialist forms instead of to the creation of a new state bureaucratic class. On the basis of the results achieved the Soviet leadership in the 1930s through the 1950s must be understood, however tenuous its *direct* (or "instrumental") connection to Soviet workers, as the authentic representative of this class. Hence, the Soviet state and Communist Party in this period must be considered to have been exercising a genuine dictatorship of the proletariat.

It is inconsistent for many Marxists to apply qualitatively different criteria to the question of whether the bourgeoisie is the ruling class in a capitalist society (or the landlord class the ruling class in a feudal society) than they do to the question of whether the proletariat is the ruling class in a socialist society. All Marxists realize that the presence of elections in which perhaps only two or three percent of the electorate are capitalists is no guarantee that the capitalists don't dominate the electoral process, i.e., that in spite of the *form* of popular rule, a whole set of instrumental mechanisms (campaign funding, candidate selection, lobbying, policy formation), as well as a whole set of structural mechanisms (the necessity to maintain "business confidence" to insure economic prosperity, ideological hegemony of the bourgeois media, the threat of military intervention) act to insure bourgeois rule. No Marxist would be so foolish as to argue that since the military took over in Brazil,

Chile, Turkey, South Korea or Argentina and installed a military junta (composed of officers of petit bourgeois class backgrounds) which rules by decree, that these countries are not essentially ruled by the capitalist class, and are not as effective dictatorships of the bourgeoisie as they would be if all capitalists (and only capitalists) composed the electorate and elected one of their own to be an accountable leader. Few Marxists argue that Hitler in the 1930s was not the instrument of the dictatorship of German capital or Mussolini in the 1920s of Italian capital merely because they were not held accountable by any *formal* instrumental process of election or control to German or Italian capital. Likewise, few Marxists would maintain that the absolutist kings of late feudal times (e.g., Louis XIV of France, Phillip II of Spain, Charles I of England) were not, in fact, exercising a dictatorship of the landed classes even while they subordinated the local autonomy of the lesser nobility.

It is clear that there are informal or structural mechanisms operating in class societies to insure that hereditary monarchy, military juntas, fascist dictatorships, as well as popularly elected officials, act in the interest of the dominant propertied class. Why, then, can we not expect that parallel structures could not exist in socialist societies to insure that those in leading positions act in the class interests of the proletariat just as surely as the Brazilian or South Korean junta acts in the interests of capital, or feudal hereditary kings acted in the interest of landlords?

Why must utopian instrumentalism dominate the discussion of the criteria of working class power which occurs among most Western Marxists? In essence, Maoists, following the path established by anarchism, syndicalism, Trotskyism and left wing social democracy before them, define socialism as *direct* and *immediate* control by workers of both their economic and political institutions.

If equivalently rigorous criteria were applied to capitalist societies (as, in fact, they often are by conservative critics of Marxism who attempt to argue that the U.S. is, in fact, a democratic pluralism), it would perhaps be shown that *none* of the major capitalist countries in the world is ruled by their capitalist class. We would then be left with the strange conclusion that neither the working class *nor* the capitalist class is in power in *any* country, i.e., all countries are either pluralistic (as in the U.S.), or run by a state bureaucratic class (the USSR) — a most un-Marxist (and pro-U.S. imperialist) conclusion.

No, the only reasonable criteria by which it can be judged whether or not the capitalist class is the ruling class is whether or not this class has power (i.e., whether the state operates in their interest, *against* the interests of other classes, *because* of direct *or* structural mechanisms which force the state to adopt pro-capitalist policies). Likewise, the only criteria by which it can be judged whether or not the working class is the ruling class is whether or not they have *state* power (i.e., whether the state operates in their interests, against the interests of other classes — or potential classes — because of direct *or* structural mechanisms which force the state to adopt proletarian policies).

To ask whether hired managers or workers run socialist enterprises is to confuse day-to-day operational decision making with questions of fundamental power, equivalent to asking whether hired managers or major stockholders and banks run the corporations. Just as major stockholders have fundamental power over corporations even though they hire managers to run their businesses for them, there is no *a priori* reason that workers cannot similarly have fundamental power, while allocating day-to-day decision making to hired managers. The question of *de facto* ownership of property, just like that of real state power, has to be addressed on the same level in both cases — are the decision making powers of the managers essentially limited by direct (i.e., incentives, the threat of being fired) *and* indirect structural mechanisms (prestige, pride in work, necessity to increase productivity and output, etc.) to do the bidding of the owning class (capitalists *or* workers), *or* do they have fundamental autonomy and thus *de facto* real ownership.

Contrary to the arguments of such conservative sociologists as Roberto Michels ("The Iron Law of Oligarchy") and Max Weber, that everyone in a position of power attempts to consolidate their personal power, the corruption of militant trade union leaders and the moderation of socialist politicians in office has nothing to do with some biological power hunger (and its corollary of striving to be led on the part of the masses). The behavior of individuals in positions of power in capitalist society is a result of the structural logic of capitalist society. There are tremendous structural pressures on both union leaders and socialist officials in capitalist societies to behave "responsibly" and constructively, i.e., to promote "business confidence," increase wages through increasing productivity, etc., with most serious negative consequences (from losing the next election to assassination) for noncompliance. Further, there are tremendous temptations to move towards pro-business policies for working class leaders within capitalism, not the least of which are the promise of high paying jobs with business (versus the alternative of going back to work in the factory), and the prestige of associating with upper class people. But both the direct and indirect mechanisms of corruption are historically specific to the capitalist mode of production. A socialist mode of production has a qualitatively different logic.

The immediate structural necessities of real post-revolutionary societies such as those of the Soviet Union in the 1920s and 1930s — building solidarity, increasing production, military defense, realizing fundamental social justice within the framework of essentially socialized industry, led to a high level of concentration of operational decision making power. The self-conception and prestige of those in the "command posts" of Soviet society during this period were thoroughly tied to both their immediate tasks and to the long term goal of building socialism. Indeed their feelings of accomplishment, as well as the threat of demotion, were tied to the progress they made in achieving these imperatives. Thus, the actual movement of Soviet society was a product of the structural logic of its social formation, not of the subjective desires of its "power elite."

In a socialist economy surrounded by a capitalist world, the necessity to develop industrially, to feed the people, to protect itself and catch up with the leading capitalist countries, imposes a fairly limited set of options on a socialist leadership. The public claim that the leaders' positions rest on their attaining progress towards communism can easily be discredited (and their positions delegitimized) in the absence of such progress. Self-serving decision making and accumulated privileges (or even systematic manipulation of the masses, as has been the case in Poland) among a leadership which bases its legitimacy on revolutionary egalitarianism and progress towards communism, leads to cynicism and eventually massive resistance

(Poland is a prominent example). Socialist economies must rely on massive grass roots participation if they are to work, especially since the control functions of markets do not operate. The productive classes must be mobilized and politically active if rapid economic progress is to be sustained. Such massive and authentic participation creates great pressure on both the selection of leading officials and the formulation of party and state policies (with or without formal elections). As Poland has made painfully clear, manipulation and lack of consideration for the sentiments (and interests) of the masses results in demoralization and depoliticization, a decline in productivity and the decay of the moral fabric of socialist institutions, and in general social breakdown — mighty structural pressures indeed — to insure that the leaders of a socialized economy, however weak their *direct* ties to the working class, take continuous measures to increase popular participation, increase equality and expand the sphere of goods distributed on the basis of need, i.e., lead their countries towards consolidating authentic socialism and perhaps even towards full communism.

INTERNATIONALISM OR SOCIAL IMPERIALISM

The remainder of this article will analyse the relationship between the USSR and both the less developed countries of Asia, Africa, and Latin America and its allies in the Council for Mutual Economic Assistance (CMEA or COMECON) (which includes Poland, Czechoslovakia, Bulgaria, Hungary, the German Democratic Republic and Rumania, as well as Cuba and Vietnam). The "export of capital," Soviet foreign assistance and Soviet foreign trade as well as the economic co-ordination that takes place between the USSR and the other CMEA countries will be scrutinized for evidence that the USSR is imperialist in its relations to them, i.e., dominates them in order to economically exploit them.

The Export of Capital

Maoists typically claim that "Soviet imperialism" is primarily driven by the need to export capital. But there is neither pressure nor mechanisms to export capital in the Soviet economy. Each Soviet enterprise or association operates according to over a dozen separate target criteria given to it by the central planning agency. The criteria of profit maximization and enterprise control over capital investment does not apply in the Soviet economy (where most investment funds are centrally allocated, and profit is only a secondary criterion of enterprise success). It should also be noted that all relations with other economies are handled exclusively by one of about 20 autonomous foreign trading enterprises which have no direct connections to domestic production companies (they operate solely by directives of the central planning agency and are concerned primarily with securing imports necessary to fulfill the state plan) (see Gregory and Stuart, 1974, Ch. 8). This means that domestic Soviet production enterprises do not have the option of deciding to open up overseas operations.

In 1979 the Soviet Union had an ownership interest in a total of 92 firms in the advanced capitalist countries as well as 25 firms in the less developed capitalist countries. The total value of its direct investments in the advanced capitalist countries in 1979 was $280 million (about $3.1 million per firm). In the less developed capitalist countries Soviet investments totaled $18 million (or about $700,000 per firm). This represented .01 percent of the estimated Soviet NMP for that year. Two things should be noted about these foreign investments. First, they are miniscule by Western standards. Two, they are qualitatively different in nature from Western investments in that they are largely oriented to facilitating Soviet trade (mostly Soviet exports) with the capitalist countries, rather than as is the case with the West, to take advantage of cheap labor or control world commodity markets (McMillan, 1979:629-33).

In 1978 the value of U.S. direct investments in the other advanced capitalist countries was $120,471 million (or 431 times more than that of the USSR). In 1978 the value of U.S. direct investments in the less developed capitalist countries was $40,394 million (or 2,200 times more than Soviet investments). Thus, it can be seen that whether in relation to the Soviet economy or to Western investments, the gross value of Soviet foreign investments is insignificant. Soviet investments can not serve as an important link between the Soviet economy and that of the West. Further, its insignificance indicates a qualitative difference between the Soviet economy and the logic of capitalism prevailing in the West.

The Soviets in 1978 had investments in 17 advanced capitalist countries. There were 12 Soviet firms in France, 11 each in Belgium-Luxemburg and West Germany, 10 in the U.K., 8 in Italy, 7 in Finland and 5 each in the USA and Canada. Of these, 47 percent were engaged purely in trading and marketing Soviet products, 7 percent in final assembly of Soviet exports and marketing, 22 percent in transport (mostly shipping), and 12 percent in finance (mostly financing of Soviet exports) (McMillan, 1979:629). Soviet investments in the West are almost totally focused on facilitating Soviet trade.

The Soviet Union in 1978 had investments in four firms in Singapore, three in Iran and two in Mexico. Thirty-two percent of the 25 Soviet investments in the less developed capitalist countries are in trading and marketing enterprises, 16 percent in financing of Soviet foreign trade, 16 percent in transportation companies, and 24 percent in natural resource extraction (a total of 6 jointly owned enterprises) (McMillan, 1979:630). As in the industrialized West, Soviet investments in the less developed countries are heavily centered in facilitating Soviet trade.

Soviet enterprises in the less developed countries are mostly either in the form of co-ownership with the local state or a minority share with the local state owning the majority interest. The $18 million of Soviet equity in the 25 firms averages approximately one half of their total value (McMillan, 1979:631). Here again, the form of Soviet investment differs radically from that of Western corporations which prefer full or majority interests.

Soviet investments in the less developed capitalist countries serve mostly to promote the sale of Soviet industrial goods. Secondarily these investments serve to gain access to fish from the world's oceans. *All* six Soviet investments in natural resource extraction in the less developed countries are joint ventures established by the Soviet Ministry of Fisheries on a 50-50 basis with locals. These joint ventures consist of port and service facilities for the Soviet fishing fleet and its factory ships. Part of the Soviet fish catch is marketed locally while the remainder is processed for shipment to the Soviet Union. The Soviets have no direct investment (majority or minority interest) in any other mining, petroleum, agricultural or other extractive enterprises in any developed or less developed capitalist country (McMillan, 1979:636-7). The Soviets differ radically from the Western capitalist countries in these regards, countries whose transnational corporations systematically exploit the primary resources of the less developed countries, as well as control the world markets in such commodities.

Soviet investments in the capitalist countries include seven banks (with three branches, for a total of 10 separate bank locations) and three insurance companies. The Soviet owned banks are located in the world's major money markets and operate to facilitate the financing of East-West trade (London, Paris, Zürich, Frankfurt, Vienna, Beirut, Tehran, Singapore). It should be noted that their assets have increased significantly in recent years. From total assets of $516 million in 1960, they grew to $2,065 million in 1970 and $7,549 million in 1976 (McMillan, 1979:637-9; Danylyk and Rabin, 1979:483-85). However, this is a small sum by international banking standards. In 1974 one U.S. bank alone, First National City, had $29.9 billion in overseas branch assets, while the nine largest U.S. based transnational banks had a total of $128 billion.

The lack of a significant direct investment presence in the less developed countries means that the Soviets have no stake in preventing a nationalist or anti-imperialist movement which would nationalize or otherwise threaten the profitability of foreign owned operations from coming to power. The U.S., whatever the level of good will of its leaders, on the other hand, *must* act to protect the billions of dollars worth of privately held transnational investment in the less developed countries. This commitment necessarily places the U.S. state on the side of those local property interests who are integrated with the U.S. owned transnationals and banks. This is a structural difference which should not be underestimated.

When forced to recognize that the Soviets have no significant investments in the less developed countries, Maoists often argue that the enterprises built with Soviet foreign assistance are *de facto* Soviet owned enterprises. But such is simply not the case, although such enterprises for a number of years after construction typically export a significant proportion of their product to the USSR (as repayment for the loans to build them). The Soviets maintain no ownership rights in such enterprises, and once the principal plus very low interest rates are repaid, the

Soviets have no more claims on the enterprises or their product. Further, the Soviets are careful to train local technicians and administrators to operate all levels of the local enterprises their foreign assistance creates. In no sense then are such enterprises in any way comparable to transnational direct investments in the less developed countries.

In summary, it is clear that there are qualitative differences between U.S. and Soviet investments in the less developed countries. Not the least important of these is the fact that the U.S. transnationals have about one-half of the total value of *all* foreign investment in the less developed countries, while the Soviets have .02% of the total (i.e., an insignificant amount). This qualitative difference in quantity has radical implications for the social forces and historical tendencies that the USSR and the U.S. can, and *do*, support in these countries. The Soviets, with no stake in profit making enterprises in the less developed countries, are structurally able to lend assistance to forces such as the National Liberation Front in Vietnam, the Fidelist movement in Cuba and the MPLA in Angola; while the U.S. state, constrained by heavy transnational investments in South Africa, Chile, Brazil, Saudi Arabia, etc., is forced to defend those interests by supporting the upper class based dictatorships with which the transnationals are so closely tied.

Soviet Foreign Assistance to the Less Developed Countries

The common Maoist assertion that there is no important difference between Soviet and U.S. foreign aid is incorrect. There are in fact a number of radical differences. U.S. economic assistance is primarily designed to facilitate the growth of local infrastructure to support transnational investments and to shore up conservative regimes (usually dictatorships based on the propertied classes and top military officers). It is normally given only to private enterprises or to encourage private enterprise (especially transnationals). U.S. economic assistance is almost never given to either state owned productive enterprises or to industrial enterprises *of any type*. The economic interests behind U.S. foreign policy do not want the U.S. state encouraging competition for the exports and locally produced industrial goods of the transnationals, nor do they want the growth of a strong state sector.

In sharp contrast, Soviet foreign assistance is given almost exclusively to state sector enterprises and is heavily concentrated in industrial production. Since the Soviets have no industrial investments in the less developed countries, they have no stake (as does the U.S.) in encouraging a division of labor, with privately owned transnationals producing the most advanced industrial goods. Further (as we shall see below) the Soviets, unlike all capitalist countries, export primarily in order to import. Thus, the Soviets (unlike the U.S.) have no interest in discouraging the development of either import substitute industries or the most advanced technological sectors in the less developed countries. There will always be goods the Soviets can exchange to meet their import requirements.

In addition to having radically different effects on the economies of the less developed countries U.S. and Soviet economic assistance also differ fundamentally in a number of other ways, including the types of regimes supported, the terms of repayment, and its domestic cost/profitability. U.S. assistance is used overwhelmingly to support conservative and pro-status quo regimes (usually military dictatorships) based on the propertied classes. The major recipients of U.S. assistance have included South Korea, pre-1975 Vietnam, the Philippines, Brazil, Taiwan, Israel, Chile, the Shah's Iran, and most recently Egypt. The Soviets, on the other hand, lend most of their support to the most progressive (socialist as well as anti-imperialist nationalist or at least neutralist) regimes. The heaviest recipients of Soviet foreign aid have been the Socialist Republic of Vietnam, Cuba, North Korea, Algeria, Syria, Nasser's Egypt, Nehru's India, Iraq, and most recently Ethiopia, Angola and Mozambique. The Soviets also tend to provide foreign assistance to conservative but influential (and normally adjacent) states for strategic regions. They sometimes attempt to pry such regimes loose from the U.S. sphere of influence, e.g., Turkey, Iran under the Shah. (See U.S. Department of State, *Communist States and Developing Countries: Aid and Trade,* various issues.)

Most Maoists merely dismiss this difference by maintaining there is no important difference between the types of regimes the U.S. favors (e.g., Pinochet's Chile, Thieu's Vietnam, Sadat's Egypt, Taiwan, the general's Brazil, etc.), and those the USSR favors, Fidel's Cuba, post-1975 Vietnam, Syria, Algeria, Angola, post-1977 Ethiopia, etc. It is doubtful that very many residents of Chile, Brazil, etc., or Iraq, Syria, Vietnam, Cuba, Angola, Ethiopia (or Afghan women) could agree (regardless of their class position or politics), that there is no real difference. One has to be blind to maintain otherwise.

In fact there are qualitative differences in their class nature, as well as in the conditions of life for the various classes, among the various countries that are off-handedly lumped together. The nature of regimes such as those of Nasser's Egypt, contemporary Algeria, Iraq, Syria, Ethiopia and Angola are qualitatively more equalitarian and qualitatively less influenced by either foreign transnationals or local wealthy classes, than as is the case with Pinochet's Chile, Taiwan, South Korea or the general's Brazil. This is even more the case for Cuba, North Korea and Vietnam.

A third major difference between the foreign assistance of the USSR and the U.S. is in its relative cost/profit. In the U.S. economy, foreign assistance is almost entirely an export subsidy for the mega-corporations that supply the recipients with the goods funded by the U.S. treasury. For example, foreign aid is immediately paid in dollars to General Electric which then exports dynamos to Brazil (with Brazil gradually paying back the U.S. treasury in dollars earned from its increased exports). Because U.S. corporations have trouble selling all they can produce at a profit, in the absence of foreign aid, capacity utilization, production, total exports, and hence profit are significantly less than they otherwise would be (e.g., Brazil would buy cheaper and probably better West German or Japanese dynamos). Thus, by increasing exports in a slack capitalist economy, foreign assistance results in the production of goods which would otherwise have not been produced at all (since they could not have been sold at a profit), without the government subsidy foreign aid represents. In a full employment planned economy such as that of the USSR, on the other hand, goods can be exported as part of a foreign assistance program only if already fully employed resources are reallocated from other uses, i.e., there is always a *real* cost to diverting resources overseas that otherwise could be used to increase domestic living standards. In summary, foreign assistance expands profits for those that control a capitalist economy, while slowing the rate of growth in living standards in a socialist economy. Consequently, what is in the *economic self-interest* of the first is not in the *economic self-interest* of the second.

A fourth important difference between Soviet and U.S. foreign assistance lies in the mechanisms of repayment. While the U.S. requires repayment in hard currency, which can generally be obtained only through expanding exports (and hence in aggravating the international division of labor), the USSR accepts repayment primarily in *goods* produced by the enterprises constructed with Soviet foreign assistance. In fact, most of the goods the USSR accepts as repayment for its export of advanced machinery and equipment could not have been sold on the world market. Datar, for example, estimates that 75-80% of the goods India used to repay Soviet loans in the 1954-1966 period could not have been used to generate hard currency (Datar, 1972:176). The advantages of the Soviet repayment requirements are obvious, both to objective economists and participants. Little hard currency is required to repay Soviet loans, the means of repayment are automatically created by Soviet assistance, and industrial enterprises, which because of economies of scale, might not yet be quite feasible otherwise, become possible because the USSR takes a major part of their output (for a period averaging 8 years) until the local economy grows sufficiently to absorb all the output.

Soviet Foreign Trade

Maoists usually claim that the nature of Soviet trade with the less developed countries is no different than that of the U.S. Both countries allegedly trade high priced, high technology exports for competitively priced labor intensive imports from the less developed countries (and accordingly make a substantial profit from unequal exchange), as well as develop and reproduce the world division of labor between the industrial and less developed countries. Once again, the Maoist argument has no empirical basis.

Soviet trade is oriented totally differently than capitalist trade. Capitalist enterprises and economies are oriented primarily to selling goods, i.e., exporting commodities. Most imports other than essential raw materials for productive purpose are thus considered necessary evils. A capitalist country is considered successful, the bigger its balance of payment *surplus* (i.e., the more its exports *exceed* its imports), while a country is considered to be in serious trouble if its imports significantly exceed its exports. In contrast, a planned socialist economy is oriented to using exports as a means to acquire necessary imports (as well as to lend political support to friendly regimes). The plan starts with an estimate of how much of which kinds of goods are needed over and above what can be produced domestically, and then figures out the quantity of exports that will be necessary to pay for the required imports at prevailing world prices. Because the Soviet trade plan is primarily geared to securing a set level of imports and to exporting only enough to ensure these imports, the resultant trade is relatively insensitive to world prices.

The Soviet economy is carefully isolated from world market forces by the system of trade planning and centralized prices. Profitability plays no role in the behavior of the Soviet trading enterprises which purchase Soviet goods at prevailing domestic prices and sell them to domestic enterprises at the prevailing domestic price. Since the Soviet productive enterprises have no economic involvement in foreign trade, fluctuations in world prices have no impact on their output plans (which are determined by the goals of the central plan).*

Soviet imports from the industrial West are oriented to accelerating the Soviet rate of economic growth by acquiring high technology (and thus saving the Soviets the expense of developing all new technology themselves) as well as to importing feed grains to accelerate the rate of meat consumption per capita (see Goldich, 1979 and Szymanski, 1983 for a fuller discussion of Soviet trade with the advanced capitalist countries). Soviet imports from the less developed countries on the other hand are oriented to lending political support to friendly countries (i.e., are the result of repayments from Soviet loans) and/or are part of essentially equalitarian trade relations designed to exchange Soviet manufactured goods for natural gas, fish, phosphates, coffee, tea or other materials *actually produced* by the less developed countries. (Goods in which they specialize because of the long standing international division of labor imposed on

---

*For a fuller discussion see Holzman (1974) and Brainard (1979).

them by the far more economically powerful Western capitalist countries.)

Overall, in 1979, 1.6% of *all* the exports of the less developed countries went to the USSR, compared to 17.9% to the USA. Further, 1.4% of *all* the imports of the less developed countries were from the USSR, compared to 16.2% from the USA (I.M.F. *Direction of Trade*, 1981). Clearly, then, the USSR can not be blamed for the world division of labor. If it is going to purchase anything from the less developed countries it must purchase what they in fact (through no fault of the USSR) produce; likewise, if it sells these countries anything, it must sell them what they need and want (to alter the world division of labor): advanced technological goods, not raw materials.

The Soviet economy is the most self-sufficient in the world. In the mid-1970s total imports equaled about 5% of its Net Material Product (significantly less than the ratio of any advanced capitalist country). The USSR has the most diverse and abundant endowment of raw materials in the world. It is in a position to provide for all of its vital needs without engaging in trade at all (if such were necessary). It has the largest reserves of petroleum in the world, and in fact is the world's second biggest exporter of petroleum. Raw material imports (excluding food and feed) as a percentage of NMP has declined since 1940 (from 1.6% in 1950-53, 1.3% in 1958-61, .9% in 1966-69 to .7% in 1970-75) as the USSR became less dependent on raw material imports (see the sources cited in Szymanski, 1979:109). In short the Soviet economy, unlike those of all Western imperialist countries, by reasons of raw material endowment and conscious planning for self-sufficiency, simply has no technologically dictated need to subordinate less developed countries to obtain raw materials.

The Soviet Union has been especially generous in its trade with Vietnam and Cuba. It has purchased these countries' exports and supplied their necessary imports on extremely favorable terms (that have amounted to a major subsidy). For example, in the 1965-70 period the Soviets paid an average 261% of the world market price for Cuban sugar. The price the Soviets pay for Cuban sugar is set by long-term agreement which stabilizes the price, except for periodic upward adjustments, when the world sugar price rises above the predetermined subsidy level price. The stable price at which the Soviets buy Cuban sugar has allowed socialist Cuba to avoid the economic dislocations that were so characteristic of its pre-1959 economic dependence on sugar exports (see Goure and Weinkle, 1973).

Asha Datar (1972) as well as others have shown that Indians usually get higher prices from the Soviets than from Western countries for their exports. Of the 12 leading export commodities studied by Datar in the 1960-69 period, six were consistently purchased by the USSR at higher than their world prices, three usually purchased at prices higher than those paid by the capitalist countries, and two purchased on a year to year basis sometimes above and sometimes below the world market price. Only one (unmanufactured tobacco) was consistently sold to the USSR below the world market price (which probably indicates more about the quality of Indian tobacco, than anything about the nature of Soviet trade) (see Datar 1972:170-172, 196-7). Another study, reported in a widely circulated booklet issued by the vehemently anti-Soviet Communist Party of India (M-L), which was designed to show that the USSR *was* "social imperialist," concluded that of 15 important Indian exports the USSR paid less than the world price in the case of only four (CPI:[ML], 1976).

Although the impact of Soviet economic assistance and trade is qualitatively less than that of the advanced countries, its impact is exerted consistently in the direction of encouraging rapid industrialization in the less developed countries, i.e., the exports of the less developed countries to the USSR are concentrated in the relatively capital intensive products produced by the economic assistance granted to the less developed countries by the USSR. Again, it must be emphasized that while the policy of the states of the advanced capitalist countries is to reproduce the world division of labor through their foreign assistance and tariff policies (restrictions on the import of manufactured goods from the LDC's), the state policy of the USSR is just the opposite, i.e., it encourages the import of manufactured goods. Again we see a qualitative difference in trade policy, hardly what Maoism claims is the case.

The Maoist claim that there are no significant differences between Soviet/LDC economic relations and Western/LDC economic ties could not be further from the truth. A careful examination of both the dynamic and effects of Soviet and U.S. economic assistance, foreign investment and trade practices indicates that there are in fact a multitude of qualitative differences between them. Soviet foreign assistance, although far smaller than that of the Western capitalist countries, is dollar for dollar considerably more beneficial to the less developed countries. This is primarily the case because it is concentrated in industry, in the public sector, and is paid for in the products of the enterprises built with foreign assistance rather than hard currency. There are no Soviet foreign investments in the less developed countries (except a virtually insignificant amount invested in trading banks and fishing enterprises) thus giving the Soviets no stake in the pro-capitalist status quo. In contrast, the U.S. transnational corporations' immense stake dictates that the U.S. state supports the pro-transnational propertied classes throughout Asia, Africa and Latin America. Soviet trade with the less developed countries is much more concentrated in the import of relatively capital intensive goods from the LDCs than is the case for the Western capitalist countries. The terms of trade of the LDCs with the USSR are by all indications more generous than these countries could obtain in the West. In summary, there is no evidence in Soviet economic relations with the less developed countries that the Soviet Union is imperialist in its relations with them.

Trade Relations with the Eastern European Countries

The six Eastern European CMEA countries primarily export industrial machinery and equipment to the Soviet Union and import raw materials and fuels in exchange. In 1966-68 48.2% of all Eastern European exports to the Soviet Union were industrial machinery and equipment and only 26.1% raw materials, fuels or food. During the same period 62.8% of all Soviet exports to Eastern Europe were raw materials and another 10.7% food, and only 24.4% industrial machinery and equipment and 2.1% manufactured consumer goods. The proportion of all Eastern European exports which is industrial machinery and equipment has tended to rise slightly over time, while the proportion that consists of raw material and fuels has decreased drastically (it stood at 43.7% in 1950-1953). The proportion of Eastern European exports which has been manufactured consumer goods has risen significantly since the 1950s (see Table One). The proportion of all Soviet exports in the form of raw materials and fuel has stayed about the same since the 1950s. The Soviet Union is the principal supplier of raw materials and fuels for Eastern Europe, while Eastern Europe is a major supplier of capital goods, and to a lesser extent, manufactured consumer goods, for the Soviet Union. This is, of course, exactly the opposite pattern of trade observed between the advanced capitalist countries, which specialize in capital goods and manufactured exports, and the less developed countries, which specialize in raw material and food exports.

In comparison with the 26% of total Eastern European CMEA exports to the Soviet Union which are raw materials, fuels or food, the percentages of total exports to the U.S. from countries often regarded as its dependencies are considerably greater, e.g., (circa 1973): Columbia 88.9%, Dominican Republic 98.0%, Guatemala 84.4%, Honduras 97.9%, Mexico 54.3%, Nicaragua 82.0%, Panama 73.5%, the Philippines 95.6% and Venezuela 98.8%. There is thus a qualitative difference in the trade patterns of the CMEA countries of Eastern Europe and the Soviet Union in comparison with the trade patterns of the dependencies of the U.S. with the U.S. The U.S. dependencies almost universally specialize in the export of raw materials to the U.S. (primarily in exchange for manufactured goods) while the Eastern European countries export manufactured goods, especially capital equipment, in exchange for raw materials. Unless the terms of trade between the Soviet Union and Eastern Europe were highly imbalanced in favor of the USSR (which, being based on world prices, they are not) it would be very difficult to interpret their relationship as imperialist.

As a rule the prices used in evaluating the commodities exchanged between the Eastern European socialist countries and the Soviet Union are approximations of the prices in the world capitalist market (with minor adjustments made for transportation costs from alternative suppliers and elimination of monopoly factors). Because the law of value is not the essential determinant of prices in the planned economies of these countries, domestic prices of commodities are in good part arbitrary. Different countries might thus price the same commodity at very

Table One

Soviet Exports to and Imports from the Six CMEA Countries of Eastern Europe
(As Percentage of Total Exports or Imports)

	Industrial Machinery and Equipment		Fuels and Raw Material (ex. food)		Foods		Manufactured Consumer Goods (ex. food)	
	Exports	Imports	Exports	Imports	Exports	Imports	Exports	Imports
1950-53	22.0%	39.2%	51.7%	43.7%	25.2%	7.2%	1.1%	9.9%
1954-57	15.5	46.8	60.7	37.1	21.6	5.8	2.3	10.3
1958-61	13.9	45.8	64.4	27.0	18.6	7.6	3.0	19.6
1962-65	19.7	49.8	65.9	20.5	12.2	7.9	2.2	21.9
1966-68	24.4	48.2	62.8	16.9	10.7	9.2	2.1	25.7

Source: Paul Marer, *Soviet and East European Foreign Trade, 1946-1969*, 1972, Table III.

different levels because of various political or long term economic considerations. Because of their arbitrary nature these prices cannot be used in inter-socialist trade without one or the other party in any given exchange complaining of "exploitation." This becomes apparent if the arbitrary price of an offered export is higher than the equivalent commodity on the world capitalist market *or* if the offered price for an import is lower. CMEA regulations specify that all prices of raw materials are based on adjusted world market prices in the previous five year period.

As is well known, the fact that a few advanced capitalist countries have a virtual monopoly on producing technologically advanced capital goods allows them to sell these goods to the LDCs at approximately monopoly prices while, except in petroleum and a handful of other crucial raw materials, overproduction, competition and foreign ownership in the raw material and food producing less developed countries depresses the world prices of most of these materials. As a result a real transfer of value occurs from the raw material/food producing countries (except the petroleum exporters) to the advanced capitalist countries, i.e., the poorer less developed raw material suppliers can be considered to be "exploited." The result of the socialist countries' using approximations of world prices for capital goods and raw materials is that the exports of the raw material exporter, the Soviet Union, tend to be undervalued; and the exports of the capital goods exporters, i.e., most of the countries of Eastern Europe, tend to be overvalued. In other words, the Soviet Union must be considered to be "exploited" in its trade with Eastern Europe in the same sense and to an equivalent degree that the LDC raw material exporters are exploited by the advanced capitalist countries.

Although the rule is that exports are exchanged at approximately world prices the Soviet Union nevertheless has, since at least the mid-1950s, been supplying crucial raw materials, especially petroleum products, to Eastern Europe at considerably below the world market price. For example, the price charged the Eastern Europeans for Soviet oil in 1974 was approximately *one-fifth* the world market price. After a substantial increase in the price of Soviet oil in 1975 the cost to the CMEA countries in 1976 was still about one-third less than the going world market price (Kramer, 1975, p. 71).

Detailed empirical studies show that the Eastern European specialist countries are not discriminated against or exploited in their trade relations with the USSR. One careful study of the prices for Bulgarian and Polish exports to and imports from the Soviet Union (i.e., their terms of trade) shows that they tend to be significantly better than those obtainable from the market capitalist countries. In 1959, of thirty-two leading categories of Bulgarian exports, the price paid by the Soviet Union was higher than that obtainable in Western Europe for twenty-four and lower for eight. In the case of Poland the Soviet price was higher in twenty out of twenty-eight categories and lower in seven. In the case of Soviet exports to Bulgaria the price charged Bulgaria in 1959 was lower than that of Western European equivalent commodities for eighteen of the thirty-two basic categories and higher for twelve; while for Poland the Soviet price was *higher* for eleven categories of commodities and lower for six (Holzman, 1974, Chapter 11).

Since it is logically possible that the few goods the Soviets trade to their advantage could represent the majority of goods traded, and thus that the Soviets could secure a net gain from trade, it is important to look at measures of trade advantage which incorporate quantity as well as price. The same study cited above found that *overall* Polish exports (measured by unit value, a concept which includes both price and volume) to the Soviet Union were purchased at 1.45 x the prevailing price for similar goods on the Western European market, and Bulgarian goods at 1.32 x. It was also found that overall Soviet imports were purchased by Poland at 81% of the price similar goods were available for in Western Europe and Bulgarian imports at 69% (Holzman, 1974, Chapter 11). Thus the net barter terms of trade (a concept which incorporates both price and volume) between Poland and the Soviet Union in 1959 were 1.8 times better for Poland (and worse for the Soviet Union) than could be obtained in trade with the West. The terms of trade for Bulgaria were 1.9 times better. Substantially identical results were found for 1960, indicating that 1959 was not a fluke year. Thus it seems clear that even though the prices of commodities traded among the non-market socialist economies officially approximate world market prices, the Eastern European countries gain at the expense of the Soviet Union in this trade (See Marer, 1974).

In addition to complaining about the cost of the subsidy to Eastern Europe through supplying such cheap petroleum, the Soviets have also been complaining of an "exploitation" effect caused by their having to undertake all the heavy investment expenditures of developing and producing oil. It was estimated that in the late 1960s the capital intensity of the basic raw materials and fuels exported to CMEA countries was 3 to 3.5 times *higher* than that of the machinery supplied to the USSR, i.e., the value of material investment (machinery and fixed facilities such as pipelines and other transport) per worker was considerably higher in raw material production than in the machine producing sectors. The Soviets have been fostering integration in the production and distribution of raw materials and fuels such that the Eastern European countries share in the costs of producing and acquiring their own raw materials. In the early 1970s the CMEA countries began to mutually finance projects to produce fuel and raw materials mostly in the USSR. In return for capital investments in raw material production enterprises, the investing countries (mostly Eastern European) are repaid in raw materials (Fallenbuchl, 1974).

The Eastern European countries depend very heavily on raw material exports from the Soviets. For example, around 1970 the Soviets provided 100% of Czechoslovakia's imports of petroleum (about 97% of its consumption), about 85% of its iron ore imports (about 75% of its consumption), 92% of its aluminum and 76% of its copper. During the same period the USSR supplied about 90% of East Germany's petroleum, 60% of its iron ore and 70% of its aluminum and lead. Hungary imports most of its petroleum, iron ore, phosphates and electric power from the Soviet Union, etc. (Mickiewicz, 1973, p. 213; *Current Digest of the Soviet Press,* July 7, 1976, pp. 12, 13). Because it is the predominant supplier of raw materials to Eastern Europe the Soviet Union *is* in a position to "exploit" them economically. That it does not take advantage of its position is indicative of the lack of a typical imperialist relation between these countries.*

---

*Things were not always so advantageous for Eastern Europe. Before the mid-1950s the terms of trade, essentially dictated by the Soviet

Economic Assistance to Eastern Europe

The Soviets extended some economic assistance to Eastern Europe in the immediate post-war period (1946-1952) mainly to relieve especially troubled situations and to convince the Eastern European countries to reject Marshall Plan aid, e.g., a $450 million loan to Poland in 1947. The most generous period of Soviet aid to Eastern Europe, however, was 1953-1958 following the rebellions and riots in East Germany, Poland and Hungary, which were in good part directed against the exploitative relations in which Eastern European countries found themselves in relation to the Soviet Union. The most comprehensive aid program of all took place in the 1956-58 period when about $3.6 billion in aid was extended in the form of about $1.5 billion in loans, $1 billion in debt cancellations, and $1 billion in free transfers of jointly-owned enterprises to the Eastern European countries. Additional generous export credits were granted to these countries during this period. (Marer 1972, p. 237; Goldman, 1967, p. 34-7; Sherman, 1969, p. 194). The 1956 period (when Maoists usually claim the USSR became imperialist) marks a watershed in the economic relations between Eastern Europe and the USSR: the remaining joint stock companies were handed over to the local countries, and much of their debt cancelled; terms of trade favorable to the Eastern European countries were established; and generous aid extended. It has been estimated that the total value of Soviet aid to Eastern Europe (including debt cancellations, turn over of enterprises, loans and credits) has been of the same order as that of the Marshall Plan aid to Western Europe, approximately $14 billion

---

Union, were overwhelmingly in favor of the Soviets. Trade with the Eastern European countries during the immediate post World War period was regarded primarily as a mechanism to reconstruct the war devastated Soviet economy. One of the clearest examples of the exploitation of Eastern Europe through unequal exchange before the mid-1950s was the export of coal from Poland to the Soviet Union. Until November 1953 Poland was supplying coal to the Soviet Union at approximately *one-tenth* of the world price. In 1956 the Soviets acknowledged that there had been "exploitation" of Poland in the coal trade and cancelled the $626 million in debts owed by Poland to the USSR as compensation for the coal subsidy supplied the USSR from 1946 to 1953. Goldman, (1967) p. 7.

(Marer, 1972, p. 240-2). The Soviet Union, at least since the mid-1950s, has thus played a central role in accelerating the economic growth and all around development of the Eastern European economies, hardly a phenomenon to be expected from an imperialist type relation such as exists between the United States and Western Europe on the one hand and most of the countries of the less developed world on the other.

Co-ordinated Planning

During the first decade of the Council of Mutual Economic Assistance the joint coordination of the economies of these countries was limited to planning trade among themselves. Since 1958, however, there has been a gradual increase in overall economic integration and coordination of production plans among the CMEA countries. While the ideal is the eventual total integration of the various economies, as nation states wither away, all parties are extremely jealous of maintaining their economic independence and all around economic development, so the process proceeds very slowly.

No supra-national planning authorities exist which can dictate to any member state what to produce or how to distribute their production; instead, totally voluntary coordinating agencies have been set up to coordinate joint efforts and integration. A Committee for Cooperation in Planning exists to promote coordination of five-year and longer plans and exchanges of information. Discussions are held among the CMEA countries while each constructs its operative plans. The primary concerns of the Committee for Cooperation in Planning appear to be systematically developing adequate supplies of raw materials and energy throughout the CMEA countries, promoting the most advanced technological processes by allowing economies of scale and developing integrated transportation networks. CMEA also continues to promote coordination of production for purposes of planning trade among the member countries. This mostly means the development of intra-industry specialization, e.g., Czechoslovakia specializes in metal pipe, East Germany in steel for bearings, Poland in thin rolled steel and Hungary in fine bore tubing. Each country decides whether or not to participate in a given integration project (of which there are many) on the basis of what it thinks it would gain from participation.

CMEA rules, deferring to the interests of the less developed CMEA countries, especially Rumania, specify that one of its goals is to eliminate differences in the levels of development of the member countries. Concretely this takes the form of the less developed countries being given preference in developing new lines of industrial production *providing* the new products are of sufficiently high quality, and the granting of economic assistance to the less developed by the most developed CMEA countries (Fallenbuchl, 1974; Goldman, 1967, p. 51-9; Wilczynski, 1970, p. 195-203).

Another form of CMEA cooperation involves leasing of land in one country by another. Bulgaria and the Soviet Union have an arrangement where Bulgaria leases forest land in the Soviet Union for purposes of building and operating a forestry enterprise for export to Bulgaria. In return for providing building materials, land, technical advice, equipment and transportation, as well as the trees, the Soviets get a proportion of the total Bulgarian enterprise's output proportionate to the relative value contributions of the two countries. (The Bulgarians provide the lumberworkers.) There is beginning to be some labor mobility among the CMEA countries from areas of relative labor surplus to relative labor shortages, e.g., Polish workers working in the Czechoslovakian construction industry. (Fallenbuchl, 1974, p. 404-5; *Current Digest of the Soviet Press*, [July 7, 1976], p. 13.)

Economic Development

That the period of socialist construction in the six CMEA countries of Eastern Europe has resulted in both industrialization and economic development of these formerly agricultural, less developed countries can be seen by comparing them now to what they were in the 1930s. In 1937 Czechoslovakia had 17.0% of its economically active population working in manufacturing, Hungary 7.3%, Poland 6.2%, Bulgaria 5.9%, and Rumania 2.7%. These figures are generally somewhat lower than for most of Latin American countries of comparable size in the 1970s. The G.N.P. per capita of these countries in 1937 (in *1973* U.S. dollars) was $440 for Czechoslovakia, $428 for Hungary, $300 for Poland and $271 for Bulgaria. These figures are comparable with or lower than many countries today. For example in 1973, the G.N.P. per capita of Columbia was $400, the

Dominican Republic $480, Guatemala $402, Chile $579, Brazil $723 and Egypt $245. In comparison the 1937 G.N.P per capita (in 1973 dollars) of the United Kingdom was $1,676 and of Italy $503. In 1974 the per capita national income of the Eastern European countries was estimated to be $3,599 for Eastern Germany, $1,812 for Rumania, $2,505 for Czechoslovakia, $1,812 for Poland, $1,520 for Hungary and $1,002 for Bulgaria (and $1,880 for the Soviet Union). These figures compare well with the relatively less affluent countries of Western Europe, e.g., Spain $1,991, Ireland $2,021, Italy $2,442 and the United Kingdom $3,016.*

Eastern Europe was truly a poor and backward area in the pre-Socialist period, fully comparable to the middle level underdeveloped countries of Asia, Africa and Latin America today. It was the 25 years of Socialist guided development policies since about 1949 that has modernized these economies and greatly increased their standard of living (especially of the working and peasant classes) in the process.

The Soviet Union does not grow rich at the expense of Eastern European countries, neither does it develop a specialization in industrial production while the latter specialize in raw materials. In large part it has been the economic ties between Eastern Europe and the USSR that have been responsible for the rapid economic growth and industrialization of the former region. In fact, Eastern Europe has consistently had the highest rate of economic growth, as well as the fastest rate of industrialization, of any region of the world.

A close empirical examination of the aggregate economic relations between the Soviet Union, the countries of the less developed world and the CMEA countries of Eastern Europe *does not* support the Maoist thesis of "Soviet Social Imperialism."

There are no mechanisms analogous to overproduction operating in the Soviet economy which force the pursuit of overseas investment outlets or trade surpluses in order to allow the accumulation of capital; Soviet trade does not disproportion-

---

*These figures come from the U.N., *Yearbook of National Account Statistics,* 1975 and Business International Corporation, *Investing, Licensing and Trading Conditions Abroad* (June, 1976).

ately benefit the Soviet Union at the expense of other countries; Soviet economic assistance is generous and not used to economically dominate and exploit other countries; the Soviets, unlike all the Western capitalist countries, do not invest in the less developed countries for profit; and Soviet economic integration with Eastern Europe is mutually beneficial to all parties and participated in freely by the Eastern European countries.

Conclusion

It is most unfortunate that the R.C.P. and the other remnants of U.S. Maoism as well as social-democrats, anarchists and Trotskyists are destructively speculating about Soviet society at the very time when the Soviet model of socialism is proving its vitality and the USSR is giving more concrete support to national liberation movements and progressive countries than at any time since the 1940s. It is truly ironic that when Soviet socialism was rather more tenuous than it is today (i.e., the 1930s and 1940s) its institutions were so widely celebrated among many in the West. This irony seems to demonstrate that the interpretations of Soviet and other socialist societies current in Western "radical" circles have very little to do with anything actually going on in the Soviet Union or any other socialist country. It is rather much more a product of the state of contradictions of, and social movements in, Western society, as well as the particular condition of the Western intelligentsia. In the 1930s when Western capitalism looked like it was collapsing and a strong working class movement was on the ascendancy, it was acceptable to be a pro-Soviet Marxist. Then Western leftists had every reason to romanticize and idealize life in the Soviet Union. In the 1950s cold war repression coincident with the rapid expansion of socialism made it quite fashionable to adopt the "totalitarian" model of Soviet society. In the 1960s, middle class student radicals and counter-cultural movements quite naturally idealized and romanticized China's Cultural Revolution, which was largely interpreted as an anarchist revolt against authority and the spontaneous self-determination of the Chinese people (contrasted with the "top down" "bureaucratic socialism" or "state capitalism" of the Soviets). Disillusionment with the Chinese in the 1970s by almost all of the 1960s generation of radicals (as well as by many of our elders such as Bettelheim and Sweezy) should have led to a more realistic (and scientific) understanding of both the nature of socialism and socialist transition. But rather understandably given the lack of a vital Marxist mass movement in the U.S., a revolutionary movement which would have required a scientific understanding of who its international friends and enemies are, a scientific understanding of the possibilities of socialism, as well as an inspiration and proof of the possibility of the socialist enterprise, a different outcome has been produced. The small and isolated U.S. radical movement, largely abandoning careful scholarship and study in favor of anti-Soviet polemics, has fallen victim to the all permeating anti-socialist propaganda machine of monopoly capital (which penetrates even the conceptual definitions employed by U.S. Marxists). ☐

References

Azrael, Jeremy
   1966   *Managerial Power and Soviet Politics.* Cambridge, Mass.: Harvard University Press.

Bettelheim, Charles
   1975   *Economic Calculation and Forms of Property.* New York: Monthly Review Press.

Brainard, Lawrence
   1979   "Foreign economic constraints on Soviet economic policy in the 1980's," in *Soviet Economy in a Time of Change.* A Compendium of Papers submitted to the Joint Economic Committee: Congress of the U.S. Joint Committee Print. 96th Congress, 1st session, Vol. 1, pp. 98-109.

Communist Party of India (M-L)
   1976   *Soviet Social Imperialism in India.* Vancouver, B.C. Indian People's Association in North America.

Conquest, Robert
   1967   *Industrial Workers in the USSR.* New York: Praeger.

Datar, Asha
   1972   *India's Economic Relations with the USSR and Eastern Europe 1953-1969.* Cambridge, England: Cambridge University Press.

Dohan, Michael
   1979   "Export specialization and import dependence in the Soviet economy," in *Soviet Economy in a Time of Change, op. cit.,* Vol. II, pp. 342-395.

Danylyk, John and Sheldon Rabin
1979   "Soviet owned banks in the West," in *Soviet Economy in a Time of Change, op. cit.*, pp. 483-506.

Fainsod, Merle and Jerry Hough
1979   *How Russia is Ruled.* Cambridge, Mass. : Harvard University Press.

Fallenbuchl, Z. M.
1974   "Comecon Integration," in Bornstein, Morris, and Daniel Fusfeld, editors, *The Soviet Economy.* Homewood, Illinois: Richard Irwin, Inc.

Goldich, Judith
1979   "USSR grain and oilseed trade in the seventies," in *Soviet Economy in a Time of Change, op cit.*, Vol. II, pp. 133-164.

Goldman, Marshall
1967   *Soviet Foreign Aid.* New York: Praeger.

Goure, Leon and Julian Weinkle
1973   "Soviet-Cuban relations: The growing integration," in Jaime Suchlicki (ed.), *Cuba, Castro and Revolution.* Coral Gables, Florida: University of Miami Press.

Granick, David
1961   *The Red Executive.* Garden City, N.J.: Doubleday.

Gregory, Paul and Robert Stuart
1974   *Soviet Economic Structure and Performance.* New York: Harper and Row.

Hill, Ronald
1977   *Soviet Political Elites.* London: Martin Robertson.

Holzman, Franklyn
1974   *Foreign Trade Under Central Planning.* Cambridge, Mass.: Harvard University Press.

Hough, Jerry
1974   "The Brezhnev Era: The Man and the System," in *Problems of Communism*, November - December.
        "Political Participation in the Soviet Union," in *Soviet Studies*, 28:1 (January).

Hopkins, Mark
1970   *Mass Media in the Soviet Union.* New York: Pegasus.

Kramer, John
1975   "The Energy Gap in Eastern Europe," *Survey* (21:1-2) Winter-Spring.

Lane, David and Felicity O'Dell
1978   *The Soviet Worker.* New York: St. Martins.

McMillan, Gail
1979   "Soviet investment in the industrialized Western economies and in the developed economies of the Third World," in *Soviet Economy in a Time of Change, op. cit.*, Vol. II, pp. 625-647.

Marer, Paul
   1972   *Soviet and Eastern European Foreign Trade 1946-1969*. Bloomington, Indiana: Indiana University Press.
   1974   "The Political Economy of Soviet Relations with Eastern Europe," in Rosen, Steven and James Kurth, ed., *Testing Economic Theories of Imperialism*. Lexington, Mass.: D.C. Heath and Co.

Matthews, Mervyn
   1978   *Privilege in the Soviet Union*. London: George Allen and Unwin.

Mickiewicz, Ellen
   1973   *The Handbook of Soviet Social Science Data*. New York: The Free Press.

Nicolaus, Martin
   1975   *Restoration of Capitalism in the USSR*. Chicago: Liberator Press.

Osborn, Robert
   1970   *Soviet Social Policies*. Homewood, Illinois: Dorsey.

Rigby, T.H.
   1976   "Communist Party Membership under Brezhnev," in *Soviet Studies*, 28:1 (July).

Revolutionary Communist Party
   1974   *How Capitalism Has Been Restored in the Soviet Union and What This Means for the World Struggle*. Chicago

Sherman, Howard
   1969   *The Soviet Economy*. Boston: Little Brown.

Skilling, M. Gordan and Griffiths (eds.)
   1971   *Interest Groups in Soviet Politics*. Princeton, N.J.: Princeton University Press.

Sweezy, Paul and Charles Bettelheim
   1971   *On the Transition to Socialism*. New York: Monthly Review Press.

Sweezy, Paul
   1981   *Post-Revolutionary Society*. New York: Monthly Review Press.

Szymanski, Albert
   1979   *Is the Red Flag Flying: The Political Economy of the Soviet Union Today*. London: Zed Press.
   1981   *The Logic of Imperialism*. New York: Praeger.
   1983   *The Political Economy of Human Rights: USA/USSR*. London: Zed Press.

Wilczynski, J.
   1970   *The Economics of Socialism*. Chicago: Aldine.

Yanowitch, Murray
   1977   *Social and Economic Inequality in the Soviet Union*. White Plains, New York: M.E. Sharp.

Soviet Economic Relations With India and Other Third World Countries

Santosh K. Mehrotra
Patrick Clawson

This paper is concerned with the aid and trade relations of the Soviet Union with Third World countries, with certain sections devoted wholly to Indo-Soviet economic relations. Trade and aid are two different aspects of economic co-operation between nations. However, in East European literature, trade with the Third World countries is regarded as a special form of aid. It would be more correct to regard aid as an adjunct to trade. Aid is rarely a gift (grant). 'Aid' usually means loans which must be repaid with interest.

It has been alleged, and rightly so, that the existence of aid from Western capitalist countries can be explained only in terms of an attempt to preserve the capitalist system in the Third World. Aid is seen as a concession by capitalist nations to enable them to continue their exploitation of the ex-colonial

---

Patrick Clawson was an editor of *The Review of Radical Political Economics* special issue on the Soviet Union and has taught economics at Seton Hall University.
Santosh K. Mehrotra studied at Jawaharlal Nehru University where he wrote his dissertation, *India's Economic Relations with the USSR, 1955-77*. This article originally appeared in *Economic and Political Weekly* (Bombay), Special Number August 1979.
Reprinted by permission of Patrick Clawson.

countries.[1] As regards trade relations between Third World and advanced capitalist countries, it is well known that the terms of trade of the Less Developed Countries vis-a-vis the Western countries have been deteriorating over the years, particularly in the era of neo-colonialism.[2]

In the light of the experience of the LDCs with aid from and trade with the West, it is important to carefully consider and scrutinise Soviet aid and trade relations with LDCs. According to a widely accepted view, the Soviet Union has had to bear a heavy economic burden in order to develop political ties with LDCs [1]. This article argues that the rulers of the USSR do in fact draw substantial economic gain from trade and aid with LDCs. Soviet trade and aid relations are largely economically motivated, although politics often determines from which country an item desired in trade will be acquired. The second section of the article shows how the USSR has drawn economic advantage from its trade and aid with India. The third section points out the essential similarity between the structure of Soviet-LDC relations and that of Western-LDC relations. The actions of the USSR since late 1950s are shown to be consistent with Lenin's description of imperialism and inconsistent with the principles of socialist trade.[3] In no sense does the article "prove" that the USSR is an imperialist power in the Leninist sense. The argument here is much more limited: the analysis is only of the

---

[1] There have been several studies of Western aid which have characterised aid as imperialism in a new garb: Teresa Hayter, "Aid as Imperialism" (Harmondsworth: Pelican, 1971); Michael Barratt Brown, "The Economics of Imperialism" (Harmondsworth: Penguin, 1974); C R Ninsman, "Rich against Poor: The Reality of Aid" (Harmondsworth: Penguin, 1971); Cheryl Payer, '"The Debt Trap: The IMF and the Third World" (Harmondsworth: Pelican, 1974).

A survey of the policies of the various Western donor countries by W G Zeylstra (a Dutch diplomat), who is surely no Marxist, shows that as a rule either aid-giving is largely dependent on considerations which have little to do with the promotion of development or its commitment as a priority is low. See W G Zeylstra, "Aid or Development: The Relevance of Development Aid to Problems of Developing Countries" (Sijtholf-Leyden, 1975).

[2] In the period of neo-colonialism, from the Fifties of the 20th century to the present day, but for a few exceptional years and commodities, the secular trend of worsening terms of trade for Third World primary goods has continued.

[3] From the 1920s through the early 1950s, the Soviet Union engaged in little foreign trade with capitalist countries. The main policy under Stalin's leadership was self-reliance. Soviet economic relations with the Third World expanded rapidly in the middle 1950s; the analysis of this article begins at that date.

character of foreign economic relations. This precludes analysing whether there exist finance capital and monopolies in the USSR. The evidence presented here is consistent with the theory that the USSR is imperialist.[4] The article closes with an examination of the effect of Soviet trade and aid on class relationships in India. It is shown that economic relations with the USSR have reproduced India's dependency on foreign powers. In other words, Soviet actions have been what would be expected from an imperialist power which is exporting capital to India.

I
ADVANTAGES TO USSR TO TRADE WITH THE THIRD WORLD

While there is much data on Soviet LDC trade, most of it is close to worthless. The World Bank, the IMF, and the US Commerce Department publish data based on the foreign trade statistics of the developing countries.[5] While India's foreign trade statistics are quite comprehensive and reliable, unfortunately most LDCs do not include in their statistics all imports financed by loans from foreign governments or exports to repay those loans. Since it is these transactions we are most interested in, the data from LDCs are not used here. The official Soviet data, which are translated and compiled by the UN, the US State Department, and the CIA, are used throughout this paper. The

---

[4] Charles Bettelheim has provided the most systematic treatment to date of Soviet capitalism; see Bettelheim, "Economic Calculations and Forms of Property" (New York: Monthly Review, 1975); and "Class Struggles in the USSR 1917-1923" (New York: Monthly Review, 1976).

The Communist Party of China has forcefully argued that the Soviet economy is dominated by capitalist monopolies. The polemical tone of the Communist Party of China's writings should not hide the theoretical sophistication of its position. See Communist Party of China, "How the Soviet Revisionists Carry Out All-Round Restoration of Capitalism in the USSR" (Peking: Foreign Languages Press 1968); and "Ugly Features of Soviet Social Imperialism" (Peking: Foreign Languages Press, 1976).

[5] A technical appendix on Soviet-Third World trade data is available on request from the authors (Department of Economics, New School for Social Research, 65 Fifth Avenue, NY USA). On Soviet foreign trade data, see Barry Kostinsky, "Description and Analysis of Soviet Foreign Trade Statistics" (Washington, D C: Government Printing Office, 1974).

Soviet data do not include arms exports. There is a substantial difference, however, between the Soviet aggregate figures for trade with the LDCs as a group and the sum of the reported trade with each LDC. This difference corresponds roughly to estimates of the arms trade.[6] There are no good data on the Soviet balance of payments as distinct from the balance of trade. It would seem that the only major transactions not reflected in the trade data are the hard currency purchases of arms by Middle Eastern countries.

(a) Soviet Imports Provide Raw Materials for Industry

Soviet trade with LDCs expands Soviet industry in two ways: (1) by providing a market for Soviet machinery, and (2) by providing raw materials for industry (including food-stuffs for the workers in industry). In this part of the article, the latter factor will be considered. Soviet imports from LDCs fall into two major categories: on the one hand, there are raw materials (such as cotton, wool, rubber, hides and jute); on the other hand, there are speciality foodstuffs (such as cocoa, rice, citrus fruits, oranges, nuts, tea and coffee). Every one of these raw materials was a major Soviet import in the 1920s; that is, until the rise of autarkic policies in the 1930s. When the USSR began to re-emerge on the capitalist world market after 1953, it was these raw materials and foodstuffs which were imported — before the USSR had any political ties with countries exporting these commodities.

When the USSR imports raw materials from LDCs, it is able to reduce the more expensive expansion of domestic output of these raw materials. For instance, the import of long staple cotton from Egypt and Sudan is less expensive than the construction of extensive irrigation systems in Soviet Central Asia.[7] By

[6] Kostinsky, *op. cit.* There are no official data from the USSR on Soviet arms shipments. The estimates from the US Arms Control and Disarmament Agency, cited below, are widely respected. The other major source is the Stockholm International Peace Research Institute.

[7] The Soviet Union has greatly expanded cotton output since World War II, and now it even exports quite a bit of cotton primarily to Eastern Europe. To some extent domestic production has replaced imports. Domestic cotton is, however, medium-staple, which is of lower quality for most purposes than Egyptian or Sudanese cotton.

exporting manufactured goods in return for raw material imports, the USSR is able to increase its rate of industrialisation. Increases in manufacturing output offer the USSR the possibility of economies of scale. A broad industrial base helps the USSR fund large-scale research and development. A rapid pace of capital accumulation allows for the constant introduction of new technology. All this enables the USSR to become a major world economic power while preserving (if not reinforcing) the subordinate role of the LDCs.

In the last decade, Soviet imports have been shifting from unprocessed raw materials to semi-processed goods. For example, Soviet imports of cotton fibre from the Third World rose only slightly from 1960 to 1972: from $145.9 million to $181.2 million. On the other hand, imports of cotton yarn and clothing went up from $1 million to $122.3 million in the same period. While Soviet imports of Indian hides declined from $16.3 million in 1966-7 to nil in 1974-5, imports of leather and leather goods [increased] from $24.1 to $58.7 million.

The shifting import pattern of Soviet trade reflects the needs of the Soviet economy. Twenty years ago, the USSR was engaged on a large scale in the basic processing of raw materials. Today, Soviet industry is shifting towards more advanced industries, using more sophisticated technologies. In order to expand the output of technologically advanced goods, resources must be shifted away from the production of semi-processed raw materials and low quality manufactured goods. For instance, the USSR used to import leather from India to manufacture gloves. Now, the USSR is exporting plants to India to produce 1.6 million pairs of gloves for export to the USSR. Instead of producing gloves, the Soviets are producing glove-making machinery, a more technologically advanced product. This process is called the product life cycle. New products are developed in the advanced countries and are initially produced there. Eventually, the technology for making these products is standardised and routinised. The products are then made in the LDCs. The high initial profits from the products pay for the costs of developing new technologies which are put into production in the advanced countries. Through the product life cycle, the basic character of Soviet-LDC trade is preserved.

It is sometimes argued that exports to the USSR are profitable for LDCs even when the Soviets pay prices below world market prices. The reason given is that trade with the Soviets represents a net increase in exports. This argument is wrong for two reasons. First, the Soviets are likely to purchase many of the same goods with hard currency on the open market if they could not obtain them any other way. Second, as Datar has shown, the Third World could have exported considerably more to the West if it had not exported to the USSR; she estimates that India could have found markets in the West for 26 per cent of its exports to the Eastern Bloc, at the same or higher prices.[8]

(b) Soviet Aid Creates Market for Soviet Machinery Exports

A principal barrier to the expansion of Soviet imports in the 1950s and early 1960s was the lack of foreign exchange to pay for imports. The Soviet exports were then largely raw materials; the demand for these in the LDCs was limited (see Table 2). The USSR ran up a cumulative deficit with the LDCs of $991.3 million from 1955 to 1962; the gap in 1960 alone was $229.3 million. The Soviet deficit stemmed primarily from large hard currency purchases of raw materials from LDCs which were not markets for Soviet exports. If the USSR were to continue its imports of raw materials, the Soviet leadership would have to find a market for some category of Soviet goods. The Soviet leaders were not satisfied with a bilateral exchange of raw materials; they wanted to increase the level of industrialisation in the USSR. In other words, the Soviet leaders wanted to reinforce an international division of labour in which a few advanced countries export advanced technology, especially machine goods, while most countries become dependent on exports of industrial raw materials and some basic consumer goods.

---

[8] Asha Datar, "India's Economic Relations with the USSR and Eastern Europe 1953-1969" (Cambridge: Cambridge University Press, 1972), pp 138-9, 259. There has been a third, quite minor, reason why Third World exports to the USSR do not represent a net increase in Third World exports. The Soviet Union has occasionally re-exported some of the goods it imported from the Third World, often making a profit from its role as middleman. After citing many of the known cases of re-exporting, Nirmal Chandra, "USSR and Third World" (*Economic and Political Weekly,* Annual Number, February 1977), correctly concludes that Soviet re-exporting has been quite small.

The expansion of Soviet machine goods exports faced a major barrier: there was no demand for Soviet machinery in the Third World, partly because of Cold War pressures but also partly because of the poor reputation of Soviet machinery.[9] One of the ways to break into LDC markets was to offer loans to finance the purchase of Soviet machinery; another way was to finance purchases by state-owned corporations which were denied access to Western credit. It was against this background of balance of payments difficulties that the Soviets began to extend loans to LDCs — loans that were then called 'aid'. Khruschev's famous declaration of 'economic warfare' against the US did not reflect a willingness to take economic losses in order to make political friends (as was widely feared among US business circles at the time). Khruschev intended to break into US-dominated markets by offering better credit terms, thereby consolidating the USSR's position as a major force on the world market. Soviet economists have gone so far as to calculate how much trade is generated by each extra rouble of credit.[10]

From 1956 on, the USSR has been extending credits on a large scale. According to US government estimates, from 1955 through 1976, the USSR extended $11.8 billion, over 95 per cent of which was loans. Eastern European countries extended $6.5 billion. 28 per cent of the Soviet aid has gone to Egypt and India. Another 43 per cent has gone to the Middle East broadly defined (Afghanistan, Algeria, Iran, Iraq, Syria, and Turkey). 10 per cent has gone to sub-Saharan Africa, and 20 per cent to the rest of the world. The credits authorised in an aid agreement cannot be used until further agreements are signed; the Soviets must approve each project for which the funds are to be used. The credits must be spent on goods purchased in the USSR. In other words, Soviet aid is 'double tied': tied as to which projects it may

---

[9] Datar, *op cit*, p 167: "The USSR and Czechoslovakia find it difficult to promote exports of machinery and equipment to Western markets and so it appears that their products are not good enough to compete with Western products. In private discussions [Indian] government officials seemed to accept this as natural." See Goldman, "Soviet Foreign Aid" (New York: Praeger, 1967), pp 69f, on the difficulties the Soviets had in building the High Dam at Aswan in Egypt; Western equipment had to be brought in surreptitiously.

[10] In documents submitted to UNCTAD, cited in Michael Kidron, "Pakistan's Trade with Eastern Bloc Countries" (New York: Praeger, 1972). The multiplier was 5.4 roubles of trade created for each extra rouble of aid.

be used on, and tied as to the origin of the goods. There is no guarantee that the credits authorised in a Soviet aid agreement will necessarily be used, nor that the level of trade called for in a trade agreement will be reached. There are only sketchy data on the actual deliveries of Soviet goods under the aid shipments to LDCs from 1967 through* below on India). The US government estimates that a little over half of the credits have been shipped.

The figures above on Soviet aid do not include military aid. Soviet arms shipments to LDCs from 1967 through 1976 are estimated by the US government at $13,460 million. From 1965 to 1974, Egypt purchased $2,400 million, Syria and Iraq together bought $2000 million, and India purchased $1,300 million. Soviet arms sales — often called Soviet military aid — are generally financed by ten-year credits (with three year grace periods) at 2 to 2-1/2 per cent interest.[11] The prices paid by LDCs for Soviet arms are 40 to 50 per cent below Western prices. Most arms sales by both the West and the Soviet bloc are of older equipment. Even if the trend towards sale of newer equipment continues, the revenue from sales to LDCs will still help fund acquisition of new equipment, especially by reducing the per unit cost of research and development.

(c) Aid, Balance of Trade, and Balance of Payments

The effects of this large credit programme on the Soviet balance of payments with LDCs have been dramatic. Soviet imports from these countries were rising rapidly. The only way the USSR could maintain an even balance of trade was by increasing shipments under the aid programme. As can be seen from Table 2, the USSR increased machinery exports, especially exports of 'equipment for complete plants' — a category which is almost completely identical with shipments under the aid programme.

---

* Words missing from original source — Ed.

[11] This information, unfortunately unconfirmed from Soviet sources, is from the US Arms Control and Disarmament Agency, "The International Transfer of Conventional Arms" (Washington, D C: Government Printing Office, 1974). The figure of 40 per cent lower prices for Soviet arms is based on a very generous evaluation of the quality of Soviet arms. Quality is a major factor affecting price comparisons.

Table 1: Soviet Imports From Third World Countries

(Millions of US$)

Year	Total Imports	Rubber	Hides, Skins, Leather	Coffee, Tea, Cocoa	Nuts, Fruits, Vegetables	Jute bags, Packing Cloth	Cotton Fibre, Yarn, Fabric, Clothing	Cereals, Sugar	Other
1955	210.4	25.5	11.7	15.3	7.7	45.2		57.8	47.2
1960	564.4	151.8	38.7	6.2	27.2	8.7	146.9	6.6	177.9
1965	814.9	137.1	34.4	119.8	65.7	45.4	209.7	47.7	155.1
1970	1215.6	140.6	66.9	156.5	122.3	38.3	356.6		334.1
1972	1613.0	77.8	52.2	166.8	149.2	66.2	342.6		808.2
1975	4280.2	141.4	124.1	469.1	292.2	86.3	551.9	676.6	1932.6*

*In 1975, imports of petroleum products totalled $802 million.
Basic Source: USSR, Ministry of Foreign Trade, *Vneshnyana Torgavlya*, various years.

Table 2 : Soviet Exports to Third World Countries

(Millions of US$)

Year	Total Exports	Machinery		Petroleum Products	Foods, Lumber	Iron, Steel	Undistributed Regional Exports†	Other
		Total	Subtotal: Equipment for Complete Plants					
1955	210.4	5.4	1.1	31.9	21.2	20.1	*	132.1
1960	335.1	125.4	68.6	53.9	71.6	30.9	*	53.3
1965	1122.7	471.7	234.1	131.6	117.0	57.8	268.8	75.8
1970	2039.7	686.5	408.1	92.3	169.3	102.9	791.8	196.9
1972	2495.7	813.8	*	115.0	114.8	105.6	1069.2	277.5
1975	3173.0	1132.4	*	803.4	303.8	116.3	453.3	363.8

* Data in this category not collected by the USSR
† As noted in the text, this category is composed mostly of arms exports and includes most arms exports.
Basic Source : USSR, Ministry of Foreign Trade, *Vneshnyana Torgavlya*, various years.

The initial impact of the aid was to improve the balance of trade, which became positive by 1965. Soviet machine goods exports offset the imports of raw materials. There was an improvement in the balance of trade which is goods exported minus goods imported, but no improvement in the balance of payments which includes the movement of money sums such as the credits extended as aid. There are no data available on the Soviet balance of payments, as distinct from data on Soviet foreign trade. Soviet foreign aid is the export of money capital; therefore it worsens the Soviet balance of payments. When Third World countries began to repay the Soviet loans with shipments of goods to the USSR, the Soviets were once again importing more than they exported: the balance of trade became negative again. Previously, the negative Soviet balance of trade was a source of worry to the Soviet leaders: it meant they were piling up a debt which they owed to the Third World governments. Now, the negative balance of trade is a sign that the LDCs are paying back their debts, or at least the interests on the debts, to the USSR. In the 1950s the negative balance of trade meant a negative balance of payments. Today, the negative balance of trade may occur simultaneously with a balanced balance of payments. The USSR can import more goods than it exports because LDCs must repay the interest and principal on Soviet loans ('aid').

Weapons shipments have been important for the USSR's balance of trade and of payments. Soviet arms shipments have been a large portion of total Soviet exports to LDCs. Soviet arms sales have been in return for commodities to be shipped back to the USSR. In other words, these arms sales have been on the same basis as economic aid, and they have had the same impact on the balance of payments. For instance, Soviet military sales to India were a large factor in improving the USSR's substantial negative balance of trade with India in the early 1960s. The USSR had to suggest prepayment of the credit for the Bhilai steel plant in the early 1960s because of India's large net surplus with the USSR. "The problem [of unbalanced trade] disappeared largely as a result of the payments for defence imports" [2]. Other Soviet arms sales have been for cash; that is, convertible Western currency. Algeria, Libya, and other Arab oil producers paid the USSR in cash for shipments to Egypt during the October War; these shipments included over 100 fighter planes, 600

Table 3: Estimates of Soviet Arms Exports to Third World Countries

(Millions of US$)

Year	Undistributed Regional Exports (from USSR) trade data	US Government Estimates
1965	268.8	260
1970	791.8	1,000
1972	1,069.2	1,205
1975	453.3	1,685

Table 4: Soviet Balance of Trade with Third World Countries

(Millions of US$)

Year	Balance of Trade	Balance of Trade Not Including Undistributed Regional Exports (ie, Not Including Soviet Arms Exports)
1955	0	*
1960	− 229.3	*
1965	+ 307.8	+ 39.0
1970	+ 824.1	+ 32.3
1972	+ 882.7	− 186.5
1975	− 1107.3	− 1560.5

*Data in this category not collected by the USSR.
+ Means Soviet exports exceeded imports; − means Soviet imports exceeded exports.

tanks, and other equipment [3]. These shipments help the Soviet balance of trade: the exports are unmatched by any imports of goods from Egypt. They also help the balance of payments. The shipments also provide the Soviet leadership with hard currency with which to purchase Western technology.[12]

While granting that the Soviet aid programme has helped the USSR's balance of payments, some observers doubt the economic advantage to the USSR of foreign aid. Their doubts are based on the low interest rates charged on loans, 2-1/2 per cent being a common Soviet rate. A major reason the Soviets charge only 2-1/2 per cent is that they have faced difficulties in penetrating LDC markets. Soviet machinery is not renowned for its high quality; to sell the machinery the Soviets must offer better terms than are available from competitors. As the USSR has established itself in a market, it has become more demanding in the terms of its loans. At the same time, the West has become more accommodating, perhaps as a response to the increased competition.

The interest rate on Soviet loans has not been as much lower than the rate on Western loans as it might seem at first glance. While the nominal Soviet interest rate has been lower than the nominal World Bank interest rate (around 8 per cent on most loans), the *effective* Soviet interest rate may be higher because the Soviets have required repayments to begin sooner and have been inflexible about stretching out repayment [4]. After examining Soviet and Western aid to India, Chaudhri concluded: "There does not seem to be any evidence that the East European countries have overall offered particularly favourable terms to India" [5].

(d) Prices at which Soviets Trade

There has been quite a debate about the prices at which the Soviets trade. Much of the debate has assumed that the

---

[12]Nirmal Chandra, *op cit*, p 350, argues that the Soviets cannot use profits from trade with the Third World to finance imports of Western technology. He is wrong on two counts: (i) Arms sales to some countries are in hard currency, and (ii) Trade and aid agreements with Third World countries reduce the amount of foreign currency the Soviet leadership must spend to import raw materials, and therefore more foreign currency is available for importing advanced technology from the West.

capitalist world market price is the 'fair price'. Soviet prices are then compared to the world price to see if the Soviets are 'fair' or 'unfair' in their pricing policy. The procedure is of dubious significance. If the Soviets are charging the same prices for their exports (and paying similar prices for their imports) as the West, and if the Soviets are able to produce at roughly the same cost as the West, then the USSR is making a rate of profit off its trade with the LDCs equal to the imperialist superprofits that the West makes from its trade with the Third World.

Comparing prices is a difficult process because there are factors which influence the price of a commodity: quality of manufacture, the precise design of the good compared to other similar goods, the time of year it was bought (especially for agricultural goods), and so on. There have been two careful studies comparing the prices the Soviets charged for their exports to the West with the prices the Soviets charged for their exports to LDCs. Both studies came to pretty much the same conclusion. Chandra writes, "The USSR generally charges the Third World prices which are higher by about a third compared to those realised in Soviet exports to the West. For the machinery group as a whole, the rate of overpricing varies between three-tenths and one-half" [6]. Carter studied the prices of 63 commodities, covering 27 per cent of the USSR's nonmilitary exports to the LDCs in 1964. He concluded that if the USSR had sold these commodities to the LDCs at the same price the Soviets charged the industrial Western countries, then the Third World countries would have paid 13.1 per cent less [7]. While it is difficult to compare machine goods because of their heterogeneity, the discrimination was substantially worse in the case of the few machine goods for which some comparison could be made: export prices to the LDCs were 34.7 per cent higher than to the industrial West.

Chandra notes that the prices used in Soviet-Third World trade are substantially the same prices used in trade among the Eastern bloc countries. From the fact that the Soviets receive lower prices for their exports from the West than they receive from either the LDCs or from the Eastern bloc, it would be possible to conclude one of two things. One possibility is that the Soviets charge prices higher than the world market price in their trade with the Third World and the Eastern bloc. The other possibility is that the Soviets received prices from the West which are below the world market price. Holzman argues that the latter is true; that is, the lower price received by the USSR in its trade with the West reflects the superior bargaining position of the West *vis-a-vis* the USSR [8]. This thesis is most unconvincing. If there has been any price discrimination, the Western European countries may have discriminated in favour of Soviet exports of raw materials in hopes of diversifying supply sources (e g, Soviet oil and gas exports).

One way to test the Holzman thesis is to compare the prices the LDCs pay for imports from the USSR with the prices the LDCs pay for imports from the West (and the prices the Third World receives for exports to the two blocs). If the LDCs pay higher prices for Soviet goods than for Western goods, then, given that the USSR receives higher prices from the LDCs than it receives from the West, it would seem fair to conclude that Soviet-Third World trade is at prices more advantageous to the USSR than world market prices would be.[13] In other words, the Holzman thesis would be incorrect. Datar has made a careful comparison of the prices India paid the USSR compared to the prices India paid the West. She concludes: "The evidence available shows that the East European countries offered higher prices for some exports and lower prices for others and, as far as the imports of raw materials are concerned the prices from the East European countries and others were comparable. Therefore, it would appear that for merchandise trade alone, India's net barter terms of trade were probably comparable, or at least not significantly worse than it obtained from the rest of the world. However, this comparison excludes imports of

---

[13] The conclusion would not necessarily follow. The correct procedure would be to compare Soviet-Third World prices with world market prices, where the world market price is the price which would rule if all trade were conducted on open markets. In the real world, much trade is conducted at regulated prices. For instance, the US sugar quota system means that there is one price for sugar which can be sold in the US and another price for all other sugar. If the US quota were abolished, then the world market price would be somewhere between the US price and the non-US price. The latter price, the non-US price, is often incorrectly called the world market price. It is very difficult to tell what the world market price for any commodity actually is. Because of the problems of estimating world market prices, complicated and indirect procedures — such as those cited in the text — are necessary for comparisons of Soviet-Third World prices with world market prices.

machinery and equipment. From the case studies presented in Chapter 5 [of excess costs, see II b below] and other evidence, such as complaints from private investors, it appears that the prices of machinery and equipment from the East European countries were higher than prices offered by other countries. Imports of machinery constituted at least 50 per cent of India's total imports from East European countries. Therefore, taking into account all imports and exports, India's net terms of trade were probably worse with the East European countries than with the rest of the world" [9].

(e) Profitability of Soviet Aid

Soviet leaders have been quite blunt in justifying their aid programme on the basis of economic profitability. If we want to learn why it took the USSR over two years to decide to finance the High Dam at Aswan after Dulles withdrew the US-UK-World Bank offer in 1956, and why the Soviets did not agree to finance the second and third stages of the Dam until *after* the West Germans had agreed to finance them, we can turn to Khruschev: "We were interested in determining whether it would be a profitable business transaction. Naturally we would be glad to have an opportunity to bolster the economy of our friends and in so doing to strengthen our relations with them. But that was a political consideration, and we also had to make sure that we would not simply be giving our money away. We had to make sure that the Egyptians could repay us in regular deliveries of their best long-fibre cotton, rice and other goods" [10].

And indeed the Dam, along with the rest of the Soviet aid programme, has been profitable for the USSR. Carter argues that the 'opportunity cost' of Soviet aid should be defined as the world market price of the goods delivered by the Soviets under the credit (aid) agreements minus the world market price of the goods delivered to the Soviets in repayment discounted at 15 per cent per annum [11]. 15 per cent is supposedly the 'social rate of return' to capital in the USSR; that is, the average rate of profit in the USSR. When Carter discounts the repayments of aid at a rate equal to the 'social rate of return on capital' inside the USSR, he is trying to compare the profitability of investing in a plant inside the USSR to the profitability of investing in foreign aid. Carter

Table 5: Terms of Aid to India from Selected Donors

	Interest Rates		Maturity (years)		Grace Period (years)	
	(1)	(2)	(1)	(2)	(1)	(2)
Czechoslovakia	2.5	2.5	4 to 6	8 to 12	1	Nil
Hungary	2.5 to 4.5	2.5	10	10	1	Nil
Poland	2.5	2.5	10	8 to 12	3	Nil
USSR	2.5	2.5	12	12	1	Nil
Yugoslavia	3.	3.0	6 to 8	11	Nil	Nil
France	5 to 6	3.5 to 8.0	10	10 to 25	Nil	Nil
West Germany	3 to 5.5	2.5	15 to 25	30	4 to 7	8
Japan	5.8	5.25	15	18	5	5
IBRD	5.5 to 6.0	7.0	10 to 20	30	Nil	10
IDA	0.75	0.75	50	50	10	10
UK	3.5	Nil	25	25	7	7
USA (1)	0.75	2 to 3	5 to 6	40	2	10
(2)	5.75	6	40	10 to 20	10	3

Notes: Column (1) up to 1966-67, Column (2) 1971. For USA, row (1) refers to DLF/AID Loans; row (2) to Eximbank loans.

Source: Government of India, Ministry of Finance, "External Assistance".

Table 6: Cost of Public Sector Oil Refiniries

(Rs millions)

Name	Capacity million tons	Total Cost	Foreign Exchange Component	Collaborator
Madras	2.50	440.0		ENI (Italy)
Gauhati	0.75	159.8	64.3	Rumania
Barauni	2.00	434.5	178.1	USSR
Koyali	3.00	307.0	150.0	USSR
Cochin	3.56	293.3	177.8	Phillips Petroleum (USA)
Haldia	2.5	460.0	230.0	Hungary

Source : "Annual Report of Public Sector Undertakings 1965/6", Chapter 1, Bureau of Petroleum Information.

finds that the 'opportunity cost' of Soviet aid from 1955 through 1968 was $441 million. In other words, if the funds spent on aid had instead been invested at 15 per cent the Soviet leadership would have made slightly more than it made from investing the funds in aid. This means that the profit rate on Soviet aid was in effect slightly under 15 per cent — not a bad rate of return, especially considering that the USSR was breaking into a new field of investment, where it would have to bear some extra costs to get established as a major competitor.

Table 7: Total Costs of Construction of Bokaro Steel Plant

(Rs millions)

Collaborator	Stage 1	Total
US	394	715
USSR	486	1027

Source: For the USSR : Dastur and Co, "Cost Reduction Study on the Bokaro Project", Calcutta, 1966; For the US: Elliot and Wagner, "Synopsis of a Techno-Economic Survey of a Proposed Integrated Steel Plant at Bokaro", Washington, DC, 1966.

It would seem that the gains to the USSR from trade with LDCs are very minor in the context of the Soviet Union's $800,000 million GNP. While it is true that the profits from the aid programme are so far only a small factor in Soviet capital accumulation, it would be a mistake to gauge the impact of Soviet-Third World trade solely by the dollar amount of the trade. Profits earned in this trade are in foreign currency — either directly as in arms sales to the Mideast, or indirectly through the reduction of the amount of hard currency the Soviets must spend to purchase raw materials. The Soviet leadership has been eager in recent years to acquire advanced capitalist technology through the purchase of machine goods from the West. The primary constraint on the import of high technology equipment has been the ability of the Soviet economy to generate enough exports to cover the costs of the imports. Since any profits earned from the aid programme (and any reduction in necessary imports costs) can be applied towards the import of advanced Western technology, the profits from Soviet-Third World trade have an importance greater than their small dollar amount would indicate.

II
SOVIET AID TO INDIA

The USSR is the sixth largest aid-giver to India — in sheer volume of financial assistance — after the USA, the World Bank group, the UK, West Germany, and Canada, in that order. From India's viewpoint, the benefits of Soviet aid have been cited as being the following. Firstly, its importance is to be judged by the fact that while Western donors were not prepared to give aid to public sector projects, all Soviet aid has gone to the public sector. Secondly, the majority of Soviet loans have been for setting up capital goods industries, which were lacking in India on the morrow of independence in 1947. Finally, the presence of the USSR greatly improves India's bargaining position with Western countries.

In order to evaluate Soviet economic assistance to India we will need to consider three issues: the terms of aid, the tying of aid and the character of the technical assistance.

(a) Terms of Aid

The USSR was the first donor to accept the principle of giving development loans on concessional terms. The concessional element depends on (i) the rate of interest, (ii) the amortisation period, and (iii) the currency of repayment. The USSR merely offered low interest rates. Loans have been given for much shorter periods of time than those offered by the US and there have not been any significant grace periods for repayment. To a large extent, the short duration of the loans offsets the advantages of lower rates of interest and overall terms do not come out very favourably. For example, if we use the grant element [14] as a ranking device (the difference between the aid received today and the discounted value of further repayment obligations as of today), the USSR terms come out very unfavourable as compared not only to the US loans, but also the loans from IDA, West Germany, and the UK.

For a country faced with a severe foreign exchange shortage, repayment in local currency would be a special concession. The Soviet loans are more accurately described as repayment in kind. To be accurately described as repayable in rupees, in the sense that there were no foreign exchange costs involved, it must be shown that India could not have exported to other countries the goods it had to send the USSR. Most studies have concluded that exports to the USSR have been by and large in addition to exports elsewhere and the terms of trade not significantly worse than India obtained elsewhere. Therefore, the burden of repaying loans has not been heavier than repayment in convertible currency. But because of other indirect costs, repayment in kind has been almost as burdensome as repayment in convertible currency. One of these costs is undesirable exports. [15] The other cost was the need to give technical credits. [16] Moreover, India had repaid only a part of its credit up to 1965-6. Since the devaluation of the rupee in June 1966, the burden of repayment has increased because India's terms of trade with the USSR deteriorated. We will return to this point later.

---

[14] The difference between the aid received today and the discounted value of future repayment obligations as of today expresses, in money terms, what different writers have called the 'grant' or 'gift' element of aid.

[15] Data concerning India's exports to the Eastern bloc show that between 20 per cent and 25 per cent of those exports were diversionary; i e, they could have been exported to hard currency areas.

[16] Datar, *op cit*, has come to the conclusion that during the period from 1953-4 to 1965-6 the need for India to give technical credit (or swing credits, as they are called) arose for two reasons: (i) India's difficulty in finding acceptable imports to absorb her export-earnings from Eastern Europe, and (ii) the slowness with which East European countries have fulfilled export commitments. And since India is a net exporter to the USSR, she accumulated idle balances. This constitutes waste of credit finance. Such a waste was a serious problem for other developing countries in their economic relations with the USSR. Because of this problem, the utility of non-convertible payment agreements is questionable.

In short, the Soviet loans have not been significantly cheaper than Western loans. The differences in interest rate and in terms of repayment have been more nominal than real. If Western loans are profitable, we would also expect that Soviet loans to India have been profitable.

(b) Excess Costs

All Soviet aid granted until 1977 was double tied. It was source-tied to the extent that all goods bought with such loans had to be purchased from the donor country. It was tied as to end use in the sense that it was all specific project aid, and not general programme aid. The result was that the choice of goods was restricted to what the donor country could offer even if some of the equipment was not always suitable to India's requirements.

The following two cases are examples of excess costs in aid projects: (i) in petroleum refining, the equipment and production processes which the Soviets offered were not suitable to India's requirements; and (ii) the costs of production in the Bokaro Steel Works and the Gauhati and Barauni refineries were higher than the private sector refineries and US proposal for Bokaro.

From Table 6 it is clear that the Soviets charged higher prices than the foreign private firms. While Philips Petroleum charged Rs 393.8 million for a 3.56 million ton plant at Cochin, the USSR built a refinery at about the same time at Gauhati with a capacity of 2 million tons costing Rs 434.5 million. Western bids revealed the high cost of Soviet aid. The Soviets were soon forced to bring down their prices in order to stay in the market. The agreement for the Koyali refinery, which had already been signed, was revised and the cost considerably reduced. It however was still substantively more than that charged by the Western firms, Rs 307 million* ton plant.

During an enquiry into this problem in the Lok Sabha, the representative of the Petroleum Ministry said, "We have to confess that whenever we invited limited tenders from a single source, whether it is an East European country or any other source, we are not able to always get a competitive price" [12]. Michael Kidron has pointed out, "India may be normally paying

---

* Words missing from original source — Ed.

Table 8: Estimates of Total Plant Costs of Different Steel Works

Steelworks	Year of Completion	Initial Ingot Steel Capacity (millions tons per year)	Total Plant Cost (Rs millions)	Plant Cost Per Annual Ingot Ton (Rs)
Fukayama (Japan)	1966	1.50	1,488	992
Spencer Works (UK)	1962	1.40	1,638	1,170
Taranto (Italy)	1964	2.50	2,153	860
Dunkirk (France)	1963	1.50	1,440	960
Bokaro (USSR proposal) (India)	Stage 1	1.70	4,860	2,860

Source: Dastur and Co, *op cit.*

anything between 6 and 15 per cent, sometimes as much as 20-30 per cent, above the ruling prices for aid supported imports" [13].

For the Bokaro steel plant, there were both US and Soviet proposals. On the basis of the estimates given in the proposals, the cost of a 4 million ton plant built by the Soviets would be about 25 per cent higher than one built by the US (see Table 7). Dastur and Co, who were commissioned to do the initial feasibility report for the project concluded that the costs of the Soviet project were too high. Thus the report says, "It is well known that steel plants designed to produce flat products with facilities comparable to Bokaro are under construction or have been completed during the past few years in Britain, France, Italy, and Japan at less than one-half the estimated cost of Bokaro" [14]. This was not an avoidable cost, says Datar, because India did not have any other sources of finance for the projects concerned. However, this is surely not adequate justification for the advantage taken by the Soviets of their position as donors.

(c) Recent Credit Agreements

One would have expected that the 'special relationship' that has existed between India and the USSR in the Seventies would have suffered a setback with the coming to power of the Janata party government. It was expected by the USSR that the Janata party government would move to the right,[17] and given the orientation of its dominant constituents, look more to the USA. To stall any such development, the Soviet Foreign Minister, Gromyko, visited India within a month of the assumption of office of the new government. The visit concluded with the signing of four new economic agreements including a Soviet credit offer worth Rs 2,250 million. This offer by the USSR can again be explained in competitive terms. It is for the first time since 1965 that a Soviet credit has been given to India. What is more interesting is that the credit has been given on much softer terms than any loan granted by the USSR hitherto. The credit will carry an interest of 2-1/2 per cent per annum and will be repayable over 20 years including an initial grace period of three

---

[17] The Janata party election manifesto for the Lok Sabha poll in March 1977 spoke against the further expansion of heavy industries in the public sector.

years. For previous Soviet credits, the amortisation period has been 12 years, and the grace period only one year. What is equally interesting is that a part of the loan is non-project aid; that is, programme aid. It is for the first time that the USSR has given non-project aid. The intention behind all this seems to be that the 'special relationship' between the USSR and India should continue.

(d) Composition of Trade

In order to evaluate Soviet trade with India, we need to consider several issues: the composition of trade, India's export and import prices, the determination of the exchange rate between the rupee and the rouble, and the creation/diversion of exports.

Indo-Soviet trade falls into the usual pattern of trade between the Third World and the Western imperialist countries — exports are dominated by primary raw materials and imports by machinery. This division of labour is even more marked in the case of India's trade with the Soviet Union (and East Europe) than in the case of India's trade with all other countries. In 1967 and 1968, machinery and such items accounted for 88 per cent and 90.5 per cent respectively of imports from the USSR, while the corresponding figures for India's world trade were 50.9 per cent and 54.6 per cent. Similarly, jute, wool, hides and skins, tea, coffee, spices, cashew-nuts and leather footwear accounted for 80.6 per cent and 66.6 per cent of India's exports to the Soviet Union in 1967 and 1968, but only for 43.4 per cent and 36.7 per cent in India's world trade [15].

This is not to say that the commodity composition of Indo-Soviet trade has not been changing at all. Table 9 shows that, between 1960-1 and 1972-3, exports of manufactured goods grew very rapidly in absolute terms. Exports of food, beverages, tobacco, etc. (a group consisting mostly of primary and semi-processed agricultural products) also increased substantially, but raw material exports were quite stagnant. However, it is the alteration in relative terms that is more significant. In the early sixties, the bulk of India's exports to the Eastern bloc countries consisted of primary and semi-processed agricultural products and raw materials (74.5 per cent). By the early seventies the

Table 9: Commodity Composition of India's Exports to Eastern Bloc

(US$ millions)

Category	Annual Average 1960/1-1963/4		Annual Average 1965/6-1967/8		Annual Average 1970/1-1972/3	
	$m	Per Cent	$m	Per Cent	$m	Per Cent
Raw and Crude material	43.5	30.0	46.7	15.0	40.1	7.7
Food, beverage, tobacco, etc.	64.5	44.5	126.2	40.7	187.9	36.1
Manufactured goods	21.7	15.0	108.3	34.9	211.5	40.6
Other	15.3	10.5	29.3	9.4	81.2	15.6
Total	145.0	100	310.4	100	520.7	100

Source: Government of India, Department of Commercial Intelligence and Statistics, *Monthly Statistics of the Foreign Trade of India*, various issues.

situation had substantially changed. Manufactured goods, which were only 15 per cent of the total in 1960-1 — 1962-3, increased their share to 40 per cent during 1970-1 — 1972-3. At the same time, the share of raw materials fell sharply from 30 per cent to a little less than 8 per cent. This diversification was largely the consequence of specific clauses about increased exports of manufactures from India in the trade and payments agreements. Despite this change, however, the Eastern bloc countries absorbed a relatively lower production of manufactures as compared to the rest of the world. Furthermore, those manufactured goods which were bought by the USSR were low-technology goods which the Soviets no longer wanted to produce internally.

As regards composition of imports, rupee trade provided India with high-priority imports. Machinery and transport equipment constituted the highest percentage of the total import bill, while intermediate goods such as base metals, chemicals, fertilisers and petroleum products constituted the second most important group.[18]

(e) Soviet Advantages in Trade

Not only does the Soviet Union profit through aid, but it enjoys considerable advantage in its trade with India on account of its superior bargaining position. The superior bargaining position is due to several factors. For one thing, the volume of Soviet trade with India forms a small proportion of the total trade of the USSR.[19] Moreover, since imports from India are dominated by comparatively simple or consumption oriented commodities, non-realisation of trade plans would create only minor disturbances in the overall development plans of the USSR. On the other hand, India's imports from the USSR form an appreciable

---

[18] In this context, it is worth noting that although the Eastern European countries provide a relatively small proportion of India's total imports, they were important suppliers in these commodity groups. For instance, in the period 1969-70 — 1971-72, the Eastern bloc countries accounted for only 14 per cent of India's total import bill, but they supplied 34 per cent of the machinery and transport equipment and 18 per cent of the intermediate goods bought by India (calculated from statistics published by DGCIS, Calcutta).

[19] India's share in the USSR's total exports ranged between 0.9 per cent and 1.4 per cent during 1970-1973; the share in imports was between 2.3 per cent and 2.4 per cent.

Table 10: India's Exports to USSR

(Rs millions)

	1973-4	1974-5
Oil cake	94.7	111.7
Groundnut	111.9	59.9
Castor Oil	122.0	67.9
Tobacco (unmanufactured)	186.0	172.3
Spices	101.4	134.3
Cashew Kernels	294.3	727.6
Tea	326.4	595.3
Coffee	8.1	187.3
Mica	52.2	71.2
Cotton textiles	158.5	266.4
Jute manufacture	325.7	590.7
Coir manufacture	4.4	12.4
Footwear	38.0	44.3
Other leatherware manufacture	429.9	323.2
Cotton apparel	57.4	29.7
Engineering goods	70.5	119.7
Iron and steel manufacture	81.5	16.2
Other	396.0	651.1
Total (including others)	2,352.9	4,181.2

Source: Government of India, Department of Commercial Intelligence and Statistics, *Monthly Bulletin of the Foreign Trade of India*, various issues.

proportion of India's total imports and these consist largely of capital goods and intermediate goods. Therefore, India's needs for trade ties with the Eastern bloc are great.

The USSR conducts its foreign trade activities through state trading organisations. These foreign trading bodies function within the framework given them by their planning authorities. Naturally they must serve the needs of the changing production system and consumption requirements of the Soviet economy. On the Indian side, the bulk of foreign trading operations is in the private sector. Thus where India's exports are concerned, the effective initiative lies with the state trading bodies of the

USSR. They directly enter Indian markets and make their own purchases.

Experience reveals that the USSR and other East European countries actually prefer to deal with private agencies in India. The problem that India faced some time ago in the case of mica is a good example. The Soviet Union is the main buyer of mica; the East European countries account for 60 per cent of India's mica exports. With many Indian firms involved in the export business, the Soviet buying agency was able to buy at the most advantageous terms. Recently, it was decided that all exports would be canalised through the mica trading agency, MITCO. The Soviet Union refused to accept the suppliers chosen by MITCO. It wanted freedom to contract the purchase with any supplier it chooses; i e, to take full advantage of competition to beat down the price. At the same time, the Soviet Union also refused to allow MITCO to inspect mica samples in the Soviet Union so that complaints about quality can be checked. This stand makes it likely that these were dubious complaints, deliberately lodged in order to beat down the price with the plea of poor quality.

It is also true that the Soviet purchasing agencies withhold their purchases and wait for good bargains, especially for commodities like pepper, oil-cakes, etc, that are characterised by seasonal price fluctuations.

Trade plans do show the value and volume of each commodity to be exported from India to the USSR. But the effective initiative in fulfilling these trade plans lies with the Soviet trading agencies. India's exports to the Soviet Union are not on the same footing as its exports to the free market economies. For the latter, reliable information regarding levels of stocks, current market prices, and anticipated levels of demand are available. No such equally reliable information is available to Indian exporters regarding the USSR. Therefore, the bargains struck by the Soviet Union with Indian exporters are likely to be to the USSR's advantage. Besides, the effective initiative regarding the overall value of exports thus remains with the Soviet Union. Since India's import capacity from the USSR is largely determined by the overall value of its exports to the latter, it means that the effective initiative regarding overall trade levels also rests with the USSR.

It must be said that India's imports from the Soviet Union

and East European countries constitute essential commodities. However, it has been pointed out that these countries are overpricing their sales to India. This should not surprise us because the bargaining strength of these countries is greater. The number of suppliers for any particular commodity in this region will be small. Because of the economic integration within the Council of Mutual Economic Assistance characterised by Soviet dominance, price competition among these countries is unlikely. Besides, these countries are aware of India's foreign exchange difficulties. In view of the balanced trade relations in which any deficit incurred by India is to be settled exclusively in terms of additional exports, these countries are conscious that overpricing of their exports to some extent would not be very much resented by the Indian traders. Thus both in regard to India's exports and its imports, the Soviet Union has the upper hand.

Once sellers are sure that certain buyers have no alternative to buying from them, they are tempted to take advantage of their position. Thus, an *a priori* reasoning would indicate that the terms of trade are likely to be unfavourable in regard to India's trade with the USSR.

As regards the quality of imports, any discussion must be inconclusive. This is because machinery and equipment have constituted the majority of the imports from East European countries. Unless the goods provided are identical to goods from other sources, comparisons are meaningless. The USSR and Czechoslovakia find it difficult to promote exports of machinery and equipment to Western markets. Apparently their products are not good enough to compete with those from Western countries. In private discussions, government officials seemed to accept this as natural. They argue that unless the East European countries have some equipment they cannot sell in the convertible currency markets (because of comparatively poorer quality), they will not find the arrangement of repayment in kind convenient. Besides, the USSR looks upon credit agreements as a measure to promote exports.

(f) India Bears Risk of Currency Devaluation

The Soviets claim that Indo-Soviet trade is conducted in rupees and therefore it is less useful to the USSR than trade in hard currency because, for instance, the Soviet Union runs the risk that the rupee will be devalued. Let us examine the question of who bears the risk of rupee devaluation, India or the USSR.

A particularly thorny issue between India and the Soviet Union is the conversion rate between the rupee and the rouble, neither of which is freely convertible into other currencies. The best way of determining the exchange rate in such a situation is the purchasing power parity (PPP) [16]. While the Soviet Union has correctly established the dollar value of the rouble in terms of the rouble's relative purchasing power, it has not shown the same readiness in pursuing this logic in relation to the currencies of its trade partners in the Third World. The Soviets have insisted on cross rates *via* the dollar as revealed by the official exchange rates of rupee and rouble. And the rupee was undervalued against the dollar to the extent of over 250 per cent.[20] Thus the Soviets are taking full advantage of the considerable undervaluation of Third World currencies, particularly the Indian rupee, imposed by the Western imperialist powers and the international agencies like the World Bank and the IMF controlled by the Western imperialists [17].

Why should the conversion rate between the USSR and India matter at all? If the two countries traded only in such commodities which have well-established international prices and if there were no invisible payments between them, then the exchange rate would become practically irrelevant. But in the case of India and the Soviet Union, none of these conditions are satisfied. To a considerable extent Soviet exports consist of goods that find hardly any outlet in the West. The use of notional

---

[20] For India the GNP-based rates are available comparing the rupee with the US dollar. For 1970 it was found that India's per capita output was 2.0 per cent of the US level at the official rate of exchange but as high as 7.1 per cent in real terms. Thus the rupee was undervalued to the extent of over 250 per cent. Indeed, while most currencies *vis-a-vis* the US dollar were undervalued, PPP-wise there is a strong tendency for conversions *via* the exchange rate to show a bigger understatement for low income countries than for higher income countries (see Nirmal Chandra, *op cit*).

world market prices for these goods, as is the current practice, technically solves the problem — to the considerable benefit of the Soviet Union. Valuation of outstanding loans creates another set of problems. Every time the rupee gets devalued *vis-a-vis* other convertible currencies, the repayment burden for India goes up *pari passu* in financial as well as real terms. The much acclaimed advantages of 'soft' rupee loans are thus considerably whittled away in practice.

(g) Trade Creation Versus Export Diversion

Whether the trade with the USSR has resulted in trade diversion or opened additional markets for Indian exports has been a debatable point. The question is worth looking at for two reasons. First, it has been argued that since Soviet imports from India represent a net increase in Indian exports, India should be content to trade with the USSR even when the Soviets pay somewhat below world market prices. Second, the Soviets have been charged with profiteering from an unseemly form of export diversion; namely, switch trading in which the USSR buys goods cheaply from India and then resells the same goods at a higher price on the Western market.

Any attempt at a quantification of how much India's exports to the USSR represented net export growth must determine at least two things; (i) the degree to which India diverted export supplies from convertible currency areas to the USSR, and (ii) the proportion of Indian products re-exported by the latter (which is the phenomenon called switch trade).

As regards the first question, the conclusion of most of the studies is that, on balance, exports to the Soviet bloc countries are mostly in the nature of trade creation. In fact one of the most important features of India's foreign trade during the last few decades is the shifting of its trade pattern away from the old association with Commonwealth countries to new trade partners such as the USSR, not to mention the US, the Asian countries, and others. And because the USSR and East European countries purchased in large quantities, their purchases on certain occasions helped to stabilise the domestic prices of certain commodities such as tea. Doubtless, there has been a certain amount of trade diversion. One commodity-wise study [18] of

India's exports to the East European countries shows that between 20 and 25 per cent of India's exports to them were diversionary: the goods could have been exported to hard currency areas. Another study [19] shows that 14.1 per cent of India's total exports to the rupee payment countries (the Soviet bloc) constituted a diversion on her part. This type of diversion arises because domestic production is inadequate to take advantage of the opportunities in all markets. This diversion by itself is a cost because it reduces the amount of free foreign exchange available. Proceeds from exports to East European countries cannot be used for importing goods and services from any other country or to settle debt repayments. Therefore, these earnings may be relatively less useful than export receipts in hard currency. But despite this diversion, India's exports to Eastern Europe were largely additional to, rather than instead of, exports elsewhere.

Once we accept the conclusion that, on balance, the markets of Eastern Europe are trade creating and have helped in supporting prices of India's exports it would not be quite logical to argue that the terms of trade have been generally unfavourable to India. The undercurrent of the trade creation *versus* trade diversion argument is that the incremental import-earning capacity gained by exporting to these countries is basically inferior because it does not earn convertible foreign exchange. At the same time, it is possible to argue that what is important is that these exports add to India's capacity for importing commodities essential for developmental purposes. Therefore, the net loss to country would be negligible even if Indian importers had to pay higher prices. Even if it were accepted that there is some force in this argument, one is still not sure whether the advantages of trade creation and the price-support effect do more than compensate for the possibility that higher prices must be paid for imports from the USSR.

Switch trading is another way in which the East European countries may have impeded a net growth in India's exports. It is well known that most East European countries have re-exported Indian goods to Western Europe in order to earn convertible foreign exchange [20]. The conclusions reached by studies in the subject are as follows: (i) the volume of switch trading is not very large in relation to the total quantum of India's trade with the

Eastern bloc countries; (ii) it is unlikely that manufactured goods imported from India could have been re-exported by the East European countries, since in such goods, product differentiation and brand names are rather important and exporting involves marketing expenses like advertising, etc; and (iii) as for primary and semi-processed agricultural products some of them were definitely re-exported, but it is impossible to assess the extent of such re-exports. A parliamentary committee specifically pointed to the resale of Indian cashew-nuts, oil cakes, hides and skins, coffee, tea, and spices by East European countries in convertible currency markets [21]. The Indian government was quite aware of this situation.[21] But since it had no definite proof it was not in a position to do much about it.

(h) Tighter Links Between Indian Production and Soviet Needs

In recent years, the Soviets have entered into a variety of agreements designed to establish closer connection between Indian production and the requirements of the Soviet economy. These agreements include conversion deals, captive plants, production co-operation, and co-operation between planning commissions. The common theme in all these agreements is to guarantee that the USSR will have access to low-cost Indian-made simple industrial goods. Once assured of long term supply of such goods as textiles, the USSR no longer needs to produce these labour-intensive or raw-material-intensive goods. The Soviets can shift their resources to producing more advanced goods, such as the machinery they export to India.

Beginning with cotton textiles, a number of conversion deals have been entered into with the Soviet Union. In the cotton deal, the Soviets supplied Sudanese cotton to Indian private mills. For turning this cotton into textiles, the Indian mills were paid a conversion charge of Rs 16.5 crores. The entire output was taken over by the Soviet Union which had provided some (although not all) of the capital and which thus got the surplus

---

[21] When in August-September 1971, customs authorities in Madras and Cochin were asked to stop all shipments they suspected were being switch-traded, all exports to Eastern Europe soon stopped. Of course this action did not last long as the complaints flowed to Delhi and the restrictions were removed.

value produced (minus part of the conversion charge).[22] The net result of such deals is that the labour of the Indian working class will not even help the process of capital accumulation in India, since most of the surplus value flows directly to the Soviet owners of the capital with which they gave employment.

While the past rate of growth of Indo-Soviet trade has been very high, the scope for further expansion along the same lines is rather limited. It was noted that India has had difficulty in finding Soviet suppliers for the goods it required most and was therefore having to extend technical credits to the USSR. The commodity composition of exports too must be widened if the arrangement of repayment of debt in kind is to be beneficial to India. Therefore, in the seventies a change in the trade policies of the Soviet Union was called for. It is for this reason presumably that conversion deals seem to have been resorted to.

But the Soviets proposed to extend the conversion deals to setting up 'captive' units. Later reports revealed that the machinery for these units would be supplied by the Soviet Union and that the bulk of the products would be earmarked for export to the USSR [22]. Here again the surplus value flowed to the Soviet Union. The captive units proposed were a 5 lakh ton alumina plant, leather goods worth Rs 4 to 6 crores annually, 5,000 tons of wood screws, 90,000 tons of nuts and bolts, machine tools, TV glass tubes, computer software, and digital machines. The interesting aspect of the arrangement for setting up an aluminium plant was that the feasibility report would be prepared by Soviet experts. If the project was found to be economically feasible, the cost of the report would be shared equally by India and the USSR. If it was proved that the project would not be feasible, its costs would be borne by India.[23]

The projects mentioned above have on the whole not yet materialised. The snag has been that, in view of India's growing production of capital goods, the Soviet contribution in the form

---

[22] It was stated on 16 May 1972, in the Rajya Sabha, that the Soviet Union would send 20,000 tons of cotton each year to India for five years. The Minister of Foreign Trade, L N Mishra, denied that some textile mills in India were unwilling to process Soviet cotton into textiles.

[23] It was rather strange that the government of India agreed to the Soviet experts preparing the feasibility reports on the aluminium plant. The project report of the Bharat aluminium plant was prepared by Indian experts.

of equipment and know-how would be small, and sizeable rupee resources would have to be raised to finance these projects. To overcome this problem, India suggested that the Soviet Union should provide minerals like crude oil and non-ferrous metals on credit, and the sale of these in India would provide the rupee funds needed. This was not acceptable to the Soviet Union [23].

During the Brezhnev visit (December 1973) to India, a fifteen-year economic agreement was signed. Besides the agreements to increase trade, the agreement had two significant features: (i) exploring the possibility of production co-operation, and (ii) co-operation in the matter of supply of equipment and services for setting up plants in third countries. Besides, a separate agreement was signed on co-operation between the Indian Planning Commission and the State Planning Committee (Gosplan) of the USSR. Production co-operation does not seem to have materialised to date. It is too early to assess the progress of joint projects in Third World countries and co-operation in planning. However, when the agreement was signed, it was pointed out, "Though the agreement with the USSR does not indicate clearly that Indian plans will be so framed that they fit in with the overall economic relations among the East European countries, a careful reading of the agreements with the USSR and Czechoslovakia are pointers in that direction. Though India will not be involved in sharing plans of the East European countries, for all practical purposes, it promises to emerge as something of an associate member of this group" [24].

It has *not* been argued here that capital accumulation in India was hurt by economic ties with the Soviet Union. It is possible that trade and aid brought profits to both Soviet leaders and Indian capitalists; this section has not provided much direct evidence on this question. The concern here has been on understanding the advantages to the USSR of trade with and aid to India. As of yet, there has been no argument here that the Soviet Union is imperialist; assuredly imperialism means more than economic advantage from trade and aid. The question of imperialism will be explored in the next two sections.

III
SOVIET IMPERIALISM?

(a) Imperialism is Export of Capital as a Social Relation

The discussion about the prices at which the Soviets trade with Third World countries has implied that "buying cheap and selling dear" is the essence of imperialism [25]. The notion of "unequal exchange" is a necessary element but is not sufficient to explain the concept of imperialism. A scientific argument that the USSR is imperialist, in the Leninist sense, must include an argument that the Soviet Union exports capital. The Communist Party of China bases its claim that the USSR is social imperialist on an analysis of Soviet capital exports — capital exports which reinforce an unequal international division of labour in which a few countries dominate the world economy and the rest are subordinate to these imperialist powers [26].

Many people who would agree that the leadership of the Soviet Union has pursued its self-interest in its economic relations with the Third World do not think that the USSR exports capital. Since the export of capital is in many ways the central element in the economic aspect of imperialism, these people would hesitate to call the Soviet Union imperialist. Much of this hesitation comes from a limited conception of what constitutes the export of capital. The export of capital to which Lenin is referring is not primarily the flow of money abroad, but it is the spread of capital *as a social relation* throughout the Third World. The 'export of capital' which is central to the theory of imperialism is the breaking down of pre-capitalist modes of production, the separation of the direct producers from their means of production, the formation of what Marx calls 'doubly free labourers' — free to sell their labour-power, free of any other means of making a living. Capital, as a social relation between wage-labourers and capitalists, was not dominant in most of the Third World before the era of imperialism. While the creation of the capitalist world market encouraged the spread of commodity production, the world market (the export of commodities) did not lead to *capitalist* commodity production. The production of commodities (especially in so far as that production remains isolated, for export only) does not in and of itself result in the emergence of capitalism.

When Lenin refers to imperialism as the stage characterised by the export of capital, he is pointing to the fact that capitalism entered a new stage in which its expanded reproduction worked to dissolve pre-capitalist modes of production and to institute capitalist relations of production on a world scale. [24] Imperialism is therefore not a matter of perfidious government policy nor a conspiracy by the monopoly capitalists (Kautsky and Schumpeter) nor a search for markets (Luxemburg); imperialism is rooted in the laws of motion of capitalism, in the nature of capital as self-expanding value. Recent works on imperialism have returned to this understanding of the roots of imperialism. Christian Palloix in particular has made substantial advances in identifying the stages by which the capitalist mode of production has internationalised itself [27].

Palloix has pointed out that the internationalisation of capital has gone through several stages, and that the *form* of capital export has changed correspondingly. [25] While the various forms of capital export each merit investigation, we must keep in mind that the export of capital has always remained in essence the export of a social relation. In Lenin's day, the principal form that the export of capital took was the lending of money-capital by capitalists (especially banks) in the imperial countries to governments and quasi-governmental agencies in Third World countries (although there was the secondary form of investment in plantations and mines). In the period following World War II, the dominant form of the export of capital has been the establishment of local subsidiaries by corporations based in the imperial countries, particularly manufacturing subsidiaries (although bank loans persist as a secondary form which has undergone

---

[24] Pierre-Phillipe Rey has pointed out in *Les Alliances de classes* (Paris: Maspero, 1972), the error in assuming that the expanded reproduction of the capitalist mode of production always works for the immediate dissolution of pre-capitalist modes. While the historical tendency of capitalism is to dissolve all pre-capitalist modes, there may be entire eras in which the opposite tendency (that of preservation) is dominant.

[25] Palloix's identification of the different forms does not correspond fully to that in this text. The brief comments in this text are not meant to imply that the process of internationalisation can be periodised by reference to some 'technical' laws of capitalism. The expanded reproduction of capitalism can not be conceived without the class struggle as an integral element.

rapid expansion since 1973). These two forms of the export of capital are substantially different in appearance. The second form represents a higher stage in the process of primitive accumulation in the Third World in that multinational corporations penetrate into the heart of the local economy, unlike bankers who had to rely on political control of the local countries (which necessitated frequent military intervention). In spite of all these differences, these two forms of the export of capital are just that: two *forms* of what is fundamentally the same process of internationalisation.

(b) Soviet Form of Capital Export

There has unfortunately been substantial confusion about the character of the new form of capital export which the Soviet Union is perfecting. The Soviet government grants credits to finance the export of capital goods in return for a flow of imports of raw materials and consumer goods. The Soviet machinery is often used to establish a production process part of whose product is then sent to the USSR in payment for the capital goods: e.g., the pipeline sold to Iran for natural gas. In Egypt there is not only the obvious example of the High Dam (which is being paid for with the expanded agricultural production the Dam allows), but also, "With Soviet economic aid, Egypt has built its largest shipyard... Egypt has been building and repairing ships for the USSR. A large part of the output of the aluminium plant that is now being built in the country is to go to the Soviet Union in repayment for its loans to Egypt" [28]. The character of Soviet trade and aid emerges: the finance and machinery come from the USSR, the wage labour and raw materials come from the Third World country, and a good part of the product is shipped to the Soviet Union.

The Soviet government justifies the financing of capital goods exports by saying that these exports help Third World countries industrialise. Industrialisation is not, however, a classless process. In countries dominated by capitalist ruling classes — such as India — 'industrialisation' means nothing more nor less than capital accumulation. It is simply farcical to maintain, as the Soviet government does, that the expansion of the 'public sector' reflects the growth of socialism. The experience of nationalised industries in the advanced countries, as well as Engels' comments in "Socialism: Scientific or Utopian", demonstrate that the collective ownership of industry by the capitalist class as a whole ('nationalised' industry) does not lead to workers' power either at the point of production or at the social level (the dictatorship of the proletariat). Soviet-financed industrialisation serves in fact to expand capitalist relations of production: Soviet-built factories expand wage labour employment (under conditions of intense exploitation) at the expense of pre-capitalist modes of production.

The discussion about 'who gains' from Soviet economic relations with Third World countries often overlooks the very foundation of Marxist theory: namely, that nations are divided into *classes*. Chandra discusses at great length "the distribution of gains" from Soviet-Indian trade [29]. It never occurs to Chandra to ask which class gains, to ask whether either the Indian working class or the Soviet working class gain from trade. So too with the leadership of the USSR. They do not discuss how they will aid the working class in Third World nations — they talk about aid to the governments of those nations. The governments of India, Egypt, Syria, and other Soviet aid recipients are in the hands of the bourgeoisie: to aid those governments is to aid the bourgeoisie.

Soviet foreign aid furthermore reinforces a division of labour on the world scale in which a few countries produce technologically advanced goods (especially machine goods) while most countries produce semi-processed or standardised industrial inputs or consumer goods. By reinforcing this division of labour, the Soviet leadership is negating one of the major hoped-for benefits of industrialisation. An industrialised Third World country which has to rely on imports of technologically advanced goods and of machine goods remains economically dependent on the ruling class of the country which provides the technologically advanced and machine goods.

A socialist foreign trade policy, by contrast, would seek to break down the international division of labour, so that economic decision-making could be concentrated at a more local level, where it is easier for the direct producers to exercise control over the production process. If one reason for socialists to support local self-reliance is to facilitate workers' control, a more important reason why socialists oppose any international division of labour is that communism is incompatible with *any* division of labour. Socialist governments aim to end the division between mental and manual labour, the division between town and country, and the division of labour on an international scale. Obviously this will not happen overnight, but this will be the goal towards which socialist governments strive. A socialist policy would encourage those sorts of trade which make countries (and local units of large countries) more self-sufficient. Much foreign trade would be necessary under socialism to achieve the goal of ending the division of labour, of communism. Given the current technologies inherited from capitalism, much foreign trade is unavoidable: given current techniques, it would be foolish to produce tea in Archangel. A socialist government would encourage the development of technologies by the workers which would reduce the need for any division of labour, including the international division of labour.

It could be argued that besides reinforcing the international division of labour and besides replacing pre-capitalist modes of production with the accumulation of capital (as a social relation), there is yet another way in which Soviet aid builds capitalist relations of production. Much Soviet aid goes towards the construction of complete factories, designed in the USSR, using machinery produced in the USSR, and (at least initially) run by Soviet technicians. The very structure of these Soviet-supplied factories may reinforce capitalist relations of production, with their rigidly hierarchical management structures and with technologies which make workers "appendages of the machine". That is, rather than the workers controlling the machines through their decision-making and through their knowledge of the production process (as would happen under socialism), the workers in the Soviet-supplied factories are controlled by the machines. The pace of the production process is set by the machines (and the capitalists who control them), not the workers. The machines break down the production process into minute tasks, so that the workers' manual labour is divorced from any mental labour. These are characteristics of the capitalist production process, as analysed by Marx in "Capital" Volume I Part IV. In short, *both* at the point of production and at the social level, Soviet-financed factories reinforce capitalist relations of production: the Soviet-supplied factories are a form of the export of capital.

(c) A More Advanced Form of Internationalisation of Capital?

The Soviet form of capital export is quite different from the main Western form of capital export, which is the establishment of manufacturing subsidiaries by multinational corporations. The Soviet form possesses some significant advantages over the Western form. For one thing, Soviet capital export is more disguised than Western capital export. Since Soviet capital export can be pawned off as aid, the USSR is less likely to be the object of local popular struggles against imperialism. The Soviet form also allows for more participation by the local bourgeoisies. The bourgeoisies of Third World countries therefore often find Soviet capital more attractive than Western capital. Because Soviet-supplied factories belong to the local government, the Soviets don't have to worry about losing their capital through nationalisation or about limits on profit repatriation — problems which plague Western capitalists.

Soviet capital exports require more open government intervention than do Western capital exports. The Soviet and Third World governments are both involved in the original credit agreement and in subsequent agreements upon the exact composition of exports and imports. The history of Western capitalism in recent decades has been a history of increased government intervention into the economy. In the last few years, there has been a significant increase in government involvement in international economic relations. For instance, there have been increases in government financing for capital exports, the signing of government-to-government barter deals exchanging oil for arms and modern factories, and 'orderly marketing agreements' among governments regulating trade. State involvement in the economy is the path of modern capitalism. The Soviet economy is clearly an economy with the most advanced and complete state involvement.

The Soviet form of the internationalisation of capital may reflect the newest stage in the internationalisation process; namely, the internationalisation of productive capital. The organisation of capitalist production on a world-wide scale has generally been identified with multinational corporations. There is significant ability of multinational corporations to internationalise productive capital. In particular, multinationals do not possess the extra-market power of a nation-state — such as military power which allows states to impose their wills upon corporations. Government-to-government agreements provide, furthermore, a more solid basis for the organisation of production on an international scale than does the operation of the market. The agreements are less subject to momentary fluctuations. It is plausible that Western imperialists may turn more and more to the form of capital export pioneered by the USSR. One small example; the recent growth in turnkey factories, in which a multinational corporation builds a factory and often runs it under a management contract while ownership is in the hands of Third World nationals.

(d) Redividing World Economy

The solid basis for the internationalisation of capital given by government-to-government agreements has the effect of creating strong ties between the economies of the agreeing nations. Lenin stated that another of the five features of imperialism, besides the export of capital, is the struggle over the redivision of the world. In the current period, that struggle does not take the form of open annexations, but rather of long-term relationships of economic dependency on an imperialist power by Third World countries. The USSR's form of the internationalisation of capital creates such long-lasting ties. The Soviet credit programme by its nature establishes a long-term relationship: the Third World country is obliged to make repayments to the Soviet Union over a period of more than a decade. Unlike a grant (which is given and then is largely done with), the credit programme allows the USSR to continue its influence over the economy of the Third World country. The Soviet intransigence over the rescheduling of loan repayments from Egypt in the Sadat era is a good example of how the Soviets use credit programmes to extend their influence long after the shipments of aid.

Soviet machinery exports also establish a long term relationship between the Soviet Union and the Third World countries. The equipment provided by the aid programme requires a steady stream of spare parts. There are advantages to the less developed country from expanding production by using more Soviet equipment rather than by using Western equipment: there are economies of scale, Soviet technology is more familiar, etc. The Third World country therefore has an incentive to make future purchases of Soviet equipment not financed by aid to complement the machinery provided through aid. Fixed capital, by its very nature as *fixed* (i e, as lasting longer than one production period) creates bonds between the manufacturer and purchaser. In the case of Soviet aid, these bonds are particularly tight because the Soviets so often provide integrated factories, not just machinery.

Rather than hiding how their trade reinforces the development of underdevelopment, the Soviet leadership lauds the emerging 'international division of labour' (a phrase they frequently use). To quote Kosygin, "The importance of a stable division of labour between socialist and developing countries must be stressed" [30]. Through this economic mechanism, as well as through military, political, and ideological mechanisms (which are often more important), the Soviet leadership has sought to tie the economies of Third World countries closer to the Soviet economy. The USSR has acted as would be expected from a classic imperialist power: it competed with the US to see which one of them would replace Great Britain, a declining imperialist power, in such major ex-British colonies as India and Egypt.

(e) Soviet Theory
of Foreign Economic Relations

While the Soviet leadership may have pioneered a new form of capital export, the Soviet leadership did not necessarily understand that Soviet aid is another form of capital export to the Third World countries. The emergence of Soviet capital export did not depend on a conscious decision by the leaders of the CPSU to sell out the world revolutionary movement.

Although the changing nature of Soviet foreign policy did not depend upon the victory of an openly imperialist perspective in the CPSU, it did depend upon — and it did call forth — a new theory of international relations. In the 1950s, the CPSU developed an elaborate analysis to justify the changing nature of Soviet economic relations with the Third World: the theory of 'non-capitalist development', as distinct from the capitalist path and the socialist path of development. Before 1955, the Soviet press described the rise of nationalist leaders such as Nasser and

Nehru as representing the decline of British imperialism (based on a formal empire) and the rise of US imperialism (based on neo-colonialism). By the early 1960s, however, there had been a complete shift. Now there were many articles in the Soviet press on 'non-capitalist development' and 'national democracy' as the route by which Third World countries could break away from imperialist domination. The conclusion was that the non-capitalist path of development led to socialism but only if there was a vanguard party to lead the process. A national liberation movement was considered able to lead the non-capitalist stage, but it would have to transform itself into a vanguard party to lead the socialist stage [31].

The theory of non-capitalist development provided a justification for Soviet capital exports. Soviet aid to public sector industries was seen as reducing the influence of the capitalists. This assumes that the public sector is non-capitalist. The public sector industries are under the control of the class which holds state power — meaning the bourgeoisie in such capitalist countries as India and Egypt. State capitalist industries reinforce the rule of capitalist social relations every bit as much as do private capitalist industries. The Soviets also justified their aid on the grounds that it built up heavy industry, thereby increasing the numbers of the proletariat and therefore increasing the revolutionary potential of the country. The immediate identification of increasing numbers of workers with increasing revolutionary potential is a crass form of economic determinism. Revolution depends heavily on the class consciousness of the proletariat and on the activities of a party. Soviet aid to capitalist states — aid which bolstered the capitalist state, such that the state could repress workers all the more — does little to build revolutionary consciousness or revolutionary parties. The 'non-capitalist road' — which in practice means state capitalist development of heavy industry — has little to do with the workers seizing state power and establishing a dictatorship of the proletariat. The latter is the Leninist theory of socialism, which has been abandoned by the Soviet leadership in favour of the 'non-capitalist road'.[26]

---

[26] On the theory of the non-capitalist path, see Indrajit Basu, "Political Theory of Soviet Economic Relations in Asia" (unpublished M Phil dissertation, Jawaharlal Nehru University, 1976). The advantages which the Soviets claim the Third World receives from Soviet aid — that is support for the public sector, support for

IV
AID AS IMPERIALISM

(a) Soviet Aid Reinforces Indian Capitalists

Underlying the Soviet notion of the non-capitalist path of development was the belief that the public sector in Third World countries was the best means for mobilising resources if the long term objective is to eradicate poverty and eliminate backwardness. This too was the belief of the Indian planners and the ideology underlying the Five-Year Plans. It is now an established fact that the principal beneficiaries of state capitalism in the Third World have been capitalists and not the masses of the people. Even Soviet theoreticians are believed to have revised their earlier view and accepted this position now.

The state sector was said to be an instrument for undermining and eliminating the hold of private foreign capital and also for curtailing and restraining the growth of Indian big business. But 28 years of 'planned development' have given the lie to such hopes. Rapid concentration of assets and the continued growth of Indian monopolies have become increasingly evident. For example, 20 family groups controlled 20 per cent of total private capital in 1951. This had risen to 33 per cent by 1958. In 1965, the Monopolies Commission discovered that 75 leading business groups owned 47 per cent of the assets of all non-government companies [32].

On attaining political independence from colonial rule most LDCs need a degree of state intervention and the creation of a public sector in order to ensure economic development. A development of this kind is progressive if, apart from bringing about rapid capital accumulation it assists in destroying feudal,

---

heavy industry, a bargaining chip to get more Western aid — are the same advantages cited by Nayyar, *op cit*. These advantages are real — but they are advantages to the capitalists of the Third World, not to the workers. Soviet aid helps development: the development of capitalism. There is no reason to expect the development of capitalism to help the working class. Capitalists including State capitalists, pursue profits and capital accumulation, not the interests of the people. The goal of a socialist movement must be the overthrow of capitalism, not its reinforcement.

semi-feudal production relations, monopoly capitalism, and imperialism. But that is precisely what the state sector in India has failed to do. State power lies in the hands of the capitalist class in alliance with the bourgeoisie. Faced with the rising struggles of the workers and peasantry, and other oppressed sections of society, the bourgeoisie cannot dump the interests of the landlord class nor alienate the interests of imperialists. This becomes evident in the weakness of the regimes' land reforms and its growing dependence on foreign aid direct investments. Soviet military and economic aid seems incapable of modifying the political orientation of the Indian ruling class, no matter what the Communist Party of India says. India's ruling class has, on the other hand, used Soviet aid as a bargaining counter with the Western countries in order to extract more aid from them. In fact Soviet aid has strengthened the position of the Indian ruling class at the cost of emerging revolutionary forces inside the country.

Deepak Nayyar, while acknowledging that India should have derived substantial benefits from its economic relations with the USSR, adds that, "Within the economy of course, the distribution of benefits might be rather unequal. This is, in fact, what did happen". And then goes on to say, "This cannot be attributed to socialist trade and aid because it was the outcome of factors internal to the Indian polity. Given the political and economic system the outcome was inevitable". In other words, Nayyar absolves the USSR of any complicity with the bourgeois Indian state, and ignores the fact that Soviet aid to State capital helped to consolidate the position of the ruling elite. A G Frank, on the other hand, hit the nail on the head when he wrote: "Aid to whom? we may ask. The only possible answer consistent with the facts is that this aid is to the big monopoly bourgeoisie, which is the main economic beneficiary, first of the Soviet-supported public sector, and now of the emergency rule by their political representatives. That the Congress regime enjoyed the political support of the Communist Party of India and that Leonid Brezhnev in his visits to India has gone so far as to call Indira Gandhi a great Socialist whose government is leading India to socialism changes nothing in these facts" [33]. As a matter of fact, it goes to show how far the Soviet Union is prepared to go in order to ensure its interests in India.

(b) Soviet Aid Reinforces Unequal Division of Labor

Datar says that while constructing the public sector plants in India, Soviet contractors were generally willing to use whatever local skills were available, "if only because of the relative scarcity of skilled manpower" in India. A comprehensive training programme of a kind that a foreign firm would not have found profitable was provided on the Soviet projects. But in all Soviet projects, the credit agreement is comprehensive so that the Soviet staff take responsibility for everything. Soviet technological and managerial control is maintained until project completion. They employ large numbers of their own nationals as necessary. In January 1964, for instance there were more foreign technicians on Bhilai's payroll than on that of Durgapur or Rourkela. One of the effects of this policy is to prevent the growth of Indian technology and knowhow. In matters like open cast coal mining, Indian technicians are fully qualified to plan and conduct the operations. But the Soviets insisted on their agencies being appointed as technical consultants as the price of aid given to buy Soviet coal-mining equipment. Even feasibility studies were to be done by Soviet experts [34]. It is also true that being concerned with the success of a project, the Soviet contractors usually insisted on doing all the pre-investment appraisals, detailed project reports, drawings and designs themselves. Technical assistance of this nature cannot serve to promote the development of Indian technology. In Bokaro we have an outstanding example.

After the US had withdrawn its offer of aid for Bokaro, Dastur and Company were commissioned to prepare the detailed project report. But very soon the Soviets insisted that they would themselves again do the Detailed Project Report. Though Dastur and Co had been working on this project since 1958 and had accumulated considerable data, their services were not utilised by the Soviet contractors from the beginning; project costs might otherwise have been considerably reduced.

In the case of Bokaro, Dastur and Co made a Cost Reduction Study which would have saved at least Rs 150 crores. The main suggestions were: (i) that larger convertors, of 200-300 tons, rather than 4 convertors in the first stage be used; and (ii) that the slabbing mill be dropped. The latest steel technology used convertors of large capacity. The Soviet side, however, held that the operation of such large convertors had not yet been fully established in the USSR and therefore they would install such convertors only in the second stage. "Continuous Casting of Steel in the USSR — A Survey" published by OECD in 1964 shows that installations had been planned in the USSR with convertors of 200 ton capacity. "It is thus clear that if a plant like Bokaro were to be set up in the Soviet Union, it would have been designed in 1964 (and definitely in 1966) when the proposals of the Cost Reduction Study were being discussed with a provision for large sized convertors and without any provision for a slabbing mill" [35].

(c) **Military Aid**

The attempt to profit and perpetuate an unequal division of labour is not confined to economic and developmental assistance. Soviet military aid exhibits the same characteristics. The USSR, like other supplying countries, tends to charge higher prices for parts than they do for complete weapons. Thus, the foreign exchange cost involved in producing MiG 21 aircraft is estimated at between Rs 6 million and Rs 7.5 million. The price of the first 39 aircrafts, which were built from major assemblies supplied from the USSR was Rs 7.7 million each. As the aircraft began to be manufactured from materials supplied by the USSR, the cost went up to Rs 12.7 million each. Of this, Rs 8.3 million is in foreign exchange, i e, payment for materials supplied by the Soviets. Thus, even leaving aside the profit from the sale of machinery for the project, it was more profitable for the USSR to have the aircraft manufactured in India than to sell the complete aircraft. Even later, when the extent of indigenous material was increased, the foreign exchange cost (Rs 7 million in 1971-72) was at least equal to that of a complete aircraft [36]. This fact indicated not only the expense of defence production to a country with scarce foreign exchange resources but also the extent of dependence on the Soviet Union.

As in the case of industry, here too the Soviet Union gained a breakthrough by offering to set up plants for the manufacture of MiG-21 fighters. With this and the sale of both the MiGs and SU-7 (mainly a ground support fighter) the Indian Air Force became significantly dependent on the Soviet Union. These two aircraft now form the main strength of the IAF.

How is the unequal division of labour in the manufacture of military equipment sustained? Complete control is maintained over the project. Complex parts — such as undercarriages, braking systems, communications and electronic equipment — are still imported. Little is learned about manufacturing aircraft from foreign collaboration since there is hesitation to part with the designs. India is manufacturing only non-essential items. If, for instance, for some political reason, the Soviet Union decided to stop supplies of components there is nothing that the Indian government could do about it, and the three plants set up at enormous cost would lie idle. As a Stockholm study noted: "India would not be in a position to undertake the manufacture of any other aircraft in these factories" [37]. Despite Indian requests the Soviets have refused to part with the detailed design drawings. Under the terms of the contract, the USSR does not supply India with any detailed design or type approval data. Requests for the supply of these from the Indian side have been turned down.

In the case of the army, new supplies of major equipment are mainly from the Soviet Union. Along with the Air Force the Navy is also almost wholly dependent on the Soviet Union for new supplies. Purchases from the Soviet Union accounted for all the Navy's submarines, half its frigates, all its missile boats, and the few landing craft in the inventory [38]. The period since the beginning of the Indo-Soviet Treaty of 1971 has only increased the Soviet Union's grip over the Indian armed forces.

In the case of naval equipment there is dependence not only for spares but even for overhaul and repairs. Thus all repair can only be carried out under the supervision of Soviet advisers.

There have been complaints that the Soviet Union was not supplying sufficient spares for the MiG-21s, Mi-4s, heavy artillery, tanks, etc. Madhu Limaye had stated in Parliament that there were sufficient stores for only 10 days conflict [39]. This statement was not contradicted by the government. It was, however, denied by Jagjivan Ram, the then Defence Minister, that the Soviet Union was withholding spares for the MiGs [40].

It appears, that apart from the MiG-21 sale, the economic gains which the Soviet Union has made by supplying weapons to developing countries are negligible for the Soviet prices have been low. It seems, that the USSR, like the US, has been mainly interested in possible political and strategic benefits from arms supplies. For instance, the Indo-Soviet Treaty of August 1971 established India's dependence on the USSR in the military sphere. Articles VIII to X of the treaty deal with co-operation between the two countries in the fields of defence and security. Article VIII provides that in the event of either country being subjected to an attack or threat thereof, both countries "shall immediately enter into mutual consultations in order to remove such threat and to take appropriate effective measures to ensure peace and security of their countries."

Comparing Soviet and American military assistance to India and Pakistan, the United States has furnished large amounts of weapons to Pakistan and more limited supplies to India; the USSR has reversed the order and favoured India with considerable military aid while limiting aid to Pakistan. As of today, India stands in almost the same relationship of military dependence on the USSR as Pakistan does with the US.

V

CONCLUSION

It has been our attempt in this paper to establish the following several propositions. We have argued that to the extent that imperialism is export of capital as a social relation, the USSR exports capital to the Third World just as much as the USA does. The USSR has been in the field just from the mid-50s onwards, when the first foreign aid programmes started, while the US has been at it from the last quarter of the 19th century. We have argued that the USSR profits from its aid and trade just as much as any imperialist power.[27] In this connection it is essential to

---

[27] The charge levelled in the CPI(ML) pamphlet mentioned earlier is similar. It is important, however, to distinguish the thrust of our argument in some important respects with the argument presented in the CPI(ML) pamphlet. In the latter, the author seems to believe that unequal exchange is what predominantly constitutes imperialism. We have, on the other hand, emphasised all along that imperialism is the export of capital, and particularly the export of capital as a social relation. Moreover, it appears that the CPI(ML) pamphlet is trying to prove, like the Chinese, that the USSR is the "more aggressive and adventurous" superpower in the world, and in that sense the worse of the two evils, US and Soviet imperialisms. We have tried to show, on the other hand, that the character of India's relations with the USSR and the US is basically the same — not that one superpower is "worse" than the other.

realise that foreign aid is usually not a grant [28] or a donation (as some people are inclined to believe); rather, it involves repayment of both principal and payment of interest (although on terms which are concessionary as compared to world market rates). And the USSR has, up to now got the highest rate of repayment to aid given to India — almost 75 per cent as against just 12 per cent for the USA, 25 per cent for the UK, and 50 per cent for West Germany [41]. Is there an opportunity cost involved for the USSR in the process of extending loans to Third World countries? We considered this question in Section I. It seems that the USSR has a rate of return on its investment in aid that is a little under 15 per cent; in other words, aid is about as profitable as domestic investment (the opportunity cost of aid is low or negative). The tying of aid with trade has meant that the USSR could export machinery and equipment, which would not have sold (for competitive reasons) in hard currency markets, at high monopolistic prices to the Third World — thus earning super profits. For the products were sold at world market prices, which are themselves not fair.

We noted too that Soviet trade with the Third World has also been profitable for the USSR. In fact, in the co-ordination of trade and aid policies they found a means of finding markets for their machinery and equipment and obtaining raw materials from the Third World. The reasons for this are partly political expediency and partly economic necessity. The main attraction of the East European credits for the Third World was that the former were willing to accept repayment in kind. This, as we saw in Section II, was no real concession. In fact, repayment in kind was as burdensome for India as repayment of loans from Western capitalist countries in hard currency.

The pattern of East-South trade and aid relations is very similar to the pattern of West-South trade and aid relations (credit terms, prices, commodity composition) [42]. And if one is imperialist, so may be the other. We have not contended that Soviet aid does not lead to development; but the vital question is: What kind of development? As we have seen, it is the development of capitalism; in fact, the development of dependent

---

[28] In fact, grants constitute only 3 per cent of aid given by the Soviet Union to the Third World.

capitalism. It is not that India, and other Third World countries which receive such aid, will not be producing more sophisticated goods as a result of Soviet aid. But as the notion of the product life cycle indicates, it is a dependent development, in which an unequal international division of labour is perpetuated. Until as late as 1970 more than 75 per cent of East European exports to the Third World consisted of manufactured goods, whereas primary products and raw materials accounted for more than 70 per cent of Third World exports to the socialist bloc [43]. This was despite the professed Soviet aim of forging a new socialist international division of labour. The Soviet theoreticians admit that "the most intricate problem is that of finding concrete ways to eliminate the adverse consequences for developing countries resulting from the international division of labour which was shaped as far back as the 19th century" [44]. But the Soviet record as regards changes in the character and commodity composition of its trade with the Third World is not merely just as bad as that of West-South trade, but in fact, it is worse. Given this record, is it at all surprising that during the 31st session (1976-77) of the General Assembly of the United Nations, the USSR and the Western countries voted together on such vital resolutions as on: (1) The Debt Problems of Developing Countries (Resolution No A/31/14); (2) Industrial Redeployment in Favour of Developing Countries; and (3) Ways and Means of Accelerating Transfer of Real Resources to Developing Countries on a Predictable, Assured and Continuous Basis.

It has been contended that the initial effect of the availability of East European credits was to break the monopoly of private foreign investors in India in, for example, steel, oil and pharmaceutical industries, and there was expectation that this would aid in the future self-reliant development of India. Apart from the question of what class in Indian society benefits from such foreign assistance, such formulations ignore many glaring facts. Such units not only remain dependent on the USSR for spares, but Indian technology is not encouraged even when indigenous technology and installed capacity are adequate to supply components of the project. More importantly, it appears that the basic consideration of Soviet 'aid' is to gain a foothold [29] and

---

[29] 80 industrial projects have been constructed or designed in India with Soviet co-operation. Of these more than 55 have already been commissioned. These

break established Western cartels and earn profits. Thus, it is not that "foreign policy considerations have been dominant in Soviet objectives of aid policy towards India", as P J Eldridge contends [45], but considerations of economic profit have been at least equally important.

We believe that this discussion should provide a basis for political strategy in Third World countries vis-a-vis the USSR. In India, particularly, it is perhaps important to begin to realize that possibly the U.S. is not the only hegemonistic superpower in the world, nor the only threat to liberation struggles in Third World countries.

However, it must be understood clearly that we have not proved that the USSR is imperialist, because we have said nothing about the character of the internal Soviet economy. We have dealt instead, primarily, with Soviet aid and trade relations with the Third World. In this sense, a direction of future research could be to critically analyse the structure of the Soviet economy. And in the light of such research, and an examination of Soviet economic relations with East European countries and with China between 1950 and 1964, a case could be built which would go to *prove* that the USSR is imperialist. Some work of this kind from a Marxist perspective is already being done.[30]

An interesting general theme which could be taken up is the particular character of Soviet 'imperialism'. For instance, could the USSR, with the apparently non-capitalistic character of its aid (not owning plants, for example) come to establish a character of imperialism which should lead the world? Are policies of repayment in kind, public sector, project loans, aid and trade to set up manufacturing industries and even capital goods, etc, all of which aid the development of the country,

---

projects at present account for one-third of India's output of steel, one-fifth of power generation, 60 per cent of crude production, 30 per cent of oil products, over 80 per cent of metallurgical products and 60 per cent of steam and hydro-power plants. They also account for large quantities of pharmaceuticals and drugs, including antibiotics.

[30] Here we refer not to the so called "convergence" theory which has become popular among certain circles of liberal scholarship. Rather we refer to the growing volume of Marxist literature which sees developments in the USSR, particularly after Khruschev, as essentially making a reversion to capitalism (see note 4).

forms of relation which will come to be emulated by Western capitalist countries? Does the 'socialist' appearance of aid and trade make it a leading form of imperialism, just as American 'anti-colonialism' was a limit which gave the US an advantage as a progressive trade and aid partner? And would this have the consequence of fostering the rapid development of capitalism in the Third World? Further research may well speak to this set of questions.

References

[1] For instance, see Walter Laquer, "The Struggle for the Middle East", New York: MacMillan Co, 1969; and Mahmoud Hussein, "Class Conflict in Egypt 1945-1971", New York: Monthly Review, 1973, p 205.
[2] Asha Datar, "India's Economic Relations with the USSR and Eastern Europe 1953-1969", Cambridge University Press, 1972, p 10.
[3] *Washington Post,* November 19, 1973.
[4] Datar, *op cit,* pp 42-5.
[5] Pramit Chaudhuri, "East European Aid to India," *World Development,* 111:5 (May 1975), p 341.
[6] N K Chandra, "USSR and Third World: Unequal Distribution of Gains", *Economic and Political Weekly,* Annual Number, February 1977.
[7] James Carter, "The Net Cost of Soviet Foreign Aid", New York: Praeger, 1969, p 38.
[8] Franklyn Holzman, "Foreign Trade Under Central Planning", Cambridge: Harvard University Press, 1974.
[9] Datar, *op cit,* p 182.
[10] Nikita Khruschev (edited by S Talbott), "Khruschev Remembers", Boston: Little Brown, 1970, p 440. The authenticity of this text has been questioned.
[11] Carter, *op cit,* pp 23, 42.
[12] Marshall Goldman, "Soviet Foreign Aid", New York: Praeger, 1967, p 93.
[13] Michael Kidron.
[14] M N Dastur and Co, "Cost Reduction Study on Borkaro Project", Calcutta, 1966. Datar's view of this is in Datar, *op cit.*
[15] Stainslaus Sebastian, "Soviet Economic Aid to India", New Delhi: N V Publications, 1972, p 175.
[16] Chandra, *op cit,* p 870.
[17] See in this context Teresa Hayter, "Aid as Imperialism", Harmondsworth: Pelican, 1971, and Cheryl Payer, "The Debt Trap: the IMF and the Third World", Pelican, 1974.
[18] Datar, *op cit,* p 182.
[19] Pramit Chaudhuri, *op cit.*
[20] Report of the Study Team on Leakage of Foreign Exchange Through Invoice Manipulation, Government of India, 1971.
[21] Eleventh Report of the Fourth Lok Sabha's Estimates Committee, "Utilisation of External Assistance", New Delhi: Lok Sabha Secretariat, 1967, pp 228-9.

[22] *Ibid*, March 2, 1973.
[23] Swaminathan S Aiyar, "Soviet Aided Projects", *Times of India*, April 29, 1977.
[24] *Economic and Political Weekly*, December 8, 1973, p 2152.
[25] Communist Party of India (Marxist-Leninist), "Soviet Social Imperialism in India", Westmount: Indian People's Association in North America, 1976.
[26] Communist Party of China, "How the Soviet Revisionists Carry Out All-Round Restoration of Capitalism in the USSR", Peking: Foreign Languages Press, 1968; "Ugly Features of Soviet Social Imperialism", Peking: Foreign Languages Press, 1976.
[27] Christian Palloix, "Les Firmes multinationales", Paris: Maspero, 1973; and "L'Internationalisation du capital", Paris: Maspero, 1975.
[28] Smirnov and Matyukhin, "USSR and the Arab East: Economic Contacts", *International Affairs* (Moscow), September 1972, p 87.
[29] Chandra, *op cit*.
[30] Cited in Frank, *op cit*.
[31] Jan Pennar, "The USSR and the Arabs: The Ideological Dimension", New York: Crane Russak and Co, 1973.
[32] Meghnad Desai, "India: Emerging Contradictions of Slow Capitalist Development", in R Blackburn (ed), "Explosion in a Subcontinent", Pelican, 1975, p 18.
[33] A G Frank, "Long Live Transideological Enterprise: Socialist Economies in Capitalist International Division of Labour", *EPW*, Annual Number, February 1977.
[34] *EPW*, January 12, 1974.
[35] P Desai, "The Bokaro Steel Plant", Amsterdam, North Holland, p 57.
[36] See Dennis Childs and Michael Kidron, "India, USSR and the MiG Project", in *EPW*, September 22, 1973.
[37] Stockholm International Peace Research Institute, "Arms Trade with the Third World", Stockholm, 1971, p 753.
[38] From Military Budget 1974-75, a study by the International Institute of Strategic Studies, London, quoted in *Indian Ex-Press*, December 4, 1974.
[39] Evidence presented to the Parliamentary Consultative Committee of the Indian Defence Ministry on July 21, 1970.
[40] Letter to Madhu Limaye, quoted in *Hindu*, September 13, 1974.
[41] All figures from Explanatory Memorandum to Central Government Budget for 1973-4, Government of India Press, New Delhi, 1974.
[42] See Santosh Mehrotra, "India's Economic Relations with the USSR, 1955-77", Jawaharlal Nehru University, Unpublished M Phil dissertation, Chapter 5.
[43] Statistical Review of Trade Between Countries Having Different Social and Economic Systems, UNCTAD, Secretariat, TD/B/410 Geneva, August 23, 1972, p 9.
[44] See a study prepared for UNCTAD by the Moscow Institute of Economics of the World Socialist System, "Innovations in the Practice of Trade and Economic Co-operation between the Socialist Countries of Eastern Europe and the Developing Countries", TD/B/238/Rev 1, New York, 1970, p 10.
[45] P J Eldridge, "Politics of Foreign Aid in India", New Delhi, 1969.

The "Tarnished Socialism" Thesis
or The Political Economy of Soviet Social-Imperialism

Revolutionary Communist Party, USA

INTRODUCTION

"The 'Tarnished Socialism' Thesis" first appeared in 1978 in the theoretical journal of the RCP, USA, *The Communist*. It must be situated in the context of an intense outburst of theoretical struggle that erupted in the wake of the revisionist coup in China in 1976. The Great Proletarian Cultural Revolution in China had been correctly seen by millions throughout the world as a bold and unprecedented attempt in practice to prevent a counter-revolutionary process similar to the one which had ultimately gripped and strangled socialist revolution in the Soviet Union. The fact that this sweeping experiment to uproot old ideas and centuries-old social relations had ended in setback could not help but have far-reaching reverberations. It inevitably brought to the

---

This article appeared originally in Vol. 2 No. 2 of *The Communist*, theoretical journal of the Revolutionary Communist Party, USA. It has been slightly edited for this publication and includes a new introduction.

fore the question of whether such a political defeat should not also be seen as a refutation *in practice* of the line and theoretical concepts that had led the Cultural Revolution.

These political conditions emboldened and strengthened former "critics" of Soviet revisionism who had reversed commonly held verdicts and who had come to embrace the Soviet Union as socialist. They argued that the sharpening confrontation between the Soviet bloc and the western imperialist bloc were signs that the revisionist line of Khrushchev had not really reversed class relations in the Soviet Union and restored capitalism. And they raised ever more strident arguments that the conclusions of Mao Tsetung were not only based on a subjective overestimation of what was *possible* in the world today, but also on an unscientific assessment of what was in fact *necessary* to decisively defeat capitalist relations and proceed on the socialist road to communism.

From two sides, "The 'Tarnished Socialism' Thesis" digs into some of the controversial questions raised by the apologists of social-imperialism. First, it reveals why the real possibility of counterrevolution persists throughout the protracted period of socialist transition to communism. Second, examining the historical development of the Soviet Union since 1956, it sketches how, in fact, such a capitalist restoration occurred and how the extraction of surplus value takes place through the still state-owned economic institutions of Soviet society. It dissects the various sociological particularities of the Soviet social formation to reveal that they are not only compatible with capitalist social relations but themselves reflect those relations. The works of two authors are taken as polemical targets. The first is Jonathan Aurthur, who fired one of the first salvoes of the ex-"anti-revisionists" in a book entitled *Socialism in the Soviet Union*. The second is Albert Szymanski, who had already published two articles challenging "Mao's restorationist thesis."

If anything, the five intervening years since "Tarnished" was written have abundantly confirmed the thesis that the Soviet Union is fundamentally characterized by the contradictions of capitalism in its imperialist stage of development. Undisguisable economic crisis grips the entire Soviet bloc. In Poland, its acuteness has intensified the political hemorrhaging of the system to reveal the unbridgable gap between the masses and the revisionist ruling class, and give apologists for modern revisionism the unenviable burden of defending the need for open military dictatorship. Within the Soviet Union itself, the much-touted process of economic growth that was supposedly inherent in Soviet institutions has faltered and sputtered as severe dislocations tear at the myths surrounding Soviet planning and force a distinctly unplanned economic contraction. Finally, the Soviet bloc now has its own lingering colonial wars in Afghanistan, Eritrea and Kampuchea, complete with "search and destroy missions" and napalm raids on villages.

Of course, exactly because facts don't "speak for themselves" such developments have not resolved the controversy over the role of the Soviet Union in the world. Indeed, they have brought the question of the basic class nature of the Soviet Union to the fore with renewed intensity. Once the Soviet Union is accepted as embodying "existing socialism," it is nothing less than remarkable how its reactionary features are then ignored, justified or embraced in a spirit of political expediency. Over and over again, the revisionists return to what they have found to be a simple and compelling argument: the very structure of modern Soviet society ensures that it is the antithesis of capitalism, hence the policies of the Soviet state must ultimately express the progressive interests of the remaining, nonexploitative strata.

Although the works critiqued in "Tarnished" have been superceded by subsequent articles and books defending Soviet "socialism," many of the basic arguments put forward in defense of Soviet social-imperialism have scarcely changed. For that reason, "Tarnished" still stands as a valuable contribution to the debate, particularly in its argument that where the lever of social production is the law of value, the planning process itself (regardless of its socialist pretenses) simply becomes the form through which capital is allocated to produce and appropriate surplus value.

At the same time, however, we have developed some new insights over the last five years of theoretical investigation and struggle which bear directly on the discussion. These ideas are developed in the recent writings of Bob Avakian, Chairman of the Central Committee of the RCP, and in various publications already or soon to be published. For the purposes at hand, we can only briefly summarize certain points, but we want to present them in this introduction, not simply as additions to the arguments "Tarnished" makes, but as an overall framework that is essential for a correct understanding of the issues raised by the debate. There are three broad, yet interrelated, themes. The first concerns the specificity of imperialism and the international determinants of the capitalist accumulation process; the second concerns the fundamental essence of the capital relation; the third, and unifying theme, concerns the international dimensions and requirements of proletarian revolution.

I

The arguments refuting the very possibility that the Soviet Union could be imperialist start from deep-seated misconceptions of how capitalism functions in this era. To begin with, their operative model is something resembling capitalism in the pre-imperialist epoch. In other words, if capitalism were restored in the Soviet Union, we should expect to find increasing immiseration of the masses, growing unemployment, and cyclical economic crises. Since these phenomena are not readily observable in the Soviet Union...end of argument. In fact, imperialist crisis need not assume the features of a rerun Great Depression. Conventional wisdom of the international communist movement has not been clear on this point. And even in our own previous writings, including "Tarnished," there has been a tendency to assume that the central manifestation of crisis is economic collapse and widespread impoverishment within the imperialist countries themselves. This is a legacy of the erroneous theory of "general crisis."

Frankly, if one examines the many pages devoted to an empirical "proof" that the manifestations of capitalism are absent in the Soviet Union — one is quickly struck by the fact that the "non-capitalist" features of the Soviet Union are quite typical for modern imperialist metropoles. There are several imperialist countries, notably West Germany and Japan, that sustained economic growth for decades, with negligible unemployment; in West Germany, over twenty years elapsed after the end of World War 2 before it experienced a real downturn. Similarly, the rise in the standard of living of the Soviet masses between the mid-'50s and '70s was both real and not particularly spectacular compared to the achievements of some other imperialist countries. Even on the question of income distribution, the ratio between the top tenth and the bottom tenth in Sweden compares quite favorably with that of the Soviet Union.

When the concept of imperialism is introduced into the discussion, the Soviet Union is stacked up against the United States. Since the external network of the Soviet Union does not match the sprawling empire and string of military bases of U.S. imperialism, then the Soviet Union does not pass muster as an imperialist power. Indeed, the apologists, as "Tarnished" points out, conceptualize imperialism in thoroughly Kautskyite terms, as an external policy (untoward treatment of other countries) or as an external additive (x amount of returns from overseas activity). The relative merits of its "internal" policies and its "external" policies are weighed against each other, as if they were easily separable. Or, alternately, it is claimed that the Soviet Union must surely be socialist since its policies in this or that country seem beneficent enough.

Marxism-Leninism, of course, analyzes imperialism as a specific stage of development of capitalism, as a structural and systemic phenomenon. Accumulation proceeds through *monopoly*, through the *division of the world into oppressor and oppressed nations*, and through *rivalry* between imperialist capitals. Capitalism has operated internationally from its beginnings, but this undergoes a qualitative change in the imperialist era. Underlying this change is the further socialization of production, the internationalization of capital, and the complete partition of the world among the imperialist powers. The world market becomes an integral and determining whole, and national economies are integrated into a *single world process*. A new international dynamic emerges in the imperialist era; it is more determinant of the structures, trendlines, and barriers to accumulation than is cyclical motion within the imperialist economies. The decisive stimulus to profitable accumulation is international expansion, particularly into the colonial and neo-colonial regions of the world. This furnishes the basis for more extended periods of growth in the imperialist countries and for the bribing of substantial layers of their populations.

Monopoly capital is an internationalized mode of production which functions according to an inner compulsion. It remains rooted in national markets, yet requires a global field of operations. These internationalized capitals press up against each other. All this defines a new matrix of accumulation. The contradictions of accumulation become concentrated in the international arena. For the imperialists, crisis can only be resolved through warfare for the redistribution of power and spheres of influence. Thus, major changes in international political alignments have marked the essential qualitative leaps in the process of imperialist accumulation. The basic laws of capitalist accumulation exert themselves in the framework of the relation of forces in the world in which interimperialist wars of redivision have been nodal points.

Politics assumes far greater importance in the imperialist era. The enmeshing of the world in the capitalist mode of production draws the masses of the oppressed nations into the swirl of history and intertwines the contradictions between imperialism and the oppressed nations and between the proletariat and the bourgeoisie in the imperialist countries. The intensification of the contradictions of a world system opens new prospects for the subjective factor. At the same time, the centrality of international relations to the accumulation process foists a new calculus on the imperialists. They must make moves and countermoves on the international chessboard; they must defend, extend, or secure integrated empires. The flow of capital, then, is not directly determined by the highest rate of return. Investments, trade and aid have geopolitical determinants as well. The Alliance for Progress cannot be understood outside the impact of the Cuban Revolution; concessionary prices charged by the Soviet Union to its East European allies cannot be understood outside the need to shore up its bloc.

At the same time, the requirements and contradictions of accumulation implicate the state far more pervasively in the reproductive process: the seeding of new, strategic industries, bail-outs, infrastructure development, etc., are integral to the role of the imperialist state. Its warfare and welfare functions express the larger needs of empire, that is, the organization of force to confront rivals and to suppress and intimidate the masses and the organization of concessionary pacification to stabilize the home front. The capacity of the imperialist state to centralize and reallocate surplus value represents a modification of the operation of the law of value.

Arguments that the Soviet Union is not capitalist because capital is steered to the less profitable heavy industrial sectors (which have obvious linkages with the military) or because the Soviets lose money in Cuba (as do the U.S. imperialists in Israel) are rather frivolous in view of the imperatives of empire. One might plausibly argue on such a basis that the war in Vietnam was not an imperialist war since its costs far outweighed the potential economic benefits that might be derived from Vietnam alone. But if the law of value is mediated through complex mechanisms in the imperialist era and if politics continually and powerfully interacts with economics, these imperialist politics are grounded in the expand-or-die nature of capital, in the regulating role of the law of value.

Only by grasping the specificity of imperialism can the dynamics and particularities of the Soviet social formation be understood. Social-imperialism emerged *out of* the reversal of socialism — and is still making use of many of the forms and structures developed under socialism — and on a foundation of a fairly high degree of development of the productive forces. On the other hand, it emerged *into* a very specific international environment, reflecting, in the main, a division of the world which had its roots in the outcome of World War 2. The Soviet Union faced a vastly more powerful imperialist network dominated by U.S. imperialism. The specific international configuration and relative strengths on a world scale impacted greatly on the structures and necessities of the Soviet Union — on the allocation of capital, the particular forms and policies adopted internally, and on the international strategy pursued by social-imperialism to extend its sway. On the latter point, Khrushchev's open betrayal of revolutionary struggles and the attempt to avoid head-on confrontation with the United States in the late '50s and '60s at the same time that the social-imperialists were making inroads into strategically key regions, corresponded to the needs and possibilities of the period. As the world situation further developed and Soviet strength increased, these policies of collaboration with and capitulation to U.S. imperialism no longer conformed to the needs of the Soviet bourgeoisie.

This international framework and rivalry with a global adversary, interacting with the historical basis of capitalist restoration in the Soviet Union (a highly centralized, planned economy) and revisionist ideology itself, has resulted in a massively bureaucratized and militarized economy. Many of the particular current features of the Soviet Union are not necessarily inherent in the nature of a restored capitalism. Had the Soviet Union been less industrially developed, or had it emerged as a junior partner to some other imperialist rather than as a head of its own distinct bloc — it is conceivable that the specific structure of its capitalist economy might have looked different. There has been a long-standing and conscious awareness among the social-imperialists that the only way out of their *cul-de-sac* will be world war, a recognition reflected in the huge military build-up since the mid-1960s. This militarized economy is at once a source of strength and an Achilles heel (greatly lopsiding development and lending a certain complexion to crisis within its bloc). The Soviet Union is not an imperialist power out of the contemporary Japanese mold, that is, a highly efficient and organized workshop or trader to the world, although the particularities of Japanese imperialism can also be understood only in the context of the specific political arrangements and international division of labor established on the basis of the resolution of World War 2 and the international alignment of forces in its aftermath.

If Soviet social-imperialism was contending in a world which was not a "blank slate," where the majority of oppressed nations were, for instance, subjugated by Western imperialism, neither was it "coming from nowhere." The Soviet Union was able to pull an entire part of the world, notably large sections of Eastern Europe which had been in various stages of political transition, into its imperialist orbit, based on the leadership it previously exercised over them in the socialist camp, a critical mass of military strength, and the forms of economic integration previously developed under socialism. Moreover, as suggested above, the Soviet Union entered into and/or transformed its relations with some "third world" countries relatively quickly, and this provided it with certain reserves that could be utilized to its advantage. These factors also impacted on the internal structure of its economy. This ability to forge its own international division of labor combined with far-ranging internal restructuring (effected by various "economic reforms") to generate a certain stimulus and momentum to the Soviet economy (and bloc) — at the same time that it imposed new requirements and created new contradictions.

The Soviet Union has extensive trade, aid and investment ties with many countries in the world, including in the "third world." Its forms of overseas activity are diverse: international banking institutions, joint East-West ventures in the "third world," barter trade, shipping, and international gold sales, to name a few. In other works, the RCP has documented the exploitative character of Soviet relations in the "third world," and another essay in this volume takes India as a case study and shows how Soviet trade and aid reinforces dependency. It must be underscored that the Soviet export of capital to the "third world" often involves complex arrangements, revolving around sale of arms, trade, aid projects, loans — all sometimes tied into "package deals." Here we can only concentrate on an important theoretical point. As an international exploiter, the Soviet Union quite clearly pales beside the United States. While it exports capital, this is not nearly as massive a phenomenon as it is in the West. How, then, is this formation to be understood, particularly in light of the methodological insistence of the apologists of Soviet social-imperialism that if capital is not being exported on a large scale, it is entirely inappropriate to describe the Soviet Union as imperialist.

The imperialist nature of its international relations has to be understood from two sides.

One, these relations are already fundamentally exploitative and involve the export of capital and extraction of surplus value through various mechanisms. Second, in quantitative terms, what characterizes the Soviet position is that it is gripped by an overbearing need to expand the scale of this international exploitation. The Soviet Union does not yet have an empire on the scale of, or with the coherence of, the U.S. empire today. But the point is that it *needs to forge such an empire* and its actions are predicated on doing so.

Let's look at these general points a little more closely:

To begin with, the role of capital export, especially investments in the colonial and neocolonial countries, must be understood in *qualitative* terms. In none of the major imperialist countries do overseas profits represent a large share of total profits. But once this is disaggregated, these profits can be shown to figure much more prominently within the operations of the decisive and leading units of finance capital. The imperialists must go after high profits to stimulate and activate their entire mass of capital, and the higher rates of return, the extra value and particular inputs (e.g. raw materials) entering into the domestic imperialist economies from the "third world," along with the transformations of productive relations possible in these backward regions, play a disproportionately important role in imperialist accumulation. On the other hand, a given imperialist country may be cut out from such opportunities. Germany, for instance, in the interwar period was not able to export massive amounts of capital. Its economy did not immediately fall apart... but it had to go to war, and it was certainly no less an imperialist power than Great Britain.

The Soviet Union is gripped by the compulsion of an internationalized mode of production. There are forces pulling capital outward, yet the present division of the world and structure of world capital does not permit either the volume of such flows or the requisite reorganization of capital internationally to fuel an expansionary process. There is a specific dynamic of crisis within the Soviet bloc — it involves a division of labor turning into its opposite, historic difficulties in agriculture, the reverberations of military spending, among other factors. This in turn interacts with the crisis in the West. Lacking the ability to expand on a new basis, the structure of capital in that bloc turns ever more wrenchingly in on itself, heightening all its contradictions.

The interplay between rivalry and crisis can be briefly illustrated. The Soviet Union has been able to make some inroads into various "third world" countries. In Egypt, it could offer military assistance and aid in the construction of the Aswan Dam. Yet the relative economic weakness of Soviet social-imperialism, *vis-a-vis* the U.S., showed itself in this particular instance of rivalry. The Soviet Union lost Egypt back to the U.S. bloc, in part, because it lacked comparable reserves and international networks (I.M.F. and World Bank-type institutions) to tear the Egyptian economy decisively away from the West and to successfully carry out the kind of imperialist-sponsored restructuring that might buoy it up temporarily. The faster growth Egypt experienced once it fell back into the Western orbit has, of course, led to more serious economic dislocations. And this speaks to a related point. The Soviet Union often makes gains in such countries at U.S. expense after several decades of distorted and disarticulated development and at a time when the world is convulsed by an unprecedented crisis. It can and does provide substantial military support and some project aid. But experiences as diverse as those of Egypt and Vietnam reveal that outside a complete recasting of international relations, the Soviet Union runs into insurmountable problems in their attempts to consummate these gains.

In Poland, a serious economic and political crisis has virtually paralyzed that country and has presented the Soviet bloc with a dilemma. On the one hand, the Soviet Union lacks the capacity to produce any significant measures and initiatives to even paper over the cracks of that economy. The situation can only grow worse. Indeed, Western financial assistance has been relied on, and this in turn increases Western leverage while compounding an already serious financial crisis in the West. On the other hand, despite a potential challenge to revisionist rule, the Soviets have gingerly avoided sending troops in, as this would not only detonate mass resistance but also jeopardize their attempts to woo some of the West European imperialists (as part of their larger strategic plans). And so, the crisis intensifies.

The point is that the Soviets cannot resolve the crisis in their own bloc within the bounds of the existing division of the world. Nor can they allow the U.S. bloc to obtain the more favorable division of the world which it just as desperately needs. This is the compulsion they face, and the same applies to the U.S.-led bloc. The severity of crisis in the Soviet Union and its bloc, like that of the western bloc, cannot be measured chiefly in terms of indices of industrial output or unemployment — although these are by no means insignificant. Rather one must look to the explosive interaction of political and economic crisis with global rivalry, to the necessities these contradictions foist on the imperialist powers.

In short, it is the presently existing division of the world that confronts the USSR as *the* central obstacle to a resolution of any of the major strands of its crisis.

II

In capitalist society, the labor process, purposive activity through which human beings make use of and transform nature, is subordinate to the value-creation process. Labor is socially useful (and employable) only insofar as it is capable of producing surplus value and meeting the demands of profitability. Efficiency and technical progress are measured in terms of their contribution to profitability. The average social profit rate on invested funds sets the norm for enterprise performance and viability, as mediated by the political factors spoken of earlier and by monopoly. Historically, revisionist political economy has held that the overarching task of socialist society is to produce in a planned way the maximum amount of products to satisfy social needs with minimum consumption of social labor: the right combination of technical efficiency and incentives (to spur greater efficiency) will lead to abundance which is the key to advancing society to a higher level. But economy of time is achieved within and serves definite production and class relations. In capitalist society, the urge to produce more with less labor is the requirement of maximizing profit with a minimum of capital. In a genuine socialist economy, the value-creation process is subordinate to the socialist labor process and the conscious activity of the masses, exchange value is subordinate to use value, and economy of time is subordinate to and governed by revolutionary, proletarian politics. What, then, is meant by the capital relation and its dominance?

In 1981, Bob Avakian posited this definition of capital in a ground-breaking work summing up the historical experience of the international proletariat:

> "Capital is a social relation and a process, whose essence is indeed the domination by alien, antagonistic interests over labor power and the continual (and extended) reproduction of that.... It means that...labor power is controlled and utilized on an expanded basis to reproduce relationships which are alien to them [the workers] and opposed to them."

As applied to socialist society:

> "If ownership has been (in the main) socialized, if a correct line is in command...which means that the division of labor as well as differences in distribution are being restricted to the greatest degree possible...if the motion is toward eliminating these things, then how can it be said that a force opposed to the proletariat has domination over its

labor power or even a force alien to it, in the fundamental sense?"*

This understanding is crucial if we are to evaluate what actually goes on in a society. The RCP has long emphasized that the existence of socialism is a question of the socialist road rather than a question of certain fixed attributes. It is a question of the direction society is moving in. In other words, in determining whether the capital relation is dominant in the Soviet Union, it is necessary, first and foremost, to examine what social labor is in the service of, whether the masses are being mobilized to transform society in the direction of communism and for the purpose of contributing to world revolution. That some of the institutional forms of monopoly capitalism in the West (juridically private ownership of means of production, stock exchanges, etc.) are absent, tells us very little. That some of the social "insecurities" of premonopoly capitalism have been attenuated, that some sections of the working class have seen their living standards rise for extended periods, that some workers may even be "happy" with their lot, is scarcely proof that socialism exists.

For the revisionists, socialism turns on a *quid pro quo*, a kind of social compact — in exchange for their labor power the workers receive a social wage: cradle-to-grave security enlivened by some perfunctory "worker participation." For those theorists who reduce the capital relation to the mere existence of commodity relations and the division of labor inherited from capitalism, a position strongly implied in the recent writings of Charles Bettelheim, the acid test of the dominance or nondominance of that relation is worker control in factories. Now the persistence and reproduction of commodity relations and a division of labor still marked by inequalities are part of the material basis for the restoration of capitalism. But the existence of these relations as such is not tantamount to capitalism. Again, capital is a *societal* relation: "what are you working for, what is your labor power being applied to?"

This brings into sharper relief the central role of the superstructure and the decisiveness of ideological and political line in socialist society. Socialism is a contradictory entity in which newly developing production and social relations are in

---

*Bob Avakian, *Conquer the World? The International Proletariat Must and Will*, special issue of *Revolution*, No. 50 (December 1981), p. 29.

conflict with regenerated capitalist relations. Socialism, as "Tarnished" stresses, is a coherent system and yet, at the same time, a checkerboard of contested zones, with bourgeois forces in control here and proletarian forces in control there. What makes such a society socialist is the fact that a proletarian line is overall in command, that society is on the socialist road, overcoming bourgeois relations, and, most important, functioning as a base area for world revolution.

III

The task of proletarian revolution is to abolish class distinctions generally, to abolish all the relations of production on which they rest, to abolish all the social relations that correspond to these relations of production, and to revolutionize all the ideas that result from these social relations. Chang Chun-chiao, in summarizing Marx on this point, concludes:

> "In all the four cases, Marx means *all*. Not a part, a greater part, or even the greatest part, but all! This is nothing surprising, for only by emancipating all mankind can the proletariat achieve its own final emancipation. The only way to attain this goal is to exercise all-round dictatorship over the bourgeoisie and carry the continued revolution under the dictatorship of the proletariat through to the end, until the above-mentioned four *alls* are banished from the earth so that it will be impossible for the bourgeoisie and all other exploiting classes to exist or for new ones to arise..."*

The material, social and ideological underpinnings of capitalism cannot be eliminated in one stroke. Further, capitalism can adapt itself to any variety of institutional forms (capitalism exists as kibbutz in Israel, workers' "self-administration" in Yugoslavia, and Committees to Defend the Revolution in Cuba). This is not because capital thrives in the celestial mists, but exactly in the "deep structure" of society. Capitalism does not reside in any single legal property relation between individual men and

---

* Chang Chun-chiao, "On Exercising All-Round Dictatorship Over the Bourgeoisie," in Raymond Lotta, *And Mao Makes Five* (Chicago: Banner Press, 1978) pp. 216-17.

the means of production. In the real world it consists of a network of relations between social classes, relations which have a material foundation in commodity production, in the differences between mental and manual labor, town and country, etc., and which are expressed through the complex, dialectical interaction between base and superstructure. Thus, there is no form or structure which, by dint of its "innate characteristics," is impervious to capitalism. For these reasons, society must be repeatedly "sprung into the air," the most thoroughgoing process of revolution is necessary if communism is to be achieved. Indeed, unless this happens, capitalism reemerges.

But all the necessary transformations of society toward communism cannot be conducted in one country alone. The contradictions between forces and relations of production and between base and superstructure and the class struggle in socialist society are rooted in the contradiction between socialized production and private appropriation, which has international motion and development. This brings us back to the dominance of the bourgeois mode of production in the world as a whole, the role of the world market, and the concentration of imperialism's contradictions in the world arena. We live in a period of worldwide transition from the bourgeois epoch to the epoch of world communism. The socialist countries that come into being in this period are integrated into this overall process of transition. The international context sets the basic parameters for revolutionary struggle. Thus, the contradictions of the world imperialist system and the international class struggle react back upon the socialist countries.

The period of proletarian rule in China furnishes some useful examples of the influence of an international dynamic. The Chinese road to socialism was associated with the policies of combining small and medium industry with large industry, of encouraging agricultural self-sufficiency and local self-reliance in industry, and saw millions go into the countryside. These policies contributed profoundly to narrowing the differences between town and country and between worker and peasant; they were seeds of the future insofar as Mao was consciously striving to avoid the trajectory of lopsided industrial development, with all its oppressive social consequences, characteristic of the West. But these policies were also influenced by the necessity of preparing to fight a people's war against imperialism on the most favorable ground. Similarly, the terms of the struggle within the Chinese Communist Party in the early 1970s were very much conditioned by the intensifying drive toward war between the two imperialist blocs. This interpenetrated with questions of economic and military strategy — how far to restrict and narrow social differences, monetary policy, etc. The real danger of war and invasion by imperialist powers with vastly more sophisticated military arsenals objectively strengthened the position of the capitulationist forces within the CPC, who eventually won out.

At the same time, a backward country like China was forced to develop within the confines of a world economy dominated by imperialism. More generally, the socialist revolutions of the twentieth century have faced enormous economic strains. Even when China's direct commercial contacts with the West were minimal, it was, nonetheless, affected by the objective structure of world capital and the international division of labor. The fact that there was a real opportunity to open its oil fields to Japanese capital, that finance capital's ability to centralize and reallocate capital results in "newly industrializing countries," à la Brazil — in a word, that internationalized movements of capital and real differences in productive efficiencies exist in the world — all this impacted on the struggle over the allocation of China's resources. The revolutionaries struggled to stick to the Chinese road to socialism while the revisionists, particularly as China ran up against certain economic difficulties, could argue for some "practical" alternatives. Which raises a far more profound question.

Since communism can only be established on a world scale, there are limits to the transformations that can be carried out in particular socialist countries. In the essay referred to earlier, Bob Avakian analyzed why breakthroughs in a socialist country can ultimately turn into their opposite unless the international proletariat seizes new ground in the world:

> "In terms of maintaining power and advancing further on the socialist road — and not just from the standpoint of a socialist state but in particular from the standpoint of the international proletariat — the question is much more that there is a limit...to how far you can go in transforming the base and superstructure within the socialist country without

making further advances in winning and transforming more of the world; not in terms of conquering more resources or people as the imperialists do, but in terms of making revolutionary transformations...[F]irst of all...there is the ideological influence, as well as the actual military and political and other pressure, from the imperialist encirclement. But there's also the fact that this is the era of a single world process and that has a material foundation, it's not just an idea. What may be rational in terms of the production, even, and utilization of labor power and resources within a single country, carried beyond a certain point, while it may seem rational for that country, is irrational if you actually look upon a world scale. And that reacts upon that country and becomes an incorrect policy, not the best utilization of things even within that country, and begins to work not only against the development of the productive forces but, dialectically related to that, against the further transformation in the production relations (or the economic base) and the superstructure."*

The imperialists, of course, have their own versions of international rationality: theories of comparative advantage, neocolonial "new economic orders," the social-imperialist "socialist division of labor," *ad nauseam*. But these are merely vehicles to export capital and dominate the oppressed nations. Avakian is talking about the transformation of the world in the image of the international proletariat.

The imperialists operate according to compulsion rooted in the expand-or-die character of capital. The proletariat has its own, qualitatively different, compulsion, rooted in the historic necessity of abolishing the four "alls" on a world scale. This is why the main energies and efforts of a socialist country must be bent towards promoting world revolution and why, during those moments when the contradictions of the imperialist system come to a head on a world scale and when it becomes possible for the international proletariat to make qualitative breakthroughs, it must be prepared to "put everything on the line."

---

*Avakian, *op. cit.*, p. 38.

That the proletarian revolution is in its historic infancy and aims at nothing less than transforming all exploitative relations and ideas means that this is an era of revolution and counterrevolution on a world scale, of protracted and tortuous struggle. This view exists in opposition to the mechanical notion, now proven incorrect by historical experience, that the ultimate victory of world revolution is an arithmetic sum of separate national revolutions where socialism was simply and decisively "secured" in one country after another. The revisionists inveigh against Maoist "pessimism," and blast us for refusing to accept that there is some elixir that "locks" a society into socialism. Needless to say, not only is this not possible, it is not desirable, in the sense that socialism is not an end in itself, but a transit point to communism and a base area for world revolution. In point of fact, no social order is "stable" in this epoch. The internationalization and intensification of capital's contradictions stamp this era as the most violent and turbulent in human history. Capitalist restoration is not the inevitable inheritor of any given revolutionary process in any given country. But if we look on a world scale, the epoch we live in is, as the Chinese revolutionaries emphasized, one of restoration and counterrestoration. Imperialism can only lead to more devastating crises and wars; capitalist roaders in power can only make a mess of things; and counterrevolution begets revolution.

Not only does oppression inevitably produce resistance, but each new advance does not start from square one. The world is not standing still. Historical development continually ripens the material basis for classless society. And with each new decisive contest, there is a deepening of the scientific understanding of the subjective forces. In a spiral-like motion passing through both victory and defeat, and punctuated on an international level by intense periods of revolutionary storms, a real historic world process is propelled forward towards communism.

The revisionists tar us with the brush of "utopianism," ascribing to us the insistence that communism be established immediately. The claim is absurd...then again if napalm in Afghanistan and the stultification of social life in the Soviet Union is socialism, the confusion is perhaps understandable. Nevertheless, the dialectics of the epoch are such that unless the proletariat dares to scale the heights, unless it dares to keep advancing and win more of the world, communism can just as well be written off as a utopian dream.

March 1983

CLASS STRUGGLE UNDER SOCIALISM AND THE NEW BOURGEOISIE

Jonathan Aurthur begins his book by straightforwardly arguing that "capitalism has not been, and cannot be, restored in the Soviet Union or any other socialist country."[1] History, he claims, moves forward in a continual upward spiral. The "form," the political superstructure of society, can be turned around; but the "content" of society, its economic base, the fundamental relations of production, cannot. According to Aurthur:

> "Once a new mode of production has taken hold, counter-revolution can still attempt to force it backward. But it can succeed, if at all, only superficially. Its content is forced, on pain of extinction, to adapt itself to the new, more advanced economic reality, the new mode of production. And why? Because new modes of production (slavery, feudalism, capitalism and socialism) do not come upon or leave the historical scene arbitrarily, accidentally, ideologically, or at the whim of this or that individual or group, but as the result of the development of social production."[2]

While it is true that history moves forward in an upward spiral,[3] this does not rule out distinct reversals of this motion. As Lenin put it, "it is undialectical, unscientific and theoretically wrong to regard the course of world history as smooth and always in a forward direction, without occasional gigantic leaps back."[4] And there is certainly no rule which states that such leaps cannot be taken in the economic base as well as in the superstructure. Socialism and ultimately communism will inevitably triumph over capitalism, since only socialist revolution can resolve the contradictions of the capitalist system. And while the proletariat is advancing and will continue to advance, its struggle has never been and never will be without its twists and turns. As Mao Tsetung said, "the future is bright, the road is tortuous."[5]

The historical epoch of several centuries which saw the development of capitalism out of feudalism also witnessed many reversals for the rising capitalist production relations. In Renaissance Italy commodity production and trade developed to the point where merchant capital was beginning to be transformed into industrial capital, but for various reasons this did not come to fruition, the Italian city-states stagnated and the bourgeois revolution did not take place for another three centuries.

Another instructive example can be found in the transition from slave society to feudalism in China. This occurred over a period of several hundred years, beginning as early as about 600 B.C. It was not until 221 B.C., however, that China was unified under a feudal dictatorship, headed by emperor Chin Shih-Huang, who upheld and implemented the Legalist line and program representing the rising landlord class, ruthlessly suppressed the counter-revolutionary restorationists and brought about the thoroughgoing triumph of feudalism over slavery throughout China at that time. Previous to that, during a long period, although the feudal class had on the whole superseded the slave-owning class well before Chin Shih-Huang came to power, the slaveowners still had power in certain areas and there were repeated attempts by the slaveowners, represented by such famous historical figures as Confucius and Mencius (and their followers), to restore the old order in China as a whole. And even after Chin Shih-Huang unified China under feudal rule there were still some attempts by the remnant forces of the slave system to stage a comeback, though they were unsuccessful.[6]

Further, the very nature of socialism as a transition between capitalism and communism makes a correct understanding of the dialectic between base and superstructure even more essential than it is for understanding capitalism or earlier exploiting systems. Because while capitalist relations developed within feudal society, feudal relations within slave society, etc. and each of these exploiting classes only came to power in the superstructure after building up their economic base, socialism cannot develop in the same way out of capitalism. And unlike capitalism and previous exploiting systems, socialism aims to make an unprecedented transformation of society, eliminating all exploitation and its superstructure, to make what Marx and Engels termed a "radical rupture" with all traditional property relations and traditional ideas.[7]

It is true that under capitalism the socialization of production creates the basis for transforming private appropriation into social appropriation, but this transformation itself cannot take place before the proletariat seizes state power. Although overall under socialism the economic base continues to determine the nature of the superstructure, the proletariat must consciously carry out the revolutionization of the economic base, the transformation of the relations of production, by exercising its state power and consciously applying its ideological and political line — in other words through the active, initiating role of the superstructure.

Citing Marx, who compared socialist revolution to childbirth, Aurthur argues that "Once a baby is born it cannot be stuffed back into the womb. Once socialist society is born out of the womb of the old capitalist society, it cannot be rejoined to its mother."[8] Let's take a look at exactly what Marx did say about this birth. He said that:

> "What we have to deal with here is a communist society, not as it has *developed* on its own foundations, but, on the contrary, just as it *emerges* from capitalist society; which is thus in every respect, economically, morally and intellectually, still stamped with the birth marks of the old society from whose womb it emerges."[9]

In other words, Marx was not emphasizing the *separation* of socialism from capitalism but the *connections* which still join the two and the *fragility* of the socialist infant. Lenin made much the same point using a different metaphor from the other end of the life cycle:

> "No, the working class is not separated by a Chinese Wall from the old bourgeois society. And when a revolution takes place, it does not happen as in the

case of the death of an individual, when the deceased is simply removed. When the old society perishes, its corpse cannot be nailed up in a coffin and lowered into the grave. It disintegrates in our midst; the corpse rots and infects us."[10]

Thus, the decisive and overwhelmingly principal task of the socialist stage, of the entire historical era of the dictatorship of the proletariat, the very purpose of that dictatorship, is to eradicate the birthmarks inherited from the old society, to transform all of society so that, as Marx himself put it, mankind may come to "the *abolition of class distinctions generally*, to the abolition of all the relations of production on which they rest, to the abolition of all the social relations that correspond to these relations of production, to the revolutionizing of all the ideas that result from these social relations."[11] (emphasis in original) This is sharply opposed to all those revisionists who argue that the historic task of the socialist period is to develop or modernize the productive forces.

To abolish all class distinctions it is necessary to abolish the production relations which give rise to them. These include three aspects, namely the forms of the ownership of the means of production, the position and mutual relations of people in production, and the distribution of the products of production. Of these three, ownership of the means of production is of decisive importance, and the key step for the proletariat in consolidating its dictatorship is to seize the means of production and place them under the ownership and control of the workers' state. But the other two aspects are also important. They react upon the system of ownership and, under certain conditions, can play the decisive role.

If the workers' state owns the means of production, but factories and enterprises are run in such a way that control is concentrated in the hands of a few leading cadres carrying out a revisionist line, if the differences between mental and manual labor, for instance, are consolidated and widened under the cover of "each keeping to his post" instead of being narrowed, then the socialist system of ownership can become a hollow shell. Similarly, while inequalities in distribution are unavoidable under socialism, reflecting the fact that distribution must be mainly according to work and not need, if it is not recognized that such distribution is, after all, a defect and that such inequalities must be restricted, then they will in turn affect the system of ownership and lay the basis for strengthening and not abolishing class distinctions. The proletariat cannot rest with transforming the forms of ownership but must also transform and eventually abolish all unequal relations as regards people's position and mutual relations in the course of production as well as all unequal relations with respect to distribution. In short, bourgeois right in all three aspects of production relations must be continuously restricted to the degree possible at each point, in accordance with the material and ideological conditions, and must eventually be eliminated altogether. To do otherwise is to strengthen the basis for capitalist restoration.

This is what it means to revolutionize the base as a crucial part of continuing the socialist revolution to the development of communism, completely classless society. And at the same time it is necessary in conjunction with this to continue the revolution in the superstructure as well. Economic relations, relations of production, while in the long run the determining and decisive relations, are not the only social relations into which people enter. There are political, ideological and cultural relations as well. These aspects of the superstructure react upon the base and they too may, under certain conditions, become decisive. Again, as Marx and Engels declared, "The Communist revolution is the most radical rupture with traditional property relations; no wonder that its development involves the most radical rupture with traditional ideas." [12]

Red Papers 7 described the importance of revolution in the superstructure and against all the ideas that arise from and serve capitalism. It pointed out:

> "Old bourgeois ideas don't instantly vanish under socialism... Bourgeois ideology remains a powerful weapon for capitalist restoration in a socialist society and must be fought by mass action and education every step of the way...
>
> "The main struggle against bourgeois ideology takes place in *concrete* struggles to replace these old ideas and methods with proletarian ideology (which is based on principles of cooperation, equality and

hatred of exploitation and reliance on the masses of people to organize production and society in general on the basis of scientific understanding of how society develops) and new methods in all the institutions of society."

Applying this to the Soviet Union, *RP7* noted that

"Socialism in the USSR, the first socialist state, had to break totally new ground, and all the tried and established methods of getting things done were inherited from the bourgeoisie. To the degree that they went unchallenged and unchanged, they slowly but surely weakened the proletarian character of the state and the socialist nature of the economic base. And this created the subjective conditions for a more or less peaceful restoration of capitalism."[13]

Now Aurthur may agree with Kautsky, Khrushchev, Liu Shao-chi and other more recent advocates of revisionist theses on socialism. He may say with them that all this can be accomplished without the sharpest class struggle over an extended period of time, indeed, over an entire historical era. But Lenin, for one, did not. He argued the opposite:

"The dictatorship of the proletariat is a most determined and most ruthless war waged by the new class against a *more powerful* enemy, the bourgeoisie, whose resistance is increased *tenfold* by its overthrow (even if only in one country), and whose power lies not only in the strength of international capital, in the strength and durability of the international connections of the bourgeoisie, but also in the *force of habit*, in the strength of *small production*. For, unfortunately, small production is still very, very widespread in the world, and small production *engenders* capitalism and the bourgeoisie continuously, daily, hourly, spontaneously and on a mass scale. For all these reasons the dictatorship of the proletariat is essential, and victory over the bourgeoisie is impossible without a long, stubborn and desperate war of life and death, a war demanding perseverance, discipline, firmness, indomitableness and unity of will."[14]

Clearly Lenin links the continuing class struggle to the continual re-emergence of bourgeois production relations under socialism. Further, in fact, the bourgeois aspects retained even in socialist production relations provide the basis for these socialist relations to be transformed back to capitalist ones. And, in general, the remnants of capitalism provide the basis not only for the continuing struggle of the old bourgeoisie against proletarian state power but, more important, the development of a new bourgeoisie. This new bourgeoisie arises from several sources. Lenin pointed to small production (a major factor in countries like Russia and China) as an important one. Technocrats, managers, the intelligentsia and the state bureaucracy are another source. This was stressed by Lenin in many of his writings and speeches, particularly during the NEP period.

But the most important source of the new bourgeoisie is the Communist Party itself. This pathbreaking discovery was elaborated most thoroughly by Mao Tsetung and those who followed his leadership in China on the basis of summing up the Soviet experience and the experience of the class struggle in China itself. As Mao put it shortly before his death, "You are making the socialist revolution, and yet don't know where the bourgeoisie is. It is right in the Communist Party."

Under capitalism the class struggle is *reflected* in the two-line struggle in the Party. But under socialism, Mao and his supporters argued, this struggle is actually *concentrated* in the Party since the most important Party leaders objectively occupy positions which can quite readily be transformed into those of a class antagonistic to the proletariat. The majority of managers, planners and leading state and Party bureaucrats are leading Communists. This is why Mao stressed that "if people like Lin Piao come to power, it will be quite easy for them to rig up the capitalist system."

Socialism is a transitional system where the rising communist relations must, through long and protracted struggle over an entire historical era, replace the declining capitalist relations. Only the correct, proletarian ideological and political line of the Communist Party, and its mobilization on this basis of the masses of people, can prevent the majority of Party leaders from degenerating, and the minority which do anyway from seizing power. Mao, of course, stressed that as long as the proletariat wields supreme power and a revisionist line is not in command overall, the capitalist-roaders (those in authority who do degenerate and on the basis of adopting a bourgeois class stand and a revisionist political line attempt to turn their positions into those of capitalists) will be few in number. But Mao did not intend this to mean that the proletariat should be any less vigilant; the revisionists after all can command a significant social base. For Mao, prevention of a revisionist coup through continually advancing the revolution and at each stage striking at the soil which gives rise to the bourgeoisie — this is the cardinal question for communists during the entire socialist period.

For Aurthur, of course, all this is just idealist nonsense. For him "once the new mode of production is established, it marks the end of the old antagonism between the proletariat and the bourgeoisie because there is no more bourgeoisie in the sense of an owning, exploiting class."[15] And as for the new bourgeoisie, he contends this whole concept makes "classes and modes of production become reflections of mental categories, not material relations among people."[16]

This was not Lenin's view. Even though he did not and could not (because of the then very limited experience of building socialism) develop the kind of understanding of class struggle under socialism that Mao did, Lenin, in true "idealist" fashion, declared quite forcefully that:

> "On the ground cleared of one bourgeois generation, new generations continually appear in history, as long as the ground gives rise to them, and it does give rise to any number of bourgeois. As for those who look at the victory over the capitalists in the way that the petty proprietors look at it — 'they grabbed, let me have a go too' — indeed, every one of them is the source of a new generation of bourgeois."[17]

Here Lenin, like Mao, seemingly makes class origin a reflection of "mental categories." But Lenin's and Mao's view is entirely correct and thoroughly materialist because the basis is there for people with such a line to put their views into practice. *Political and ideological line are decisive in the class struggle under socialism.* This is not idealism but an expression of the contradictory nature of socialist society. As Lenin put it, "politics is a concentrated expression of economics."[18] Aurthur explicitly rejects this scientific approach since to him it equates "what is capitalist or socialist with 'line' or ideology. The 'line' of this or that department or unit will determine 'the nature of ownership of it.'" He asks: "Under such circumstances, how can one call a country socialist at all? Rather it reduces itself to a giant checkerboard of 'units' which are now capitalist, now socialist, depending on which 'line' the management carries out."[19] But in a certain sense it is precisely such a "checkerboard" which does exist. For given the transitional nature of the socialist mode of production there is a basis in every unit for leadership to restore certain bourgeois production relations by implementing a revisionist line. This does not deny that socialism is a coherent economic system which marks a decisive break with the capitalist mode of production. But the internal contradictions of socialism, which mark it as necessarily only a transition to the ultimate goal of communist society, mean that it will have such a "checkerboard" character and that throughout all spheres of society there will be a constant struggle between the proletariat and the bourgeoisie over which class is in command there.

Even though a revisionist line may lead in certain factories, perhaps even in the majority, if the Communist Party leadership sticks to the proletarian line and mobilizes the masses in struggle against the revisionists, the socialist system will continue to develop and advance — but only, of course, through defeating the revisionist line and toppling from power those who stubbornly persist in fighting for this line. This is why, in 1969, in speaking of the situation that existed before the start of the Cultural Revolution, Mao stressed that "According to my own observation I would say that, not in all factories, nor in an overwhelming majority of factories, but in quite a large majority of cases the leadership is not in the hands of true Marxists, nor yet in the hands of the masses of the workers."[20] Yet Mao was not arguing that China was no longer a socialist country. He was pointing out that despite the great changes in the situation he described above, through the Cultural Revolution, still to continue the revolution was a real struggle: "the revolution has not been completed."[21]

Of course it is not just that the Communist Party is hierarchically structured or that a few bad eggs sneak in. There is a close dialectical connection between leading capitalist-roaders and their social base among other sectors of the new and old bourgeoisie. Besides the old exploiters, the intelligentsia, technocrats, lower level enterprise managers and administrators in socialist society provide a social base for capitalist restoration. The capitalist-roaders in the Party leadership are their commanders but must also reward sections of this base with added privilege and power.

This can be seen in the transformation of the Soviet Party Central Committee under Khrushchev. Under Stalin there arose a certain tendency to select Central Committee members and other political leaders on the basis of technical expertise, organizational "efficiency" or the achievement of "practical results" in production instead of according to grasp of and ability to apply and develop a proletarian political line. This was a serious counter-current to an overall correct policy of putting politics in command. Under Khrushchev, however, this incorrect tendency became the general rule. Proletarian fighters were expelled from the Central Committee and political middle forces swamped by a rapid expansion of that body's membership. New capitalist blood joined the ranks of the leaders. From the 19th Congress of the CPSU in 1952 to the 22nd Congress in 1961 there was a drastic change in the composition of the Central Committee. This period saw an influx of "practical men": educated technocrats and managers replaced the supposed "ideological hacks" of the Stalin era.

In 1952, 24.6% of the Central Committee consisted of members who had been recruited into Party leadership from leading posts in administrative, managerial or technical affairs relatively late in their "careers." By 1961, however, this proportion had more than doubled to 50.3%.[22] In the Politbureau the change was more drastic. Where in 1951 only two of eleven Politbureau members had some higher technical education, by 1971 ten of fifteen possessed diplomas in one or another kind of technology.[23] To make success in raising production quotas or prestige among members of the scientific community a basis for promotions into *political* leadership is a policy characteristic of revisionism and capitalist restoration.

Aurthur opposes placing "a large share of the responsibility for capitalist restoration on the intelligentsia or even the more advanced strata of the working class under socialism."[24] In socialist society, he claims, such people exist in harmony with the masses of workers and there is no antagonism between them.

Now surely these strata, especially the intelligentsia, do not deserve "a large share of the blame"; this must fall on the top revisionists in the Party leadership. But this must not justify the failure to recognize how these strata, especially the more privileged sectors of the intelligentsia, do provide a crucial social base for restoration. As previously discussed, such people exist in a different relation to production and a different position in society than do the workers and peasants. Differences between mental and manual labor and in distribution of wealth provide the basis for the perpetuation and development of potentially antagonistic class distinctions between them and the masses of working people.

To support his view Aurthur digs up an interesting quote from Stalin. Arguing against those who stressed the danger of the bourgeoisification of educated workers who increasingly occupied positions formerly held by bougeois intellectuals, Stalin declared:

> "These people, it appears, assert that workers and peasants who until recently were working in Stakhanovite fashion in the factories and collective farms, and who were then sent to the universities to be educated, therefore ceased to be real people and became second-rate people. So we are to conclude that education is a pernicious and dangerous thing. We want all our workers and peasants to be cultured and educated, and we shall achieve this in time. But in the opinion of these queer comrades, this purpose harbors a grave danger; for after the workers and peasants become cultured and educated they may face the danger of being classified as second-rate people."[25]

At the time it was certainly correct to recruit a new working class intelligentsia; this was a tremendous advance which strengthened the proletarian dictatorship. But still it must be said that, looking back on the whole Soviet experience and the history of socialism in general, it was an error, even a serious one, on Stalin's part to ignore the fact that the basis for antagonistic class distinctions exists in the difference between mental and manual labor and in the relative privilege in distribution and social position enjoyed by the intelligentsia regardless of the class origin of individual members of this group. Education is a powerful weapon of liberation for the proletariat, and if a correct line is in command the relations between workers and intellectuals in socialist society will overall be characterized by comradely cooperation. But if a proletarian line does not lead, education will be bourgeois education, distinctions between mental and manual labor will be expanded not narrowed and all this will serve only to perpetuate privileges and class division.

It is not that Communists wish to deny the masses an education. But education cannot stand above the ideological and political line. As Mao put it: "Some whose technical and cultural level is high are nonetheless neither diligent nor enthusiastic; others whose level is lower are quite diligent and enthusiastic. The reason lies in the lower political consciousness of the former, the higher political consciousness of the latter."[26]

Just as revisionism can arise regardless of the class origin of the revisionist (Khrushchev himself was, after all, a coal miner's son), it is also not a matter of intent. And this is Aurthur's final argument. He is forced to accept the obvious fact that there is, at the least, a privileged elite in the USSR. But, he argues, this is precisely why this group would never restore capitalism. His argument would be funny, if it wasn't so backward:

> "But why would a Brezhnev or even a Khrushchov want to restore capitalism? They have arisen under socialism, and the privileges they have gained were gained under, and in a certain sense because of socialism. The elite *like* socialism because it means that they can have their privileges *and* a working class whose standard of living is constantly rising, who are not likely to go on strike, riot, or overthrow the gov-

ernment — as long, that is, as the leadership guarantees their well-being. Brezhnev and Company have no desire to restore capitalism; instead they want, and have been able, to skim the cream off socialism, to have their cake and eat it too."[27]

Truly an amazing statement, is it not? Aurthur, who accuses us "restorationists" of idealism and contempt for the working class, puts more of both in this one statement than could ever be found in all the publications attacking Soviet social-imperialism put out by Marxist-Leninists worldwide. Imagine, the Soviet workers are content to live under the boot of these "cream-skimmers" so long as the benevolent despots guarantee their "well-being." And as for Khrushchev or Brezhnev what need have they for capitalism? As if it was ever a matter of personal desires in the first place! One might ask just who is the real idealist here.

Moreover, the vulgar economism behind this whole statement must be noted. According to Aurthur the working class will always be satisfied, will always accept whatever oppression the rulers dish out, so long as the economy is booming and wages are going up. Never mind the historic mission of the working class to liberate itself and all mankind from the exploitation and oppression of class society. Never mind the need to continue the revolution to the elimination of all class distinctions. Behind his openly contemptuous assault on the Soviet workers lies Aurthur's version of the revisionist "theory of the productive forces" which declares that the purpose of socialism is only to develop the productive forces and not to continuously revolutionize the relations of production and the superstructure and on this basis expand production and move forward to classless society, communism.

Aurthur does not recognize socialism as a society defined by the relationship between classes — and principally between the ruling proletariat and the bourgeoisie over which the proletariat exercises dictatorship. He refuses to accept the fact that this society will be moved one way or the other — forward to communism *or* backward to capitalism — and that the direction of this motion will be determined by the development of the class struggle between the proletariat and the bourgeoisie. Instead, in essence, he identifies socialism only with state ownership and views this not as a social relationship but as a thing — a static absolute without internal contradiction and motion.

PROFIT IN COMMAND OF THE ECONOMY

The intentions of any specific revisionist are not at all the decisive thing with regard to the restoration of capitalism. By championing a bourgeois line even the most dedicated of proletarian revolutionaries, who have devoted their lives to upholding the banner of communism, may degenerate into capitalist roaders and, indeed, if this happens the very prestige such people have accumulated makes them even more dangerous. Economic laws and the necessity posed by their operation *force* the revisionists to ultimately restore the capitalist system. This was stressed in *RP7*, which is worth quoting at some length on the subject:

> "It is impossible for some classless group of 'bureaucrats' to rule society in the name of the proletariat, because in order to maintain such rule these 'bureaucrats' must organize the production and distribution of goods and services. If bureaucratic methods of doing this prevail and come to *politically characterize* the planning process under socialism; and if a group of bureaucrats, divorced from and not relying upon the masses, makes the decisions on how to carry out this process; then inevitably this will be done along capitalist lines.
>
> "In the final analysis, the revisionists can only fall back on the law of value as the 'lever' which organizes production. They must reduce the workers to propertyless proletarians, competing in the sale of their single commodity — their labor power — to live. They must appeal to the narrow self-interest of the worker in this competition, backing this up with the power of the state, as a force standing above and oppressing the workers, a weapon in the hands of the owners of the means of production. They must do this because they must find some way to organize production which they cannot do consciously in a planned

way by themselves. *They have no choice but to become a new bourgeoisie...*

"Once this road is taken, the planned relationship between various sectors of the economy, according to the socialist principle of subordinating profitability — at the enterprise level, and in society generally — to the objective of all-round and constantly rising development must also come under the regulation of the law of value. And this means that profit must be put in command."[28]

Which brings us to the second argument raised by the apologists: their contention that the Soviet economy has not been reorganized along capitalist lines and that the profit motive is not in command.

In his review, Al Szymanski is careful to differentiate *RP7* from the work of Martin Nicolaus, stating that "The Nicolaus work thus focuses almost exclusively on economic relations (narrowly defined). *Red Papers 7*, on the other hand, rejects this way of posing the problem..." Szymanski applauds *RP7* for centering "instead on the question of 'who owns the state,'" and for maintaining that "the *plan* rather than markets is the decisive economic question." But he goes on to claim that "while the main thrust of the RCP work is to show that the working class does not control the state, virtually all the points made by Nicolaus about the operation of capitalist economic principles are also made (in a sort of overkill argument) — only later to be called irrelevant..."[29]

This is not the case at all. The argument presented in much detail, with extensive citation and analysis of works by Soviet economists, in Chapter III of *RP7* does not by any means mirror Nicolaus' shoddy presentation; in fact much of it was consciously aimed at refuting precisely the kind of thinking Nicolaus later raised to an opportunist principle (see especially the section "Will the Real Bourgeoisie Please Stand Up?" on pages 49-52). Our differences with Martin Nicolaus have been outlined in full in an article in *The Communist*, Vol. 1, No. 1 and the reader is encouraged to refer to this for clarification. But while it is unnecessary to repeat the whole argument here, a brief summary of just what it is that does make the Soviet economy function according to the laws of the capitalist system will be useful.

The response to Nicolaus defended *RP7*'s definition of socialism. This definition reads:

> "We can say that *socialism exists where the working class actually holds state power, where the sphere of operation of the law of value is being reduced to the maximum degree permitted by economic and political realities, where the initiative of the working class in developing new relations of production including a new division of labor is actively fostered by Party and state, and where the revolutionary transformation of all aspects of society is vigorously carried out under the leadership of the working class and its Communist Party.*" (emphasis in original)[30]

This definition correctly puts stress on the political leadership of the proletariat and not on any particular stage in the development of socialist production relations, including state ownership of the means of production, nor on planning.

While it was entirely correct to defend this definition against Nicolaus' criticism and his crude attempt to equate socialism with "planning" and capitalism with the "free market," it must still be recognized that the definition is actually more a description of what has come to be known as "the socialist road." The question of whether to remain on the socialist road or not is, of course, the decisive one. If leadership is seized by capitalist roaders representing a new bourgeois class who mobilize the Party to implement a revisionist line, then a socialist country will abandon the socialist road for the capitalist one and capitalist restoration is inevitable. In a certain sense it can be said that such emphasis follows the lead of Lenin who declared that use of "the term Socialist Soviet Republic implies the determination of Soviet power to achieve the transition to socialism, and not that the new economic system is recognized as a socialist order."[31]

However, though keeping to the socialist road is central and decisive, there are also actual socialist relations of production which define socialism as a particular transitional system standing between capitalism, the highest stage of commodity production, and communism, classless society based on the advance beyond commodity categories. Capitalist production relations are characterized by exploitation and inequality. Communist production relations have abolished both exploitation and inequality. Socialist relations are no longer exploitative but they still contain elements of inequality; hence, their contradictory quality. Under socialism both the proletariat and the bourgeoisie attempt to transform these relations in directions opposite to each other. The proletariat tries to restrict and eventually eliminate the vestiges and remnants of inequality that persist under socialism in order to advance the struggle toward communism. The bourgeoisie, however, will continually try to seize upon the bourgeois aspects of these relations in order to restore capitalism.

This latter is what has been going on in a thorough way in the Soviet Union since 1956, under the conditions where the bourgeosie has seized power in society from the proletariat. And though, in essence, and for all practical purposes, the process of restoring a capitalist economic base was completed with the economic reforms of 1965, it is in many respects continuing against important residues of the formerly socialist base and superstructure.

In short, to build socialism and communism the proletariat must seize state power in order to carry the *revolution* into the economic base while, at the same time, continuing to deepen the revolution in the superstructure. To restore capitalism, the revisionist new bourgeoisie must also seize state power and then carry the *counter-revolution* into the economic base. On the basis of this counter-revolutionary transformation the superstructure will also be further bourgeoisified.

While the key overall counter-revolutionary step took place 10 years earlier with the revisionist seizure of power in the superstructure, the key "moment" in the thoroughgoing counter-revolutionary transformation of the economic base as it unfolded in the specific conditions of the Soviet Union was the restoration of the profit motive as the main motivational force in the economy. According to Szymanski the crux of the 1965 reforms was not this but instead "simply a reduction in the number of criteria used by the central ministries to evaluate enterprise performance..."[32] But a writer on whom Szymanski relies at a number of points for support, the prominent academic defender of the "New System" in the Soviet Union and Eastern Europe,

Jozef Wilczynski, makes clear in his work *The Economics of Socialism* that this is hardly the case. According to him, "profit was officially accepted in the USSR in 1965 as the main criterion of enterprise performance... before the reforms it was treated merely as an accounting device to ensure that enterprises endeavored to cover their costs out of their own resources where possible, and to hand over the surplus to the State."[33]

Moreover, Wilczynski reveals that it is not just the amount of profit that is taken into account but the *rate of profit* as well (called "rentability" according to Soviet economic newspeak and reflecting the fact that most profit must be turned over to the central state monopoly capitalists as if it were "rent"). Wilczynski presents the following formula for computation of the profit rate:[34]

$$R = \frac{Q(P - C)}{F + V} 100$$

where R = rentability, or rate of profit
 Q = quantity of output actually sold by the enterprise
 P = price at which the output delivered is sold
 C = average prime cost
 F = average annual value of fixed assets
 V = average annual value of variable (circulating) assets

This is really not much different from how capitalists compute the rate of profit, as a rate of return on investment. And, indeed, his description of the significance of the profit criterion under "socialism" is also similar to descriptions of the role of profit under capitalism offered by bourgeois economic theorists:

> "The significance and success of the profit criterion consist mainly in the fact that a direct link has been established between profit and incentive payments, so that it is in the interest of the enterprise personnel — and at the same time society — to strive to maximize enterprise profits. But profit can achieve more than

merely a better utilization of resources at the operational level. Trends in the levels of profitability of different branches of the economy provide guidance to central planners in their endeavor to optimize the allocation of resources on the macrosocial scale. Thus profit provides that unique bond of union between micro and macroeconomic interest — the missing link from which Socialist economies had traditionally suffered."[35]

Adam Smith, of course, referred to this "missing link" as the "invisible hand."

Wilczynski does try to differentiate what he calls "socialist profit" from profit under capitalism, enumerating seven "significant" differences between the two. But are these really so "significant"? Let's see.

Wilczynski says that under socialism:[36]

(1) "Profit is not an objective but a means." But this is true under capitalism too — it is a means of capital accumulation. And anyway, how is one to differentiate the means from the end here? After all, don't the capitalists always claim that profit is merely the most efficient measure of productivity and the effectiveness of investment?

(2) "Profits cannot be increased by restricting production." Under certain monopoly conditions the capitalists can sometimes make short-term windfalls by restricting production, artificially driving up prices, and then selling dear what has been produced cheap. But this is by no means the essence or normal functioning of capitalist production. Indeed, Marx argued that to point to such instances as the source of capitalist profit places exploitation in the sphere of distribution and not production. Marxists argue — against all sorts of bourgeois economic theories — that capitalist profit arises from production, as surplus value. Thus, for the capitalist a greater mass of profit can only come from either greater production or a higher rate of exploitation, and usually some combination of both. Restricting production to raise profits is an exceptional practice under capitalism stemming from the development of certain monopoly situations. It hardly pertains to the essence of capitalist profit, including in the imperialist stage. And besides, such incidences of restricting production to increase

profit do occur, as the exception, in the Soviet Union too. The Soviet press has at times run reports of managers who find it more "profitable" not to overfulfill the plan.[37]

(3) "Profits are not owned by private persons." So what? Just look at the nationalized steel industry in western Europe — is it not capitalist? Moreover, the truth of this contention is itself highly questionable since the Soviet rulers lead quite a privileged life (as we shall see) and it is exclusively they who have control over how profit is to be reinvested (under the present system it is to make more profit), which is what happens to the lion's share of profit under capitalism in all its forms.

(4) "Profit is only one of several driving forces behind Socialist production. Planning must still be regarded as the main driving force." But the question is what guides planning, profit or the revolutionary interests of the proletariat?

(5) "Profit is not necessarily an objective measure of efficiency." On this we agree. It is one of the criticisms which has been offered of the profit system for generations — even before Marx. What's the point?

(6) "Differences in the profit rate do not necessarily determine the distribution of investment." In some cases this is true in the USSR. After all in the U.S. too the capitalists are forced to invest in some very unprofitable things to keep their system running. Witness Amtrak, the postal service, some corporate research and development projects, etc. But in the Soviet Union profitability is still the principal and dominant determinant. Wilczynski argues this himself — remember the "missing link"?

And (7) "Flows of capital to foreign countries are not determined by profit." This may be true in many cases in the short-run, as it is for much U.S. and West European investment, but don't count on it holding up after time. More on this subject later.

Finally, in defense of "socialist profit" Wilczynski quotes the famed revisionist economist who more than anyone else came to symbolize the principle of "profit in command" under socialism, Yvesei Liberman. And not surprisingly (if still ironically), Liberman's words have a familiar sound to them, reminiscent of our "Stalinist" friend, Mr. Aurthur: "Rivers do not flow backward," Liberman assures us. "And if, at high water, rivers make turns, they are simply cutting better and shorter channels for themselves. They are not looking for a way to go back."[38] While this may be true of rivers, it can hardly be said to also be true of revisionists.

The difference between *RP7* and Martin Nicolaus was that *RP7* saw adoption of the profit motive as the key element in the "reforms," but also as something distinct from the much-trumpeted abandonment of "planning" in favor of the "market." The aspect of the reforms' restoring autonomy to individual enterprises did not, *RP7* argued, return the Soviet economy to the stage of competitive capitalism. Thus, its much ballyhooed "failure" is on this score beside the point.

RP7 argued that after the reform the plan came to be guided, not by politics, by the ever-increasing mastery of the proletariat led by its Party and achieved through continuing class struggle, over the spontaneous pull of the economic laws of commodity production which continue to function but are restricted under socialism. Instead it was guided by subordination of the plan to the demands of these laws themselves, especially the law of value, the fundamental law of commodity production, and by abandonment of their restriction and an exaltation of their role. In other words, "plan" and "market" were, in a sense, merged, with the "market" thus regaining dominance over the plan but *inside* the planning process itself and not independent of it. This was reflective of the highly developed monopoly nature of the Soviet economy.

Indeed, this was evident in the price reform which necessarily followed introduction of the profit motive. Under the profit system prices have to more closely reflect their determination by the law of value so that profitability in different industries and enterprises can be measured on a common basis. Thus before the Soviet wholesale price reform of 1967 the profitability of different industries ranged from -17% in coal mining to +30% in light industry with an average of +13%.[39] But after the price reform the range was narrowed to a low of +8% for coal mining to +16% in the iron and steel industry.[40] This is a reflection of the influence of commodity market *categories* on *planned production* under state monopoly capitalism.

Here it will be useful to digress somewhat and discuss various Soviet economic theories since it is often thought, and has recently been put forward, that criticism of Liberman's "market socialism" is by itself an adequate critique of revisionist economics. This view is closely akin to Nicolaus' theories. But it would be a serious error to limit revisionist economics to the theory of "market socialism."

"Market socialism" advocates free trade and competition among state-owned enterprises under the plan. It has been put into practice (but only partially, since the development of monopoly, including state monopoly, is inevitable under capitalism) only in Yugoslavia but has been advocated ever since the '30s when its theory was devised by the Polish socialist economist Oskar Lange. Today "market socialism" is associated in one form or another with such prominent revisionist economists as W. Brus in Poland, Ota Sik in Czechoslovakia before the invasion, Branko Horvat in Yugoslavia and, to some extent, A. Birman and Liberman in the USSR.[41]

But the other main trend of thought in revisionist economic "science," the theory of "optimal planning," which denies the free operation of market factors, also rests on the assumption that market exchange of equivalent values is the most "rational" means of allocating resources and goods. The "optimal planners" seek to plan out the workings of market forces in advance through employment of mathematical planometrics, input-output techniques and the use of computers. The ideas of this school of thought have much in common with the thinking of the U.S. bourgeois advocate of capitalist planning Wasily Leontief. Its primary Soviet advocates have been the Nobel prize winner L.V. Kantorovich, V.S. Nemchinov, V.V. Novozhilov and N. Fedorenko.[42] This is pretty much the group identified in *RP7* as the "prices of production" school, although *RP7* fails to give Kantorovich and his planometrics the deserving revisionist credit he received in Stockholm. They have enjoyed increasing influence in Soviet planning in recent years.

Both these theories are based on the erroneous premise that, protected from the obstruction of monopoly, the capitalist economy can operate smoothly according to the law of value. It is not this law, these theories fundamentally argue, which leads to the irrationality, crisis and exploitation of the capitalist system but the obstruction of its smooth operation by personal greed and other "excesses" stemming from individual appropriation and leading to monopoly. The function of socialism becomes to make Adam Smith's "invisible hand" really work. This is not an application of the revolutionary theories of Karl Marx but is based upon assumptions taken from David Ricardo, the 19th century bourgeois economist criticized by Marx.

Nearly all significant Soviet economists reflect, in one way or another, the ideas of one of these two revisionist schools — "market socialism" and "optimal planning" — much as in the U.S. economists divide into monetarists, those who believe that control of the money supply is the best way to regulate the economy, and Keynesians, those who believe government spending and budgetary policy may be employed to "fine-tune" the economy. But, as in the U.S., the system does not and cannot fully match up with any of these theoretical models. This is because the assumption is incorrect that capitalist crisis, etc. is not intimately tied into the very nature of the laws of the commodity system, but is a product of "interference" with such laws. As Marx and Lenin both stressed, speaking of pre-socialist society, monopoly and competition are two sides of the same coin and must coexist under commodity production. This is a unity of opposites expressed in the contradiction plan-market. Thus it is no wonder that nearly all revisionist economists, no matter what school they espouse, accept the thesis that "There is no real justification for treating plan and market under Socialism as mutually exclusive."[43] In a sense they are correct; both aspects of this contradiction must exist so long as the commodity system operates whether it takes on a "free market" form or not. As in any contradiction the two aspects interpenetrate, there is a "market" in any plan and "planning" in the market. But the revisionists raise the interpenetration of the two aspects of this contradiction exactly to disguise its contradictoriness, just as Nicolaus undialectically ignores the interpenetration. As Mao put it in his criticism of a Soviet economics text:

> " 'Spontaneity and *laissez faire* are incompatible with public ownership of the means of production.' It should not be thought, however, that spontaneity and *laissez faire* do not exist in a socialist society."[44]

For Marxist-Leninists this contradiction must be dialectically *resolved* through continued revolutionary struggle to restrict the sphere of operation of the law of value and finally eliminate it.

Revisionism, on the other hand, "accepts" this contradiction.

This is why Nicolaus is wrong to reduce the whole question to one of plan = socialism, market = capitalism, but also why Szymanski is wrong to caricature *RP7* as declaring the whole question of captialist economic laws irrelevant, *reducing* the matter to a simple question of "who owns the state" instead of *basing* the analysis on this key question and proceeding from there.

According to Szymanski, the 1965 reforms were "rescinded" anyway in 1971 and 1973, and he credits this unique discovery to the authors of *RP7*.[45] But nowhere does *RP7* make any such claim, mainly because such a startling series of events never took place outside Szymanski's imagination. What did occur in 1973 was the institution of the Production Association or "trust" as a new form of organization in the economy. The Production Association combines, in various forms, numerous enterprises in much the same way as a conglomerate does in the U.S.

The decree establishing the Production Associations was issued while *RP7* was in preparation and its final impact was not clear when the book was published. But it is now apparent that these Associations have become an important phenomenon in the Soviet economy; indeed, they increasingly represent the basic unit of state monopoly capitalism. By the beginning of 1976 there were some 2,300 Production Associations operating in the Soviet Union accounting for some 24% of industrial production.[46] While the individual enterprise has lost most of the semblance of autonomy it gained under the 1965 reform, these larger "trusts" are another matter. The Production Associations are formidable concentrations of capital and represent the development of specific competing capitals within the state capitalist system.

Szymanski is apparently not aware of the work of the French expert on the Soviet economy, Marie Lavigne, who has compared the Soviet "trusts" to Western monopolies and in a very interesting study has shown how their role in the economy is increasingly to modify the workings of market laws (within and without the plan) in a way similar to monopoly corporations in traditional capitalist economies.[47] Indeed, at least one prominent Soviet economist has applauded the advent of the Association for, among other things, its ability to engage in self-financing (and thus self-expansion of value, i.e., the ability to behave as an independent capital within the overall plan). The logic of this development leads to two possible results. One is the transformation of the state economic ministries into large-scale enterprises themselves similar to the Associations; the other is the elimination of these ministries, which under socialism in the USSR were the heart of proletarian plannned economy, and their replacement by the Production Associations.[48] Another Soviet economist has picked up on this and suggests that the economies of the Soviet bloc must limit the responsibility of the state ministries and reduce their number.[49]

In other words, what has happened as a result of the development of the Production Associations on the basis of the restoration of profit is not just an end to the "free market" pipe dreams of the enterprise managers. No, what has happened is that, on the one hand, there is increasing concentration and centralization of state monopoly capital coupled, on the other hand, with the continuing centrifugal pull of capitalist anarchy and competition. In other words, what was predicted in *RP7* is coming to pass:

> "Even where a capitalist 'plan' for development exists, including a state 'plan' designed to ensure the profitability of key monopolized industries, the laws of commodity production/exchange, including especially the law of value — the blind force of the market — will still remain dominant. This means that competition between various capitalists, controlling different sectors of the economy and different 'pieces' of the surplus will inevitably develop too...
>
> "The creation of the large-scale Production Associations reveals that this is developing rapidly in the Soviet Union. These Production Associations will inevitably compete with each other in pursuit of profit. An association centered around the production of steel, for examle, will attempt to branch into coal mining. Soon the Production Associations will not only be set up according to industry but will — and to some degree, no doubt, they already do — come to represent competing groups of capitalists whose interests are quite varied; equivalent, say, to the Morgan or Rockefeller groups in the U.S. These competing groups

will in turn fight it out for political influence and control in the Communist Party.
"It will be impossible for these competing capitalists to peacefully divide the wealth. They will try, but their eternal quest for ever-greater profit will always create new contradictions for them. It will always smash to smithereens whatever agreements they succeed in reaching among themselves. This is directly due to the fundamental contradiction of capitalism and imperialism everywhere — the contradiction between private appropriation and social production of wealth."[50]

Like Szymanski, Aurthur also minimizes the importance of the reforms in a mirror-image of the Nicolaus idiocy. To him Khrushchev's early decentralizing efforts were simply a series of measures designed politically to "weaken the Molotov grouping,"[51] which, not coincidentally, was based in the central state ministries. The 1965 measures continued in this vein. Their purpose, he says, was to "raise productivity by giving local enterprise leadership more leeway in their use of resources, more incentive to conserve capital, rationalize their operations, etc." But, Aurthur contends, the reform failed because it came into conflict with the fundamental laws of socialism. "Objective laws of political economy," he argues, "cannot be changed, radically changed, abolished or negated by decrees, resolutions, maneuvers, schemes, 'economic levers,' bargaining, or the changing of a political 'line' in a factory, farm or mine."[52]

But, as seen earlier, it is precisely by seizing the superstructure in order to transform the base that the capitalist-roaders carry out the counter-revolutionary restoration process. To deny the possibility of decrees, etc. changing the economic laws — or really, changing their sphere of operation and in what way they operate (or do not operate) — is not only reflective of an undialectical view of the relationship between base and superstructure but it also denies that the proletariat can transform the capitalist base into a communist one by wielding its state power.

On the other hand, in the Soviet Union today the new capitalist economic relations come into contradiction with remnants of the former socialist superstructure. This is revealed most graphically in the discussion of the "rules of the game" initiated in the journal *Ekonomika i organizatsiia promyshlennogo proizvodstva* (Economics and the Organization of Industrial Production) in 1975. In the course of this debate a number of prominent Soviet managerial personnel and economic experts raised complaints about petty regulations and interference in management by state administrators and others. While this complaining mainly reflected the struggle of lower-level management against their state-monopoly superiors, the discussion also exposed how remnants of real socialist planning were very much seen as an obstacle to the more "efficient" (in the capitalist sense, i.e. "profitable") functioning of the present economy. As one participant in the discussion put it:

> "Economic legislation as it exists in our country today is not fully in keeping with the goals of economic development. It is a vast systemless mass of legal norms issued at various times and under various conditions of our economic development. I agree with G.A. Kulagin that it is necessary not only to do away with certain outdated norms but also to implement a system of measures that will make economic legislation an effective tool of socialist economic development."[53]

Here we find "reform-minded" managers and experts, carrying out their revisionist economic tasks with the obvious support of prominent authorities, coming into direct conflict *not* with the socialist base, but with outdated and ineffective *laws*. And, Aurthur and his crew of reformist-dogmatists notwithstanding, Marxists have always seen laws as part of the superstructure.

While Aurthur recognizes the growing stagnation in the Soviet economy and the real problems which that economy faces but blames this on the Khrushchev-Brezhnev "policies" being out of step with the needs of the socialist base, Szymanski informs us that ever since the reform all has been well with the Soviet economy. He claims (with no statistical confirmation) that in the period 1965-73 the Soviet economy functioned more smoothly than before and that there has been no evidence of the kind of crisis characteristic of capitalism. Space is lacking here to go deeply into the nature of the developing crisis of the social-imperialist economy, or to discuss some of the empirically discernible effects of capitalist restoration. But it would be sensible to give a warning: Don't speak too soon. Clearly the growth rate of the Soviet economy has been declining. Agriculture, a problem which the new Czars inherited from the socialist period, has only worsened. The problem of productivity is an extremely serious one. Indeed, another French economist has recently tried to show, in a very perceptive and pathbreaking (though not revolutionary) analysis, that the problems of the Soviet economy bear a striking resemblance to problems caused under capitalism by the tendency of the rate of profit to fall. Indeed, this observer identifies such a tendency developing in the Soviet Union since the 1950s as a chronic problem and points to this as the cause of a distinct and serious crisis, although his analysis is not thoroughly predicated on a Marxist analysis of capitalist crisis.[54]

Before concluding this section some comment is called for on one last important point raised by Aurthur (and less completely by Szymanski) — the question of whether labor power is a commodity in the Soviet Union. Now this is a good question, since capitalism is that stage of commodity production where labor power itself becomes a commodity. Aurthur adds that "the question of whether or nor the worker sells his labor power as a commodity in the Soviet Union can be stated in another way. Does he get paid according to the market price of labor power..."[55] This is also a pretty good way to put it except that the "market price of labor power" need not be determined on the open market. Labor power will be a commodity so long as it is "alienated" by the working class to the capitalist class in exchange for its equivalent value, i.e., the cost of the existence and reproduction of the worker.

Now if goods and services can be priced basically according to the dictates of the law of value without a free market as we have shown is the case in the Soviet Union (and is also sometimes the case in the older capitalist economies at least in some aspects — for example, airline fares in the U.S.) then so can labor power. As a writer put it in the pages of *Pravda* describing the implication of reforms in the wage system, "With the introduction of new wage rates, the pay categories of most workers are determined according to uniform wage-rates and skills manual; this ensures a uniform approach in evaluating the complexity of the labor of workers in all occupations represented in various enterprises and branches."[56]

A completely free and competitive labor market is not a precondition for the development of wage labor; the fundamental basis of wage labor is that the *working class* depends upon its ability to sell its labor power to an alien *capitalist class*. For example, under the Nazis German capitalism implemented draconian labor laws which virtually chained workers to their employers like slaves. In this manner the price of labor power (wages) was held down at or even below its value despite the virtual elimination (temporarily and on a war basis) of unemployment. And Hitler's Germany was most assuredly a capitalist society.

Indeed, the comparison with Nazi Germany is, as *RP7* indicated, most appropriate. For in the Soviet Union labor power is exchanged approximately at its value mainly through a complex process of wage determination through planning and this is secured mainly through non-economic pressures. While in doing this the Soviet capitalists are able to rely to some degree on their carefully maintained socialist cover, which they are willing to make significant concessions to preserve, they too can resort to open terror. Terror, of course, was openly used by the Soviet working class and its Party when it held state power. This was, however, directed — overwhelmingly and despite certain errors — against the counter-revolutionary enemies of the working class and socialism. The Soviet social-imperialist rulers today use open terror to suppress the masses, but they also revive and proclaim the words "dictatorship of the proletariat" where it is useful to cover their sanguinary suppression of the working class and people of the Soviet Union — and other countries. This is a trick that many revisionists have found to their advantage since the fall of Khrushchev.

Actually there is more labor fluidity, more of a labor "market," in the "socialist" Soviet Union today than there was in capitalist Germany under Nazi rule. An appendix to *RP7* described the extent of this labor fluidity and the text noted the important role of the notorious "Shchekino experiment" as a model in intensifying the exploitation of the working class by driving down the value of labor power through a combination of lay-offs and speed-up.

Aurthur's "proof" that labor power is not a commodity is twofold. First, he poses the truly ridiculous argument that labor power cannot be a commodity because wages and living standards are rising. How many times do we have to hear this kind of thing from the bourgeoisie?! Is one to suppose that because many workers in the U.S. now own color television sets and because according to the government personal income has risen since WW2, the U.S. is not a capitalist country? That labor power here is not a commodity? How ridiculous! And in fact much of the Soviet wage increases have been designed specifically to bring wage levels into closer correspondence with the actual value of labor power as part of restructuring planning in such a way that profitability can effectively function as the key indicator of economic success. The *Pravda* writer cited above notes that

> "The process of increasing minimum wages and basic wage and salary rates for personnel in middle pay categories that is currently being carried out in the branches of material production provides not only for wage increases but also for the *establishment of greater correspondence between wages and the quantity and quality of labor expended.*" (emphasis added)[57]

In other words, a general hike in wages can also mask a step backward into greater reliance on value categories. Under socialism it is necessary to pay "each according to his work." But, as noted previously, this is, after all, a bourgeois principle — that is, a principle based on bourgeois right, which masks actual inequality in formal equality — and is still linked to commodity categories. It must be consciously restricted. Linked closely to this is the question of material incentives to motivate labor. The Soviet revisionists rely on material incentives to increase productivity. But this elevates a necessity, the fact that payment according to value produced can only be restricted, to a positive principle. Mao sharply criticized the whole view of reliance on material incentive, arguing that it

> "makes it seem as if the masses' creative activity has to be inspired by material interest... 'From each according to his ability, to each according to his labor.'

The first half of the slogan means that the very greatest effort must be expended in production. Why separate the two halves of the slogan and always speak onesidedly of material incentive? This kind of propaganda for material interest will make capitalism unbeatable!"[58]

Perhaps sensing the feebleness of his argument on rising wages Aurthur falls back on the line that "Without the reserve army of unemployed there cannot be competition for jobs and therefore no possibility of setting a price (wage) for a labor power that is not yet expended."[59] Here we might return again to the Nazi Germany comparison to note that unemployment there was virtually eliminated (this was also true of a number of capitalist countries, including the U.S. during WW2), yet capitalism certainly flourished. Japan after WW2 is another example. Between 1954 and 1967 the Japanese gross national product adjusted for inflation grew at an average rate of 10.1% and disposable income almost tripled. During this period of phenomenal capitalist development, the unemployment rate was by all accounts extremely low despite a continuing stream of new workers pouring into industry from the farms and fisheries.[60] No sooner was a reserve army created than it was gobbled up by the capitalist employers. Faced with what they perceived as a labor shortage which might limit the extent of rapid growth and embolden the working class to fight harder around economic demands, the Japanese capitalists followed a policy of "paternalism" aimed at virtually "guaranteeing" employment (in the short run) in exchange for gains in labor productivity and increased exploitation, a policy not dissimilar to that being followed by the Soviet capitalists today.

In other words, Aurthur is totally off base when he indicates that "unemployment is the fundamental condition of capitalist production."[61] Unemployment is an inevitable *product* of capitalist exploitation and *RP7* showed how the internal dynamic of Soviet capitalism must also lead to the development of this phenomenon on a mass scale (although it must be noted that the political constraints on the Soviet rulers to keep unemployment low and disguised are, due to the socialist past, much greater than those faced by the bourgeoisie in the U.S.).*

And it must also be stated that there is already some unemployment in the Soviet Union, although it is masked and its extent is presently limited. True, the Soviet press is filled with complaints of a labor shortage stemming in part from the demographic factors but even more from the failure of Soviet agriculture to free adequate labor resources for industrial development. Yet at the same time there is serious and chronic under-utilization of labor which, in effect, disguises unemployment. Is a woman simply sitting at the doorway to a public building as a "gatekeeper" really much different from a welfare mother getting "relief" in the mail? Can this be called "employment" in any meaningful sense? Yet the phenomenon is often noted by visitors to the USSR. Moreover, Aurthur and Szymanski both ignore the problem of "youth unemployment" which ranged as high as 22% in Moscow *oblast* at one point in the early Khrushchev years.[62]

The recent debate among Soviet sociologists on the role of women is also revealing on this question. For these Soviet experts are trying to figure out how to involve women in production at skill levels profitable for the economy while, at the same time, getting them back into the home to work on improving the sagging Soviet birth rate. An increasingly heard proposal is the institution of part-time work.[63] But, of course, Soviet literature has for sixty years correctly attacked the expansion of such employment in capitalist countries as often disguising unemployment and as a means to drive down the living standard of the working class. (It might also be added that in this case it takes on the additional aspect of strengthening the subjugation of women to male domination by removing them from production.) Quite a bind these revisionists are in!

THE SOVIET RULING CLASS

According to Al Szymanski, "While the RCP is correct in focusing on the question of which class has state power [rather than on the role of markets/plan], its authors are unable to

---

* Aurthur's arguments on the role of unemployment in the capitalist system are closely akin to the incorrect theories of Ray Boddy and Jim Crotty which were criticized in *The Communist*, Vol. 1, No. 2.

demonstrate that there has developed in the Soviet Union a new class of state bureaucratic capitalists who live off the profits of exploited wage labor and control the state."[64]

Having severed the question of a new ruling class from the question of this class' relation to the means of production by dismissing most of *RP7*'s arguments on this score as Nicolaus-type "overkill", Szymanski must refute the existence of a bourgeois ruling class on bourgeois sociological grounds. Completely ignoring the Marxist method of class analysis (which is probably better for him, since Szymanski is a pitifully poor Marxist), he instead uses bourgeois categories to "prove" the nonexistence of a new bourgeois class. He claims there is very little social inequality in the Soviet Union and those differences which do exist are "quantitatively and qualitatively less than in the West, *and for the most part are rapidly diminishing."* (emphasis in original) He cites figures to show that the spread in wages between lowest and highest paid has declined in the past decade and points out that anyway "the highest paid people in the Soviet Union are not industrial managers or state and party bureaucrats, but prominent artists, writers, university administrators and professors and scientists."[65] Moreover, Szymanski contends, in one of the more laughable notions of recent years, that "there is broad and authentic participation of the people in decision-making and control bodies in the Soviet Union."[66]

Now to focus only on these two questions, inequality and political participation, especially in the way Szymanski does, avoids the heart of the matter — relationship to production. The bourgeoisie is not defined by its income superiority over other classes; to be rich is not the same as being a capitalist. One has only to recall the reams of bourgeois literature of the 1950s in this country which over and over "proved" Marxism wrong by "empirically" illustrating how inequality is disappearing in the U.S., how the rise of the new "middle class" has created the best of all possible worlds, how the combination of free elections and democratic "pluralism" guarantees citizen control, to realize how trivial the Szymanski method of "class analysis" really is. Such bourgeois analyses were often filled with falsehoods, but often they weren't. The problem was always with their basic method and approach, which the "radical sociologist" Szymanski should know. Facts are just that — simply facts. And they will remain such unless they are synthesized, concentrated into a higher truth. To do this fully requires Marxist theory.

Leveling of income differentials and other indicators of social status can mean many things. In Britain they tax the rich so much as to force some into emigration. In Sweden the "welfare state" has narrowed income inequality quite a bit. Yet in these countries there are still capitalists who accumulate capital and still workers who sell their labor power and this whole process is still called exploitation. Reggie Jackson, Elvis Presley and Elizabeth Taylor — leaving aside what they invested as capital with their earnings — all accumulated more wealth than a good many capitalists. Does this prove that the U.S. is not a capitalist society? Of course not! Yet this is the kind of "fact" Szymanski wants us to accept as proof that socialism is alive and well in the USSR.

But even given these essential methodological objections, it is still possible to refute Szymanski on his own terms, since the evidence of diminishing inequality and growing popular control he cites doesn't really paint a true picture.

First, on inequality. Szymanski is certainly correct in noting that there is less inequality in the Soviet Union than in the West. It would be quite a surprise if this were not the case, since the Western capitalist countries have been dominated by the bourgeoisie for a long time while the Soviet Union was socialist until some twenty years ago. And although socialism does not yet eliminate inequality, and while there were serious errors made in the Soviet Union under Stalin which actually contributed to exaggerating such inequality, the expropriation of all the old exploiters and the fact that the new exploiters have only recently arisen from the ranks of the people themselves, are important factors shaping Soviet society today.

Moreover, that the Soviet capitalists do not yet appropriate large amounts of wealth for their own personal use only reveals what good capitalists they are. For the "ideal" capitalist, unlike the feudal lord, would keep nothing for himself (other than what he needs to live) and reinvest all; this is the logic of the system. The new and rising capitalists of the Soviet Union may, to some small degree here, resemble more the new and rising capitalists of 17th century Britain, puritanical in their zeal for business and contemptuous of vulgar consumption. Although as we shall see this is true only relative to their rivals in the West.

For the Soviet bourgeoisie does pretty well for itself. The figures Szymanski cites showing a narrowing of income differences are very general and tell us little about *which* differences have been narrowed. Indeed, the narrowing of differences which has definitely taken place in recent years has been mainly within the ranks of the people, between collective farmers and industrial workers, between skilled and unskilled, between higher and lower-paid industries. The migration of Soviet collective farmers to urban areas since WW2 has been the main equalizing factor. Another factor has been the development of the Soviet petty bourgeoisie which marks the Soviet Union as essentially the same as advanced monopoly capitalism everywhere.

Szymanski presents no evidence that inequality between the masses on one side and the elite ruling class of state capitalists on the other side has decreased. Nor can he, because most of the information available on social inequality in the USSR comes from the work of Soviet sociologists who are *forbidden* to examine the life of the rulers. Szymanski offers a small bibliography of bourgeois authorities to back his contentions. One of these, Murray Yanowitch, states that

> "The upper reaches of the social structure have been systematically excluded from even the best of the Soviet studies... empirical studies of what is acknowledged to be a hierarchical social structure are essentially confined to the primary units of economic organization... Personnel employed in the higher levels of government ministries, planning agencies, the scientific establishment — not to speak of the Party organization — are not included in the 'continuum' of socio-occupational strata whose incomes, life styles, and opportunities for inter-generational transmission of status are investigated..."[67]

And another expert notes that only "snippets of information on the salaries of some of the top-most earners have been collected by a few Western observers, but no one, as far as we are aware, has attempted to systematize them." Nonetheless, he concludes: "That the top salaries can be extremely high is beyond doubt."[68] In short, it is completely dishonest for Szymanski to present information and cite sources which show only a decrease in inequality among different sections of the popular masses as evidence of decreasing and limited inequality between the masses and the ruling class.

Further, even if we exclude the rulers themselves for a moment, it is clear that Szymanski downplays the inequality which does exist. Yanowitch has shown that Soviet statistics on income differentials often conceal more than they reveal since "they fail to distinguish the specific positions to be found at the poles of the occupational hierarchy and thus tend to understate the range of inequality in earnings."[69] For example, one study of an individual plant showed the average earnings of the highest-paid stratum to be only two to three times greater than those of the lowest. Yet it turns out that this highest stratum is itself quite differentiated, since it is defined simply as "managerial personnel" including everyone from foremen up to the plant director. And even plant directors are pretty small fish in the Soviet capitalist sea.

Szymanski plays a similiar sleight-of-hand game. He notes that the income spread between the highest paid sectors (education and culture) and the lowest (collective farmers) dropped from 3.2 times in 1963 to 2.2 times ten years later. But what does this show? The education sector includes everyone from school janitors to major educational adminstrators and the category collective farmers means, according to Soviet statistical methods, everyone from rank and file farm workers to highly trained agronomists and even farm chairmen.

Szymanski cites a number of figures showing wage rates for managers and other lower-level bourgeois and acts as if these were the highest pay anyone could get. But even these figures are low, for in the Soviet Union everyone from the managerial level on up is generally paid not at the assigned rate for the position but at "personal rates" (*personal'nye oklady*). These are not established for the office but for the individual who holds it, supposedly in recognition of "outstanding knowledge and experience." By definition, these rates are considerably higher than the officially authorized and recorded norms and Soviet sources make clear they are a "mass phenomenon."[70]

Also noted by Szymanski is "the fact that children of the intelligentsia (about 15% of the population) in the Soviet Union have 3-4 times better chance of graduating from college than the children of unskilled workers." "This is a serious inequity," he admits, but "the Soviet press has been criticizing it for years."[71] Well, the capitalists everywhere are always open to this kind of "criticism"; but what has happened is that the situation is getting worse. Over the past two decades the capacity of the university system to accommodate high school graduates has not kept up with the development of secondary education. Where, in the years 1950-53, 65% of high school graduates went on to higher education, by 1970-73 this had dropped to 19%.[72] This can only mean increased competition to enter college which will inevitably favor the children of the intelligentsia and those generally having more advantages, including the families of the top strata of the Soviet party and state.

The new Soviet ruling class cannot be defined simply by looking at money wages and other such indicators. Constrained to keep their socialist cover, the Soviet rulers hide their wealth and power from the light of day. But word of the privileges they enjoy sneaks out.[73] Szymanski may cite figures and wage rates but he fails to inform us of all the special things which accompany high position, particularly if one is on the Party *nomenklatura*.*

There is, for instance, the network of *Beryozka* shops and other special stores where only the elite rulers can shop, where prices are way below what the masses pay and where high-quality and imported goods rarely, if ever, seen in ordinary markets are available. There is the *kremlevskii payok*, the "Kremlin ration": each high-ranking member of the Communist Party, the cabinet and the Supreme Soviet receives enough high-quality food to feed their families luxuriously every month — free. An entire department of the Party Central Committee, the *upravlenie delami*, "Administration of Affairs," operates and equips an extensive empire of special apartment buildings, country dachas, guest houses, rest homes, car pools, domestic servants and special stores.

Szymanski doesn't tell us about *Zhukovka*, the luxurious series of small towns outside Moscow reserved exclusively for members of the political, industrial and academic elite. Here the leaders, and those scientists, artists, writers, etc. who have con-

---

* The *nomenklatura* is the official list of high Party office-holders at all levels. It is estimated to number up to two million names. All receive privileges appropriate to their station on the list.

tributed to the continuation of their rule, live in special dachas — rent free — and shop at special stores with special prices and goods. As one Soviet citizen complained, "A Central Committee member does not get much pay but he gets all kinds of things free. He can get his children in the best universities or institutes, or get them abroad. *They* [the leaders] are all sending their children abroad now, exporting them like dissidents."[74]

Of course, at this point Szymanski will complain that this kind of thing started under Stalin, that Brezhnev and Co. are just continuing what began under socialism. To a significant extent this is true. But two points must be made about it. First, this was a weakness of socialism under Stalin. The system of *nomenklatura* may or may not have had a certain necessity to it in the 1930s (most likely it was designed to keep graft under control; in a sense regulated rather than spontaneous), but very clearly it was a grievous error. Socialism must seek to narrow the inequalities between classes and strata on the basis of developing the productive forces and, most important, carrying out revolution in the economic base and the superstructure. And proletarian political leadership should not be rewarded materially. Stalin was correct in combatting "petty bourgeois equalitarianism," but clearly he went much too far in this and the Soviet people are paying a price for it today. This error contributed to the restoration of capitalism in the USSR.

But it is also essential to recognize that such inequalities have greatly expanded since the mid-'50s and that, more important, these privileges were not, under socialism, based on capitalist relations of production as outlined earlier. Unlike today, under Stalin the bureaucrats were closely watched. They would gladly have traded privilege for security and power; but this the proletariat would not and, to a great extent, did not give them. The difference between privilege then and privilege now was graphically delineated in a simple but revealing statement an old woman made to the wife of an American reporter one night outside one of the special stores serving the New Czars. "We hate those special privileges," she said. "During the war when they were really our leaders, it was all right. But not now."[75] Of course, it is not necessary to accept that these privileges were proper under Stalin as this woman seems to spontaneously conclude, to recognize the main point here: what was a mistaken policy and a weakness under socialism has become integral to the exploitation and oppression of the masses under social-imperialism today.

So much for diminishing inequality.

As for Szymanski's ridiculous argument that there is extensive participation of the masses in Soviet political life, one is tempted to advise him to enroll in a class on the fundamentals of Marxism. Here he might encounter works like Lenin's *Proletarian Revolution and the Renegade Kautsky* which make clear the Marxist stand on democracy. Here Lenin notes that "It is natural for a liberal to speak of 'democracy' in general; but a Marxist will never forget to ask: 'for what class?' "[76] Lenin urges us to penetrate beneath the kind of *formal* equality and participation exalted today, for instance, by the "pluralist" school of bourgeois political science. Indeed, he points out that "the *more highly* democracy is developed, the *more* the bourgeois parliaments are subjected by the stock exchange and the bankers."[77]

The point then, is not whether there are electoral forms or whether the social origin of the bureaucrats is working class or whether "mass organizations" are consulted by the leadership. All these things exist to one degree or another in the U.S. and where they do it is usually a sign that the bourgeoisie is more effectively employing a democratic cover in exercising its dictatorship. For Marxist-Leninists political participation is and must be linked to the question of proletarian dictatorship, and the substance of mass control must be expressed in the correct proletarian political line of the Communist Party. As Mao put it, referring specifically to the Soviet situation:

> "The paramount issue for socialist democracy is: Does labor have the right to subdue the various antagonistic forces and their influences? For example, who controls things like the newspapers, journals, broadcast stations, the cinema? Who criticizes? These are a part of the question of rights...Who is in control of the organs and enterprises bears tremendously on the issue of guaranteeing the people's rights. If Marxist-Leninists are in control, the rights of the vast majority will be guaranteed. If rightists or right opportunists are in control, these organs and enterprises may

change qualitatively, and the people's rights with respect to them cannot be guaranteed."[78]

Under Khrushchev there was a minor explosion in the number and influence of new organizations ostensibly designed to bring citizens into public activity. These have continued under Brezhnev and Kosygin, though the pace of their expansion has slowed. The main point of such institutions has been to bring *professional* opinion to bear on decision-making and has gone hand in hand with robbing the masses of their effective representation through the leadership of a revolutionary party.

For example, in 1969 a Kolkhoz Council was created to better involve collective farmers in policy formulation. But, as *RP7* noted, this "democratization" created little more than a chamber of commerce for the agrarian bourgeoisie. Of its 125 members only eight were rank and file *kolkhozniki*.[79] As the bourgeois expert T. H. Rigby has noted, "in more and more areas of Soviet life, effective decision making is coming to mean professional decision making, and this is clearly incompatible with the detailed supervision and control by party officials or by the 'party masses.' "[80] Contrast this situation with Mao's comment that "The non-professional leading the professional is a general rule."[81]

But Szymanski also cites figures indicating increased working class participation in public affairs, for instance, that in 1954-55 workers were only 11% of Soviet deputies, but in 1972-73 they were 40%. These figures must be taken with more than a grain of salt. First of all it is common knowledge that the Soviets themselves are not real decision-making bodies. For this, it is necessary to turn to the Party leadership units. And, according to one fairly sympathetic bourgeois account, the number of workers and peasants identified among full members of the Party Central Committees of all the constituent republics in the USSR increased only from 5.2% in 1961 to 7.6% in 1971.[82] It is also well-known that Soviet figures tend to inflate the number of active members of Party and especially Soviet organizations. And the category "worker" is usually defined by Soviet statisticians to include large numbers of white-collar technicians and Party bureaucrats of working class origin who may not have actually worked in a factory for decades. But more important than the class origin — or even the current class position — of a particular leading person is his line. Trade unions — and even certain so-called "communist" organizations — in this country provide rich examples of individuals who were (or in some cases still are) workers and occupy some leadership position yet represent and uphold the outlook and interests of the capitalist class against the masses of workers.

Involvement of the masses in participatory organizations may actually increase the influence and power of an individual bureaucrat or manager. This has been recognized even by U.S. political scientists. For instance, the description of the PTA offered by Robert Dahl, a notorious apologist for U.S. capitalism, could well be transposed to describe the role of numerous "mass organizations" in the USSR:

> "Ostensibly...a Parent-Teachers' Association is a democratic organization of parents and teachers associated with a particular school, brought into being and sustained by their joint interests. In practice, a PTA is usually an instrument of the school administrator. Indeed, an amibitious principal will ordinarily regard an active PTA as an indispensable means to his success. If no PTA exists, he will create one; if one exists, he will try to maintain it at a high level of activity."[83]

That this is also the purpose of most Soviet institutions of "popular participation" is clear if one looks at how the principle of one-man management has developed in recent years. This principle is applied to all economic units from the lowest to the highest levels and was instituted under Stalin (at that time, however, the power of one-man authority was checked somewhat by the commissar system and, more important, by the political police, though there were clearly problems with this latter method in particular). Soviet management literature defines one-man management as:

> "the leadership of each production unit (enterprise, shop, section) is assigned to a single executive who is endowed by the state with the necessary rights to manage, and who bears full responsibility for the

work of the given unit. All individuals working in the unit are obligated to fulfill the instructions of the executive.

"To correctly implement the principle of one-man management it is of great importance that there be a clear demarcation of obligations, rights, and responsibilities..."[84]

One-man management was instituted in Lenin's time as a means of stabilizing the economy in response to serious syndicalist and ultra-democratic deviations. But this principle has proven incorrect as a method of management in socialist society because it stifles the ability of the working class to control the means of production in reality and holds back the development of new communist production relations. Mao Tsetung criticized the principle of one-man management and its concomitant principle of personal responsibility (each to his post), and defended the system of revolutionary committees instituted in China under his leadership as collective organs of management. Of one-man management he said, "All enterprises in capitalist countries put this principle into effect. There should be a basic distinction between the principles governing management of socialist and capitalist enterprises."[85]

Recently Soviet leaders have called for more "collegiality" and the "humanization" of management. Kosygin himself noted that "Better management is impossible unless it becomes more democratic and unless the participation of the masses is considerably extended... Every worker should be made to feel that he is one of the owners of the factory."[86]

But experience has shown that use of the word "feel" here was not accidental. For it has been managerial *style* rather than the *substance* of decision-making that Soviet management experts have endeavored to change. According to one Soviet advocate of "collegial" management, the manager lets his subordinates "participate actively" in decision-making but "leaves to himself the right of final decision." "His art consists of the ability to use power without appealing to it."[87]

A significant example of how the Soviet rulers look at real mass participation was the attitude they took toward the Akchi experiment in agriculture. Akchi was a state farm in Kazakhstan which during the late '60s achieved astounding success in production by instituting a new system of work organization wherein "the functions of production and management were not divided" between different occupational strata. The farm's white-collar administrative apparatus was reduced to an absolute minimum and everyone participated in both productive labor and decision-making. In the words of the experiment's organizer, "it is important in our methodology that all people should manage in turn."[88]

In some ways, though not fundamentally, Akchi indicated what was demonstrated by the famous Tachai farm brigade in China under Mao's leadership — that high levels of mechanization, long hours of hard work, or the presence of technological experts were not the key factors in developing production. Rather, the conscious activism of the masses in waging the class struggle and revolutionizing the relations of production and the superstructure is the only basis for successfully pushing the economy forward. Despite the fact that Akchi promised the new Czars a possible improvement in their chronically bad agricultural situation, its political implications were far too ominous. The final verdict on Akchi concluded that

> "we must see two features of it: on the one hand an attempt to 'drag' into being a communal form of work collective — clearly in conflict with the collective and state farm forms — known in Russia since prerevolutionary times and representing a rudimentary form of organization of work collectives on democratic principles, and on the other hand a more or less successful form of organization of production utilizing value levers. The first clearly has no prospects for its development, but the second is being used and deserves wider application..."[89]

In other words, the only thing the Soviet rulers found productive in this was the fact that work teams were reimbursed according to the value of their product. What made Tachai a pacesetter in China was not simply its terraced fields and higher labor productivity, but the revolutionary organization of production based on raising the consciousness of the masses and advancing the class struggle to transform the production relations, which were responsible for achieving these things. Yet it was just this aspect of the Akchi experiment that the Soviet rulers scorned, much as revisionists like Liu Shao-chi in China sought to tear down the red banner of Tachai and, failing this, paint it white. For capitalist roaders everywhere models like Tachai, or even — under very different conditions, where capitalism has been restored but the appearance of socialism is retained — experiments like Akchi, are only models insofar as they prove effective gimmicks to get the masses working harder.

The question of political participation is thus a question of line. And it is clear that the line of the Soviet revisionists leaves the masses as essentially powerless as in any other capitalist country.

SOCIAL-IMPERIALISM: A SYSTEM, NOT A POLICY

Szymanski's article in the *Berkeley Journal of Sociology* seeks to show "empirically" that the Soviet Union is not an imperialist country, although its foreign policy "might well be hegemonic and oppressive."[90] But page upon page of facts and figures assembled by him are mostly irrelevant since the author's version of imperialism is an un-Marxist, eclectic jumble of bourgeois nonsense in the first place.

In what follows it will not be possible to fully refute all of Szymanski's empirical "data" fact for fact. Rather, what will be concentrated on is his anti-Marxist method with more specific refutation of only several illustrative points. For more detail on the actual workings of Soviet imperialism around the world, concrete examples and explanation of how the Soviet state-monopolists extract surplus value from the working people of other countries, and an analysis of how the Soviets use the *form of* trade to mask the content of capital export, the reader is advised to see *RP7*, Chapter IV.

Szymanski defines imperialism as "the political and economic domination of a nation or region in order to economically exploit it in the interests (normally of the ruling class) of the dominant nation."[91] This, despite Szymanski's claim to the contrary, has nothing to do with Lenin's definition of imperialism. (Incidentally or not so incidentally — imperialism, in the Leninist meaning, is *always* in the interests of the ruling class of the "dominant nation" as opposed to the fundamental interests of the masses of people of this nation as well as those nations oppressed by imperialism.) Most essentially, Lenin demonstrated that imperialism is a *stage* in the development of capitalism, its highest and final stage. For Lenin imperialism was no more an economic policy aimed at the subjugation of specific nations than it was a political or ideological policy. Imperialism in Lenin's view was intimately tied to the development of monopoly and the merger of bank and industrial capital in finance capital, which brought to the fore the parasitic nature of capitalism and demanded the outward expansion of national capital which comes in conflict with both the economic and national development of nations in less developed parts of the world and the ambitions of rival imperialists.

There isn't space here to go deeply into the correct understanding of the imperialist system and its laws, but it should be noted that Szymanski follows the lead of a number of fashionable petty-bourgeois "Marxists" (Paul Baran, Paul Sweezy, Samir Amin, Andre Gunder Frank, Harry Magdoff) who examine imperialism essentially from a Ricardian under-consumptionist view of capitalist crisis and on this basis focus on unequal trade relations and "dependency" as the essence of imperialist economics. Szymanski notes that

> "In capitalist economies profits are to be made by securing overseas markets for individual enterprises, while maintaining overall economic prosperity and the continuation of the capital accumulation process requires finding export markets for the system as a whole to counter the inherent tendency to underconsumption (promoted by workers not being paid enough to buy back everything that they produce)."[92]

This is a completely wrong approach. First, there is no "inherent tendency to underconsumption" in capitalism unless one is a follower of Paul Sweezy's neo-Keynesian brand of bogus

Marxism.* There is rather the tendency for the rate of profit to fall, leading to crises of *overproduction*, which, Marx stressed, means mainly overproduction of *capital* and only consequent to this the overproduction of goods which appears on the surface as an inability of the working class to buy back what it has produced. Further, under imperialism, because of the monopolization and high degree of concentration of capital, there is what Lenin called a "superabundance of capital" which can't be profitably invested in the home market and must be invested abroad. Under imperialism, Lenin showed, the key to relations with other countries is not the export of *commodities* but the export of *capital*. Though they do swindle others where possible, the imperialists do not exploit the people of other countries essentially through cheating in trade — selling commodities abroad that they can't sell at home and at an inflated price relative to what they purchase from those countries. Instead it is the investment (direct or indirect through loans, etc.) in the economies of those countries and the accumulation of surplus value produced by the working people there that constitutes the imperialist robbery. The backwardness of many such countries does in various ways enable the imperialists to secure a high rate of profit there, but here again, export of capital, not unequal trade, is the essence of the matter.

In another article published elsewhere Szymanski has the gall to attribute his erroneous views to Lenin whom he claims got them from the English liberal critic of imperialism, J.A. Hobson.† Szymanski advises his readers to look at Lenin's notebook on Hobson for confirmation of this. And turning here one does find Lenin has copied out Hobson's statement that *"if* the consuming public in this country raised its standard of consumption to keep

---

* For a critique of underconsumption theories of crisis see "Against Sweezy's Political Economy," *The Communist,* Vol. 2, No. 1. Ironically another very good refutation of underconsumption by John Weeks, "The Sphere of Production and the Analysis of Crisis in Capitalism," appeared in the same issue of *Science and Society* as Szymanski's review of *RP7*.

† Szymanski advanced his anti-Leninist "theory" of imperialism in an article called "Capital Accumulation on a World Scale and the Necessity of Imperialism," *The Insurgent Sociologist,* Spring 1977 prompting a debate with Magdoff in *Monthly Review,* March 1977 and May 1978. Both authors are, however, trapped in the underconsumption-dependency model, though Magdoff's relatively greater sophistication enables him to make mincemeat of Szymanski.

pace with every rise of productive powers, there could be no excess of goods or capital clamorous to use Imperialism in order to find markets." But Szymanski has apparently neglected to note that in the margin next to this statement, underlined twice, Lenin acidly remarked: "ha-ha!! the essence of philistine criticism of imperialism."[94] Further on in the notebook Lenin approvingly quotes Hobson's statement that the essence of imperialism *"consists in developing markets for investment, not for trade,* [again underlined twice in the margin by Lenin] and in using the superior economies of cheap foreign production to supercede the industries of their own nation, and to maintain the political and economic domination of a class." (emphasis in original)[95]

For Lenin imperialism does not simply hold others down nor is it the ripping off of wealth from poor countries by the rich through unequal trade, although it may include this. Imperialist investment abroad can, and in the long run must, develop the economies of the countries it dominates but it must do so on a capitalist basis — in particular on a basis favorable to the foreign capital — and in contradiction to both the welfare of the broad masses of workers and peasants and to the development of the independent home market in these places. As Lenin put it in an earlier work still applicable to the analysis of imperialism, "The development of capitalism in the young countries is greatly *accelerated* by the example and aid of the old countries." (emphasis in original)[96]

Szymanski's efforts to present empirical "proof" that imperialism is not profitable to the Soviet bourgeoisie are in line with a long tradition of bourgeois criticism. In every case, these bourgeois writers examine one or another colony or some instance of imperialist aggression and attempt to show that the imperialists lost money there. Leaving aside the veracity of these attempts, their method — and it is Szymanski's method as well — is to confound the profit motive with the actual realization of profit itself. It is as if the failure of Lockheed Aircraft to return a profit were offered as "proof" that Lockheed could not be a capitalist enterprise. Moreover, Szymanski ignores the fact that competition between imperialist countries, like competition between rival capitals domestically, involves preventing rivals from securing important markets, raw materials, etc., even where doing this means a short-term loss of profit. Economic interests in the final analysis determine political, military and ideological policies but these in turn react back upon the economic interests. This is the Marxist, the dialectical materialist, view which is opposed to the mechanical economic determinism which writers like Szymanski set up as straw men to knock down in their "refutation" of Marxism.

On this account it is enlightening to turn one last time to the work of Jonathan Aurthur, who agrees with Szymanski but documents his case on this point more weakly. Aurthur applauds Soviet attempts to push out the U.S. imperialists from where they are well entrenched: "Brezhnev's foreign policy," he assures us, "far from being a continuation of Khrushchev's capitulationism, is a reaffirmation of the correctness of Stalin and Molotov."[97] Brezhnev has certainly abandoned the largely limp-wristed stand of Khrushchev who, despite his famous shoe-banging, caved in to the pressure of U.S. imperialism left and right. But this is no return to Stalin's revolutionary foreign policy. It only signifies that the Soviet Union has become the "hungry" imperialist power, seeking to muscle in on the U.S. and gain a new redivision of the world. By and large the Soviet Union does not yet have an empire, it does not yet earn much from its still beginning exploitation of the world's people. But the point is that *it wants and needs such an empire* — and, it must be said, is rapidly acquiring one. And it is this drive, together with the equally essential drive of the U.S. to defend its own empire and, ultimately, to also expand, which is pushing the world toward a new world war.

With this understanding in mind the reader of Szymanski's article will quickly see that most of his arguments are at best irrelevant to the essence of the Soviet Union's international actions and relations. But some specific comments are still called for on a few of his contentions.

According to Szymanski profitability plays no role in Soviet foreign trade. Since Soviet trading corporations purchase goods for export from the producing enterprises and the state budget pockets all profit from overseas sales, Szymanski contends that the sphere of production is insulated from the world market, that "Soviet productive enterprises have absolutely no connection with foreign trade."[98] This was the case under socialism when a mainly proletarian line guided the activities of these trading units and their relations with production enterprises. Under Stalin, as

Szymanski admits, Soviet foreign trade was geared to strengthen the autarchic (or self-reliant) nature of the economy and it was only after Stalin's death that the USSR entered into world markets on a broad scale.

But, putting aside the fact that imperialism does not mainly operate through trade, this argument today is based on the assumption that the production enterprises are themselves independent of the state monopoly. In other words, it is based on the straw man of the "free market" model of Soviet capitalism. The point is that both producer and exporter are linked through state-capitalist ownership and control.

Moreover, Szymanski's point is just plain false. For if Soviet industry is sheltered from the effects of foreign trade how is one to explain the following complaint of a Soviet production executive:

> "Economically accountable foreign trade associations are in an even more privileged position. If such an association's agents abroad are not able to sell machinery the association has ordered and paid for, it has the right to return it to the manufacturer, even after several years, and demand its money back immediately. Industry bears all losses connected with reconditioning the machinery, storing it and searching for a new buyer."[99]

This executive did not, by the way, request an end to industrial responsibility for such foreign losses. He merely requested that industrial enterprises share also in the profits from foreign trade.

Szymanski also claims that were the Soviet Union really imperialist "we would expect that the favorable balance of trade (a surplus of exports over imports) would represent a significant proportion of capital formation."[100] Nonsense! If this were necessarily so how would one explain the unfavorable balance of trade (and even more unfavorable balance of payments) of U.S. imperialism during part of the post-WW2 period? And such a view would make the most imperialist segment of U.S. capital the wheat farmers because the U.S. exports a surplus of grain!

On Soviet aid to developing countries Szymanski comments:

> "The interest rate on U.S. loans is now the same as on Soviet loans; but the forms of repayment are very different. Repayment to the Soviets is in the form of locally produced goods, often the goods produced by the enterprises developed with foreign assistance."[101]

But isn't this just like investing in whatever product is being produced? How is it different from a banker who loans out capital and expects repayment in the product of the enterprise? South Korea has received a great deal of U.S. "aid" and now ships a lot of light industrial products to the U.S. from Korean-owned factories financed by U.S. capital. Does Szymanski mean to argue that this kind of aid has benefited the people of south Korea? In fact the kind of aid by the Soviets ties the recipient to the Soviet Union almost as if the "aided" enterprises were directly owned by the USSR. That direct ownership is often not employed simply reflects the struggle against imperialism world-wide which often forces the imperialists to abandon direct and open *forms* of control while retaining the *content* of imperialist domination.

Szymanski also points out that "Soviet aid is exclusively to the state sector with very few exceptions."[102] Although in some cases this simply represents the Soviets bringing the existing comprador bourgeoisie in a colonial (or neo-colonial) country into its orbit, it also brings up the question of the national bourgeoisie discussed in *RP7* which explains such aid on the basis of a *class analysis* of the oppressed nations (an analysis sorely lacking in Szymanski's presentation). The national bourgeoisie is that section of the capitalist class in the oppressed nations which opposes imperialism because it cannot compete with the foreign monopolies and is driven down in its attempts to expand and conquer the home market. The national bourgeoisie has, to varying degrees, played a positive role in the anti-imperialist struggle and where it has come to power it has often struck real blows against imperialism and won significant concessions which even may benefit the masses of workers and peasants. But, as *RP7* stressed,

> "...history has also shown that once in power, the national bourgeoisie may often fall under the sway of

one or another imperialist power and sections of it can be transformed into a comprador bourgeoisie dependent on imperialism. This can occur even where the national bourgeoisie has played an independent anti-imperialist role for some time. Only a revolution led by the working class and the establishment of a socialist society can finally and fully free Third World countries from the rule of foreign imperialism."[103]

Soviet aid to the "state sector" is thus only an indication of the Soviet strategy of trying to dominate these countries by winning the allegiance of the national bourgeoisie and thus, step by step, transforming it into a new comprador bourgeoisie. Again to quote *RP7*:

"The strategy of social-imperialism is to encourage such development of the public sector, while at the same time maneuvering the countries of the Third World into dependence on the USSR for loans, military shipments, etc.... The fact of the matter is that the 'state sector' is not necessarily 'anti-capitalist,' as any worker in the post office can readily testify."[104]

Believe it or not, Szymanski even applauds the Soviet Union's emergence as a major arms merchant, arguing that "Modern military establishments can now be created by the less developed countries without promoting dependency on the U.S., France or Britain."[105] What a contribution to world peace and the liberation of nations! Szymanski even has the nerve to mention Somalia and Ethiopia as positive examples. What possible benefit to the masses of oppressed people anywhere has come from Soviet fueling of *both* sides (at different times) in the recent war between these two countries? What can by any stretch of the imagination be called "progressive" about the use of Soviet arms by the phony-Marxist but authentically fascist Ethiopian junta against the just liberation struggle of the Eritrean people and against the Ethiopian masses themselves? And look at Afghanistan, another "positive" instance of Soviet military aid cited by Szymanski. The recent pro-Soviet military coup there (hardly a mass revolution) reveals just what kind of "independence" the Soviets aim for with their military aid.

Finally Szymanski discusses the relationship of the Eastern European states to the Soviet Union, contending that the USSR has "played a central role in accelerating the economic growth and all around development of the Eastern European economies."[106] Marxist-Leninists must still develop a more thorough understanding of the capitalist workings of the Eastern European economies and their relationship with the Soviet Union, a task called for in *RP7* which is, along with a full response to Szymanski on this subject, beyond the scope of this article. But it must be said that even the most superficial look shows that Szymanski's line is a fairy tale. Besides the abundance of facts and analysis, some of which is in *RP7*, which demonstrate Soviet robbery of its East European "allies," apparently Szymanski has even "forgotten" Czechoslovakia 1968 and Poland 1971 and 1975. Perhaps he studied under ex-President Ford whose campaign statement that "there is no Soviet domination of Eastern Europe" provoked laughter everywhere, especially in Eastern Europe itself.

In particular, Szymanski's attempt to compare Soviet relations with COMECON to Western relations with the third world is no more than a cheap debater's trick. Obviously these groups of countries are very different from each other. The Eastern European countries are not mainly semi-feudal oppressed nations. They are developed capitalist countries, at least some of which (certainly East Germany) have reached the imperialist stage themselves. If a comparison is to be made, it would be to U.S. domination over its bloc of imperialist allies in Western Europe and Japan, although quite obviously Soviet control over Eastern Europe is at present firmer than U.S. control in the West.

FOOTNOTES

1. Jonathan Aurthur, *Socialism in the Soviet Union*, Chicago, 1977, p. v.
2. *Ibid.*, p. 6.
3. See "History Develops in Spirals," *Peking Review*, No. 43, 1974.
4. V.I. Lenin, "The Junius Pamphlet," *Collected Works*, Vol. 22, p. 310.
5. An often used expression of Mao during the Chinese revolution. During the Cultural Revolution he wrote, "The conclusion is still the two familiar comments: The future is bright; the road is tortuous."
6. See numerous articles on the struggle between the Legalists and the Confucianists in *Peking Review*, 1974.
7. Karl Marx and Friedrich Engels, "Manifesto of the Communist Party," *Selected Works*, Vol. 1, p. 53.
8. Aurthur, *op. cit.*, p. 8.
9. Karl Marx, "Critique of the Gotha Programme," in Marx and Engels, *Selected Works*, Moscow, 1962, Vol. 2, p. 23.
10. V.I. Lenin, "Report to a Joint Session of the All-Russia CEC...", *Collected Works*, Vol. 27., p. 434.
11. Karl Marx, "The Class Struggles in France," in Marx and Engels, *Selected Works*, Vol. 1, p. 223.
12. Karl Marx and Friedrich Engels, "Manifesto of the Communist Party," *Selected Works*, Vol. 1, p. 53.
13. *Red Papers 7*, Chicago, 1974, p. 12.
14. V.I. Lenin, "Left-Wing Communism: An Infantile Disorder," *Collected Works*, Vol. 31. pp. 23-24.
15. Aurthur, *op. cit.*, p. 11.
16. *Ibid.*, p. 17.
17. V.I. Lenin, "Report to a Session of the All-Russia CEC...," *Collected Works*, Vol. 27, p. 300.
18. V.I. Lenin, "Once Again On The Trade Unions, The Current Situation And The Mistakes Of Trotsky And Bukharin," *Collected Works*, Vol. 32, p. 83.
19. Aurthur, *op. cit.*, p. 17.

20. Mao Tsetung, "Talk at the First Plenum of the Ninth Central Committee of the Chinese Communist Party," in Stuart Schram, ed., *Chairman Mao Talks to the People*, New York, 1974, p. 283.
21. *Ibid.*, p. 284.
22. David Lane, *The Socialist Industrial State*, Boulder, Colo., 1976, pp. 125-26.
23. T.H. Rigby, "The Soviet Politbureau: A Comparative Profile, 1951-1971," *Soviet Studies*, Vol. 24, No. 1, July 1972, p. 11.
24. Aurthur, *op. cit.*, p. 20.
25. J.V. Stalin, "Report to the 18th Congress of the CPSU," in J.V. Stalin, *Leninism: Selected Writings*, New York, 1942, p. 477.
26. Mao Tsetung, *A Critique of Soviet Economics*, New York, 1977, p. 83.
27. Aurthur, *op. cit.*, p. 36.
28. *Red Papers 7*, pp. 55-56
29. Al Szymanski, "Socialism or Capitalism in the USSR?," *Science and Society*, Vol. XLI, No. 3, Fall 1977, p. 339.
30. *Red Papers 7*, p. 9.
31. V.I. Lenin, " 'Left-Wing' Childishness And The Petty-Bourgeois Mentality," *Collected Works*, Vol. 27, p. 335.
32. Szymanski, "Socialism or Capitalism," *op. cit.*, p. 341.
33. J. Wilczynski, *The Economics of Socialism*, 3rd ed., London, 1977, p. 49.
34. *Ibid.*, p. 51.
35. *Ibid.*, p. 50.
36. *Ibid.*, pp. 56-57.
37. P. Volin, "When the Profitable is Unprofitable," *Literaturnaia Gazeta*, October 6, 1976, pp. 10-11.
38. Y. Liberman, "Are We Flirting With Capitalism?," *Soviet Life*, July 1965, p. 39. Quoted in Wilczynski, *op. cit.*, p. 58.
39. Y.M. Zinoviev, *Prybyl i povyshenie effektivnosti sotsialisticheskogo proizvodstva* (Profit and the Increase in Efficiency of Socialist Production), Moscow, 1968, p. 102.
40. *Ibid.*, p. 103.
41. Writings of "market socialism" theorists in English include: Wlodzimierz Brus, *The Market in a Socialist Economy*, London, 1972; Branko Horvat, M. Markovits, and R. Supek, eds., *Self-Governing Socialism: A Reader*, White Plains, New York,

1974; I. Konnik, "Plan and Market in the Socialist Economy," *Problems of Economics*, Dec. 1966, pp. 24-35; and Ota Sik, *Plan and Market Under Socialism*, White Plains, New York, 1967.
42. Writings of "optimal planning" and planometric theorists in English include: N.P. Fedorenko, *Optimal Functioning for a Socialist Economy*, Moscow, 1974; L.V. Kantorovich, *The Best Use of Economic Resources*, Cambridge, Mass., 1965; I. Kotov, "Some Problems in Applying Mathematical Methods to Economics, and the Political Economy of Socialism," *Problems of Economics*, August 1966, pp. 3-14; V.S. Nemchinov, *The Use of Mathematics in Economics*, Edinburgh, 1964; V.V. Novozhilov, *Problems of Measuring Outlays and Results Under Optimal Planning*, New York, 1969; Albina Tretyakova and I. Birman, "Input-Output Analysis in the USSR," *Soviet Studies*, April 1976, pp. 157-88.
43. V.A. Volkonskii, *Model optimalnogo planirovaniia i vzaimnosviazi ekonomicheskikh pokazatelei* (A Model of Optimal Planning and the Interdependence of Economic Indicators), Moscow, 1967, p. 68. The author is not a "market socialist" but a planometrician.
44. Mao Tsetung, *A Critique of Soviet Economics*, p. 75.
45. Szymanski, "Socialism or Capitalism," *op. cit.*, p. 340.
46. Marie Lavigne, "L'Oligopole dans la planification" (Oligopoly in Planning), *Economics et Societes*, T. XI, Nos. 6-9, June-Sept. 1977, p. 1033.
47. *Ibid.*, pp. 991-1042.
48. L. Abalkin, "Perfection of Financial Autonomy in Conditions of Developed Socialist Society," *Izvestiia Akademii Nauk (ekonomika)*, 2, 1976, pp. 26-36.
49. G.V. Aristov, *Predpriiatie v sisteme upravleniia promyshlennostiu evropeiskikh stran SEV* (The Enterprise in the System of Administration of Industry Among the European Countries of COMECON), Moscow, 1975, pp. 34, 45.
50. *Red Papers 7*, P. 56.
51. Aurthur, *op. cit.*, p. 40.
52. *Ibid.*, p. 53.
53. V.V. Laptev, "Make Economic Legislation a Tool of Economic Efficiency," *Ekonomika i organizatsiia promyshlennogo proizvodstva*, 6, Nov.-Dec. 1975. Excerpts from this

discussion in English translation may be found in American Association for the Advancement of Slavic Studies, *The USSR Today: Current Readings from the Soviet Press*, Columbus, Ohio, 1977, pp. 47-50.
54. V. Vassilev, "Caracteres et specificites des crises economiques de type sovietique" (Character and Specificity of Soviet-type Economic Crises), *Economies et Societes*, T. XI, Nos. 6-9, June-Sept. 1977, pp. 1377-1442.
55. Aurthur, *op. cit.*, p. 80.
56. L. Kistin, "Questions of Theory: The Measure of Labor and the Measure of Consumption," *Pravda*, June 28, 1975, p. 3.
57. *Ibid.*
58. Mao, *A Critique of Soviet Economics*, p. 79.
59. Aurthur, *op. cit.*, p. 76.
60. Hugh T. Patrick, "The Phoenix Risen from the Ashes: Postwar Japan," in James B. Crowley, ed., *Modern East Asia: Essays in Interpretation*, New York, 1970, pp. 311-31.
61. Aurthur, *op. cit.*, p. 80.
62. Mervyn Matthews, *Class and Society in Soviet Russia*, New York, 1972, pp. 311-19.
63. Two surveys of the debate are Murray Yanowitch, "A Note on Sexual Stratification," in his *Social and Economic Inequality in the Soviet Union*, White Plains, 1977, pp. 165-86 and Gail Warshofsky Lapidus, "The Female Industrial Labor Force: Dilemmas, Reassessments and Options in Current Policy Debates" (unpublished paper at a conference on "Problems of Industrial Labor in the USSR," Washington, September 1977).
64. Szymanski, "Socialism or Capitalism," *op. cit.*, pp. 341-42.
65. *Ibid.*, p. 342.
66. *Ibid.*, p. 343.
67. Murray Yanowitch, *Social and Economic Inequality in the Soviet Union*, White Plains, 1977, pp. 9, 10.
68. Matthews, *op. cit.*, pp. 92, 93.
69. Yanowitch, *op. cit.*, p. 38.
70. *Ibid.*
71. Szymanski, "Socialism or Capitalism," *op. cit.*, pp. 342-43.
72. Yanowitch, *op. cit.*, p. 80.
73. This account of special privileges is taken from Chapter 1 of Hedrick Smith, *The Russians*, New York, 1976, an accurate

and readable introduction to the phenomena of Soviet life. A more thorough factual account by Mervyn Matthews, *Privilege in the Soviet Union*, London, 1978 is scheduled for publication this summer.
74. *Ibid.*, p. 59.
75. *Ibid.*, p. 66.
76. V.I. Lenin, "The Proletarian Revolution and the Renegade Kautsky," *Collected Works*, Vol. 28, p. 235.
77. *Ibid.*, p. 246.
78. Mao, *A Critique of Soviet Economics*, p. 61.
79. Jerry F. Hough, "Political Participation in the Soviet Union," *Soviet Studies*, Vol. 28, No. 1, January 1976, p. 7.
80. T.H. Rigby, *Communist Party Membership in the USSR*, Princeton, N.J., 1968, p. 525.
81. From a U.S. government collection of Mao's post-1949 writings.
82. Hough, *op. cit.*, p. 11.
83. Robert A. Dahl, *Who Governs?*, New Haven, 1961, pp. 155-56.
84. F.F. Aunapu, *Chto takoe upravenie* (What Management Is), Moscow, 1967, p. 16.
85. Mao, *A Critique of Soviet Economics*, p. 73.
86. Quoted in Yanowitch, *op. cit.*, p. 146.
87. I.P. Volkov, "The Style of Management in Solving Problems of the Social Development of Enterprise Collectives," in E.S. Kuz'min and A.A. Bodalev, eds., *Sotsial'naia psikhologiia i sotsial'noe planirovanie*, Leningrad, 1973, p. 89.
88. On Akchi see Yanowitch, *op. cit.*, pp. 157-60.
89. Quoted *ibid.*, p. 160.
90. Albert Szymanski, "Soviet Social Imperialism, Myth or Reality: An Empirical Examination of the Chinese Thesis," *Berkeley Journal of Sociology*, XXII, 1977-1978, p. 165.
91. *Ibid.*, p. 131.
92. *Ibid.*, p. 135.
93. Al Szymanski, "Even Mountains Are Moved: A Response to Magdoff," *Monthly Review*, Vol. 30, No. 1, May 1978, p. 54.
94. V.I. Lenin, "Notebooks on Imperialism," *Collected Works*, Vol. 39, p. 414.
95. *Ibid.*, p. 430.

96. V.I. Lenin, "The Development of Capitalism in Russia," *Collected Works*, Vol. 3, p. 490.
97. Aurthur, *op. cit.*, p. 122.
98. Szymanski, "Myth or Reality," *op. cit.*, p. 133.
99. G.A. Kulagin, "My Partners, The Authorities and the 'Rules of the Game'," *Ekonomika i organizatsiia promyshlennogo proizvodstva*, 2, March-April 1975, translated in AAASS, *The USSR Today, op. cit.*, p. 47.
100. Szymanski, "Myth or Reality," *op. cit.*, p. 137.
101. *Ibid.*, p. 141.
102. *Ibid.*, p. 143.
103. *Red Papers 7*, p. 62.
104. *Ibid.*, p. 63.
105. Szymanski, "Myth or Reality," *op. cit.*, p. 147.
106. *Ibid.*, p. 156.